Praise for *Shunned*

"What a pleasure to journey with Linda Curtis in her brave, captivating story of really growing up all the way. I read this book deep into the night and picked it up in the morning, unable to turn away from the unfolding adventure of a young woman determined to live a true life."
—SHERRY RUTH ANDERSON, coauthor of *The Feminine Face of God* and *The Cultural Creatives*

"You can't read *Shunned* without realizing that Linda's story is, writ large, the primal story of leaving home, in which you can't become yourself without betraying your family. A wonderful book that is about so much more than the Jehovah's Witnesses."
—ADAIR LARA, longtime columnist for the *San Francisco Chronicle* and author of *Hold Me Close, Let Me Go*

"*Shunned* is a beautiful and moving account of discovery, awakening, and courage. Linda's candor, insight, and warmth are a gift."
—MARC LESSER, author of *Less: Accomplishing More By Doing Less*

"A profound, at times fascina   d with meticulous detail. The   – from dogmatism to relativisn   – ance—unfolds gradually. Be   g look at her former religious community, this memoir subtly encourages readers to challenge childhood views in search of chosen beliefs."

—*KIRKUS REVIEWS*

"This memoir of faith, struggle and rebirth will have you on the edge of your seat. It's brilliant, respectful, insightful and most of all hopeful."

—OPENLY BOOKISH

"Linda's brilliant writing lights up the page. She speaks with great authenticity, insight, and candor. This book is a wonderful inspiration for anyone who has been trapped in religious dogma or constricted by social and family pressures. Her courageous journey beautifully illuminates the path to find one's freedom in the face of being shunned."

—MARK COLEMAN, Mindfulness Meditation Teacher, author of *Awake In The Wild*

Shunned

Shunned

How I Lost My Religion
and Found Myself

Linda A. Curtis

SHE WRITES PRESS

Published April 17, 2018
Printed in the United States of America
Print ISBN: 978-1-63152-328-1
E-ISBN: 978-1-63152-329-8
Library of Congress Control Number: 2017959980

For information, address:
She Writes Press
1563 Solano Ave #546
Berkeley, CA 94707

Interior design by Tabitha Lahr

She Writes Press is a division of SparkPoint Studio, LLC.

Names and identifying characteristics have been changed to protect the
privacy of certain individuals.

For my mother, Ruth, who nurtured my reverence for the Divine, and my father, Frank, who instilled in me an appreciation for the well-told story.

Contents

PART ONE: Portland, 1993 ix

PART TWO: Chicago, 1994 123

PART THREE: The Death Exemption, 2006 241

EPILOGUE: The Death Exemption, 2010 289

PART ONE

Portland, 1993

Chapter 1

Jehovah's Witness: n. (1931): a member of a group that witness by distributing literature and by personal evangelism to beliefs in the theocratic rule of God, the sinfulness of organized religions and governments, and an imminent millennium.
—Merriam Webster's Collegiate Dictionary, 10th Edition

It started on a Saturday. The alarm blasted at 7:30 a.m., jolting my husband and me awake. He made the coffee as I laid claim to the first shower. We began our standard weekday routines: Grape-Nuts eaten over the kitchen sink, bed made, cats fed. Ross's off-key James Brown rendition of "I Feeeeeel Good!" floated through the bathroom walls.

I pulled up the kitchen blinds to see another overcast Portland day, the sky familiar shades of gray. The brittle orange leaves of our maple tree clapped in the wind, urging me to rally. The folded chairs needed to be pulled from the closet and set in tidy rows in the living room, across from the couch, facing the television cabinet.

By nine o'clock, we were ready. Ross went to the back office to organize his briefcase, preparing for the morning by reading and highlighting talking points from the latest issues of *The Watchtower* and *Awake!* magazines. I settled onto the couch, waiting for the caffeine to kick in.

1

Todd Sterling arrived first. He smiled at me as he let himself in through the front door, then removed his shoes and sat in his chair, the one I had set out in front, facing the others. He was wearing the standard Portland uniform: a tan trench coat. Todd was a longtime friend of the family and an elder in our congregation. Still trying to wake up, I didn't feel like making small talk and was grateful to Ross as he walked into the room, red hair damp from the shower, hand outstretched, making some good-natured joke about Todd's tie.

Within five minutes, the rest of the Friends had arrived. Besides Todd, there was Hannah Thomas and her husband, Patrick. With shoulder-length salt-and-pepper hair, she had the warm, buttery eyes of a deeply caring person. As always, Patrick sat down on one of the outer chairs, shoulders hunched. The Schiller family came, too: Bob and Vivian, with their teenage daughter, Chloe, and ten-year-old son, Michael, wearing a bow tie just like his dad.

Todd led the meeting. First, we read the Daily Text, a spiritual thought for the day. Then Michael Schiller volunteered to read the Bible verse it was based on, a passage from Matthew: "He that has endured to the end is the one that will be saved."

I unbuttoned the sleeves of my starched cotton shirt and rolled them up into neat cuffs at the elbow. I was having a hard time paying attention. Thoughts about my job were knocking around my mind like pinballs. That week I had interviewed eight candidates for our training staff and had narrowed the choices down to two people. We were in the middle of a rapid national expansion. Could I convince my boss to hire both, or would I have to choose between the two?

The meeting moved on to what the brothers and sisters would say at the doors, should we find a listening ear. The Watchtower Society provided weekly suggested talking points. This week's topic was international peace and security, something people have longed for throughout time. We would acknowledge the complete failure of all human governments and man-made organizations to bring true and lasting peace.

We would then point out—using our Bibles—that only Jehovah God could make it happen, empowering his reigning son, Christ Jesus, to bring a New System to our Earth. There were many prophecies pointing to now as the Last Days of this wicked world. Our preaching was a fulfillment of prophecy and an act of love for the people in our communities. Before God set up his righteous government on Earth, those not willing to bow to his divine sovereignty would be destroyed at Armageddon, the righteous theocratic battle that would precede the millennium. It was our Christian duty to warn our neighbors before it was too late.

After about twenty minutes, Todd concluded the meeting with a prayer. We all stood and bowed our heads as he gave thanks to Jehovah, requested forgiveness for our sins, and asked that we be guided to the humble and openhearted people in the community. "We are honored to be used by you, Dear God, to help separate the sheep from the goats. And please, Father, protect us from Satan, who walks about like a roaring lion, seeking to devour someone. In Jesus' name we pray. Amen."

We organized into our car groups. Enthusiastic about working with Todd, Ross had a twinkle in his eye. "I folded some tracts for you." He kissed me on the forehead and slipped the pamphlets into my book bag, next to my Bible and *The Watchtower* and *Awake!* magazines. Usually I carried other Bible study aids, but that morning I hadn't taken the time to gather them.

I was the last person to slip into Hannah's ten-year-old Toyota Corolla. I was grateful for the familiarity of the crew, sisters with whom I had been in service innumerable times before. Vivian Schiller was in the front passenger seat, Chloe and I in the back. Vivian was discussing our wonderful "sweater weather" and then turned a motherly glance my way.

"Linda, you're quiet this morning."

"Just a bit tired is all," I said. "I should have taken the morning off, but Ross and I made a family goal to get eight hours each this month in the field service."

"We missed you Thursday night," Vivian continued.

3

"You've been traveling a lot lately," observed Hannah, glancing at me in the rearview mirror. "You must find it hard to manage that schedule and still keep up with *The Watchtower* and book study."

"I don't mind," I said. "The long plane rides give me quiet time to read the magazines." The second the words left my tongue, I was startled to realize this was a bald-faced lie. I had not been reading the magazines on those flights at all. Instead, I usually prepared for the training sessions it was my job to facilitate.

We lived in the suburb of Beaverton, Oregon, about five miles west of Portland. Hannah headed closer to the city and the affluent Skyline neighborhood. The Watchtower Society organizes the preaching work by putting congregations into circuits, and circuits into districts. Each congregation is responsible for evangelizing to all the households in its assigned territory, by breaking down the designated area into smaller, manageable sections, with maps cut and pasted onto numbered cards. Hannah had checked out this territory and over the coming weeks would do her best to find everyone at home, even if it meant coming back two or three times.

She had turned onto a windy, well-manicured lane that could have been the inspiration for any Norman Rockwell painting. I had been here many times before. Passing a certain Frank Lloyd Wright–style home in the middle of the block stirred my memory.

"Does everyone here know about Mr. Gavros in that brick house on the left?" I asked, as Hannah parked on the side of the street.

"No," said Hannah. "What about him?"

"He's a retired PSU professor and a hospitable intellectual. He always asks for the magazines, and I know he reads them because he likes to discuss points from past issues. But he's never accepted my invitations to come to the Kingdom Hall. He's a die-hard Methodist with no intention of doing anything else but talking. I saw him the last time we worked this. Can you two take that side of the street?"

Vivian and Chloe agreed.

"If you disappear for an hour, we'll know Mrs. Gavros is serving you tea," I said. "She's a peach."

The sun had burned through the nimbus haze, and the humid smell of rotting leaves wafted around us. Hannah agreed to talk at the first door. I caught myself hoping no one was home on our side of the street, so I wouldn't have to talk at all but could still get credit for doing the time—two hours closer to our family goal.

The first house was a white colonial with a winding, tree-lined driveway. Two Mercedes were parked in front of the garage, and we heard music drifting from a back room. Surely Hannah saw this as a positive sign, but I was hoping the music was too loud for anyone to hear her knocking.

Standing on the bristly WELCOME mat, we did not speak. After a second knock, Hannah looked at me and shrugged her shoulders. I pulled out one of the tracts Ross had given me. The caption read: "Life in a Peaceful New World," accompanying a picture of a young girl feeding a bear in a beautiful park. It felt trite and distant, someone else's idea of utopia, not mine. Still, I envied the exuberance on the girl's face. An aura of content-ment and full engagement surrounded her. I slipped the tract under the door. Hannah wrote down the address so we could attempt another visit.

For the next twenty minutes, I got my wish: there was no answer at any of the houses we called on.

"Linda, my knocks aren't rousing many people. Are you ready to jump in here? Maybe you'll have better luck."

I had been too occupied with my work to read the current issues of *The Watchtower* and *Awake!*—nor had I spent any time thinking through what I might say if someone answered the door. But I had been preaching month in and month out since I was nine years old, and was well trained to walk blithely by NO SOLICITING signs hammered to fence posts. In my late teens and early twenties, I had spent five years as a full-time pioneer, ded-icating ninety hours each month to the ministry. It's a volunteer ministry, so I supported myself with part-time clerical work. I attended the Pioneer School, which deepened my spiritual practice and expanded my repertoire of effective ways to reason and dialogue. My dad said I was born with the "gift of gab." I found it exhilarating to engage with strangers, to skillfully bring them to an "aha moment" that could change their lives, or persuade them at least to consider a new possibility. Over the years, I conducted hundreds of home Bible studies and played a role in the formal dedication of eight people. I wasn't the least bit nervous about talking. I could fall back on twenty-two years of experience.

I gathered my thoughts as I led the way up the next driveway. I reached for the brass knocker that hung on the large oak door and gave it a rap.

A dog burst into a high-pitched barking frenzy, and I heard paws clicking against a wood floor as it approached the other side of the door. A man's voice got closer and shushed the dog away. The door opened wide.

"Linda!"

A shot of adrenaline passed through my chest. I wasn't expecting to see someone I knew.

"Nick! I didn't know you lived here."

It was Nick Marshall, one of the executives from my office whom I most admired.

"You have a beautiful home," I continued. Until that moment I had seen him only in suits and ties, but now he stood before me, wearing gray sweats, leather slippers, and Ben Franklin reading glasses. As he bent down and forced the dog to sit, I noticed the black curly hairs on his ankles between his sweats and the fleece lining of his slippers. He folded the sports section of the *Oregonian* underneath one arm.

"You look like you're dressed for the office," he said.

Nick managed a team that worked closely with my boss's group. My religious affiliation was common knowledge around the office.

"Indeed I am, Nick, but engaged in a different kind of work this morning. This is my friend Hannah."

Hannah and Nick nodded at each other; then his eyes shot

back to me. The initial shock of seeing someone familiar was wearing off, and my mind was accessing words I had said a million times before.

"As you know, Nick, I'm one of Jehovah's Witnesses. On most weekends I volunteer to talk to people about the meaning of world events in light of Bible prophecy. I see you're reading the paper. I don't suppose you're finding much good news in there?"

The words felt like wooden alphabet blocks dropping awkwardly from my mouth to the floor. This conversation was very different from our usual water-cooler banter, which ran the gamut from the Portland Trail Blazers to the state of the world to why his teenage daughter hadn't spoken to him for days.

"Good news! Are you kidding?" replied Nick. "The Trail Blazers just gave up their draft pick position. But I suppose that's not what you meant, is it?"

"As disturbing as that is, no—I was thinking bigger picture. We've talked many times, but I've never asked you what hope you have for things—world conditions—to improve."

"Well, as much as I gripe, I doubt things are any worse today than they were when my parents raised me. Each generation has its ups and downs. Why? Do you guys think you have the answer?"

"Well, yes." As I said this, I was struck by how arrogant it sounded. "The Bible suggests God has a purpose for the earth, that there is a reason why, generation after generation, He allows so much suffering. We're living in a unique time in human history, when God will bring about His original purpose for the earth."

"And what is that purpose?" His voice had tightened, and he glanced down at his watch.

"To destroy all man-made governments and to set up His own government that will solve all of man's problems."

I had a cadre of Scriptures at my fingertips and was capable of using my Bible to build a case for this bold statement, but the moment I heard the word "destroy" cross my lips, embarrassment swept over me. I'd uttered that sentence many times before, but this was the first time in my life I had noticed how harsh and partisan I sounded. My face felt so hot, I wondered if it glowed. Did Nick notice my fleeting, stunned expression, the discomfort I suppressed? I babbled and hoped the dog would start barking again so I wouldn't have to keep going. Hannah stood off to the side and said nothing.

A few years earlier, Nick had taken a three-month leave of absence. He wanted to spend time with his father, who was diagnosed with a rabid, rare form of brain cancer. Nick was already on the corporate fast track by then, closing some large deals and showing promise for more. Others might have feared that taking time off could delay the next promotion or cause management to question their dedication. For all I know, those thoughts did cross his mind, but Nick felt compelled to play an omnipresent role in his dad's final days. "You can always make money," he said. "But you can never go back and get more time."

Now, as I stood on his doorstep, I heard a condemnation in my words that did not line up with my personal experience of Nick. Ordinarily, this was when I would read a passage from The Book of Revelation about the Last Days, or something from the Gospels about seeking first the Kingdom, but now, an unfamiliar reticence stopped me. Standing before this well-informed and worldly, wise man, I had nothing new or useful to say. The story line I came with seemed fanciful and egotistical. How silly of me to think I could offer him—or anyone—some definitive method for salvation. I couldn't even look him in the eye.

I had to get out of there, the sooner the better. I handed Nick a tract, saying something about how he might enjoy reading it in the privacy of his own home. His shoulders dropped as a glint of relief passed through his eyes. I turned and fled to the street.

$$\backsim$$

My Bible lay open on my lap, the gold leaf long since worn from its pages. I struggled to concentrate. My haunting, awkward conversation the day before with Nick Marshall kept forcing itself into my mind's eye. Ross sat next to me, eyes focused on the speaker, occasionally nodding his head. We were at the Kingdom Hall, in our usual seats, four rows from the front. Vince Lloyd, one of our favorite elders and a talented orator, was delivering the Sunday sermon: "Beware of Subtle Worldly Influences."

"Remember, friends, that Jehovah is a God who exacts exclusive devotion. It's important to regularly reflect upon our lives and see where our loyalties lie. It is not enough just to be separate from the world, but to hate the world, abhorring what is wicked."

He had just finished reading from Genesis the story of Dinah, whose life was ruined when she gave her heart to an unbeliever. Dinah didn't just bring suffering on herself; her brothers got into the mix, murder and mayhem ensued, and an entire family was undone, all because Dinah spent too much time with her worldly neighbors.

Nick's creased brow, a mix of patience and pensiveness, dominated my thoughts. Each time I thought of our exchange on his doorstep, I was riddled with tension. My entire life was spent secure in the knowledge that I had The Truth. Witnesses refer to people as being either "in" or "out" of The Truth. The "T" is always capitalized. Jesus said the truth would set you free, and I had always felt lucky to be born into the one true way. And when we knocked on doors, we were bearing witness to the One True God, Jehovah. "'You are my witnesses,' says Jehovah." I understood my role in the world to be one of telling The Truth about Jehovah and his purposes, like a character witness in a court of law. ("Do you swear to tell the whole truth and nothing but the truth, so help you God?" "I do.")

From my earliest days, I was certain of my religious beliefs. During my grammar school years, my convictions for political neutrality excused me from things like saying the Pledge of Allegiance and standing for the National Anthem. I didn't attend birthday or Christmas parties because their pagan origins could poison my worship of the Almighty. When it came time for the annual school holiday program, I would venture off to the library, reading a book while "Silent Night" floated through the hollow halls. Crouched in a wooden chair of the fiction section, I sat, a lone soul among a sea of books—a bit lonely, yes, but innocent the hypocrisy of false Christianity, which had bastardized true worship by embracing heathen rituals. Lucky for me, I liked to read.

During the third grade, I found a wise and sympathetic teacher in Ms. Levy. She was pretty, kind, and smart. All the girls wanted to grow up and be just like her, driving a convertible VW bug and wearing hoop earrings. Every boy had a crush on her. When it came time for that year's holiday program, which would be held in the gymnasium, she invited me to stay in the classroom. She reserved a film projector to play cartoons and gave me a fresh box of colored chalk and free rein over the long blackboard.

As the other kids lined up to leave for the program, I slipped into the bathroom, hoping no one would notice I was staying behind. Being a Witness often meant being different and standing out, but there was no need to call undue attention to myself. My ear to the door, I prayed for a clean exit. If anyone found out I was in there, they might feel sorry for me, or I'd have to explain myself.

When all was quiet, I emerged into the room, now empty. The only movement was the class's pet gerbil spinning on her wheel. My steps echoed against the linoleum as I crossed the room and turned off the lights, keeping open the window blinds that lined one side of the room. Taking my seat next to the projector, I clicked it on. The sprockets combed through the film as it transferred from reel to reel, a cone of light delivering images to the screen. After a few episodes, I lost myself, isolation trumped by laughter as Bugs Bunny taunted the Tasmanian Devil and massaged Elmer Fudd's scalp to the rhythms of *The Barber of Seville.*

A few hours later, when my classmates returned from

the auditorium, I was amusing myself by telling the gerbils make-believe stories as I changed the water in their cages.

"Where were you?" asked Julia, a new girl I had befriended. She rushed over to stand next to me and seemed relieved that I was okay. "I thought we would sit together."

"She's one of those Jehovahs!" answered Billy Gustafson, the class smart aleck with a butch haircut. "She doesn't get any presents at Christmas."

Everyone in the class heard him and turned to look at me. In a split second, my biggest fear was realized: I had become the center of attention. I wanted to disappear, but I swallowed hard and stood taller. I didn't have anything to be ashamed of.

Ms. Levy entered the room and sensed something was up.

"Is that true?" asked Julia. Her eyes were peering and curious.

"Yes," I said. "It's true. I've never celebrated Christmas. It's against my religion."

"Never, ever?" asked Julia. When she had chosen me as her new friend, she had never imagined such a dire reality as this.

This was one of those moments we discussed at the Kingdom Hall, and for which my mother had prepared me. There was no use avoiding the inevitable. Jesus was also ridiculed. When you are a true Christian, people make fun of you. It comes with the territory. My actions had created an opportunity for everyone in the room to hear Jehovah's name, and that was a privilege. But the only thing I wanted to do was crawl behind the coat rack.

"Isn't that weird?" Billy shouted this question to the whole class.

The knot that churned in my stomach started to unravel. I wanted to smack Billy Gustafson right upside the head.

"Everyone find your seats," Ms. Levy said, as she walked to the front of the room.

Billy stuck his tongue out at me, then obeyed. Julia moved slowly, apparently trying to take in this news, to understand.

Ms. Levy went up to the board and started erasing the doodles I had made earlier. I was grateful the attention had shifted away from me.

"There is something I want all of you kids to remember," she said. "There are all kinds of different religions in this world. Linda happens to be a Jehovah's Witness."

My stomach tightened back up. *Is she going to make me stand up and say something?* She wrote "Jehovah's Witness" on the blackboard in large letters.

"Are there any Catholics in this room?" she asked. Five hands went up. She wrote "Catholic" on the board.

"How about Protestants?" she asked, as she twirled around to count the hands.

"We're Lutherans," said one of the kids.

"Thank you, Sean." Ms. Levy wrote "Lutheran" on the board. "What other religions can you think of?"

And it went on this way until six or seven religions were recorded on the board. My nerves were on edge and my breath was shallow.

"Now, I happen to be Jewish," said Ms. Levy. She wrote "Jewish" on the board, set the chalk down, and, one by one, looked us each in the eye. "I don't celebrate Christmas, either. Jews have other celebrations throughout the year."

Discovering there was another religion that didn't celebrate Christmas was a flat-out revelation. This meant I wasn't the only person in the room who was different, and it was comforting that the other person happened to be the coolest teacher in school.

"Everyone, please look at this board. In our classroom we have all kinds of different religions, and these are just a few of the religions in the whole world. As you grow up, you'll run across even more: Episcopalians, Hindus, Buddhists. They're all just different paths to God. None of them is wrong or something to make fun of."

With that, Ms. Levy asked us to open our math books. I took a deep breath and began to relax, another test of faith endured.

That evening, as we washed dinner dishes, I relayed the entire scene to my mother in great detail.

"'Different paths to God.'" As she echoed Ms. Levy's words, she shook her head. "'None of them is wrong.' Ha! They can't all be right."

Her movements under the sudsy water became more rigorous. "She rescued you with lies," she said.

Her words stung. Mom was insulting me and my new hero. I was aware that we didn't agree with Ms. Levy's logic, but it didn't seem like the time to nitpick. Scanning my mother's profile, I saw her jaw shoot out as it hardened. Was she disappointed that I had not confronted Ms. Levy?

"Mom, please don't say anything to her." I grabbed her arm and summoned a whiny, pleading tone. "I don't want to make a big deal about this. Ms. Levy is my favorite teacher, and I don't want to upset her."

"Well, of course not, Lindy. Ms. Levy may be misguided in her religious perspective, but she's very kind. I'll send her a thank-you note for being so thoughtful. And I'm very proud of you. Jehovah is proud of you, too."

These words were sufficient to comfort me, and I started to relax. I finished drying the dishes, basking in maternal and celestial approval.

Several incidents like this occurred throughout my school years, and I continued to feel the isolation of being different from my classmates. But even stronger than that powerful discomfort was the deeper satisfaction of knowing in my heart that Jehovah was pleased with my faith. A momentary good time wasn't worth my everlasting life. Over time, this separation from the rest of the world became a badge of honor as I refrained from participating in all sorts of activities, like birthday parties, my high school prom, and dating. It wasn't that I didn't prefer to fit in; it was that I never questioned I was doing The Right Thing, avoiding worldly celebrations that had roots in ancient pagan rituals and traditions that could lead to unwholesome alliances with the world. By adulthood, I had squelched all fears of standing out at work. My siblings and friends all shared the same experience: we found understanding and our sense of belonging in the safe embrace of our family and the Witness community.

Ross nudged me with his elbow. Another Scripture had been cited. I found it and followed along, more by rote than by awareness. Nick's words kept reverberating like a catchy radio jingle: "Do you think *you* have the answer?" they echoed now. "Yes," I had said. The audacity made me cringe.

For the very first time in my life, I wondered. I was watching a relentless slow-motion replay of the scene, with cymbals crashing the instant I used that gritty "d"-word: "destroy." If you stripped away all the pleasantries of that conversation, I had looked this man in the eye and said definitively that he would be destroyed if he didn't believe a certain way and join the right team—*our team*.

I squirmed in my seat. Why hadn't I ever heard it this way before? Was Jehovah really that ruthless? That severe? Of course not. Jehovah was the epitome of love. Everything He did was grounded in higher wisdom and righteous principle. And yet. Nick *seemed* like one of the good guys. No. Scratch that. Nick *was* one of the good guys. And yet. If he didn't embrace The Truth, was he worthy of salvation? And yet. Nick was a man of great integrity. Everyone in the office knew of his penchant for honesty. And yet. The Bible was filled with stories of people with good intentions who still failed to meet Jehovah's high standards. And yet. I remembered the way Nick's eyes crinkled upward whenever he spoke about his daughter, his hopes for her future. And yet. The Bible was clear about the requirements for God's approval. This newfound skepticism seemed to emerge from someone else, another, small, distant version of me.

"Do not be misled. Bad associations spoil useful habits." Vince was quoting First Corinthians as he pushed his wire-rimmed glasses up the long bridge of his nose. He had a good point. I needed to watch my line of thinking and keep it in check. Maybe some of my long work hours were starting to affect me. Vince was reminding us that too much time spent in worldly environments, like work, was one way our thinking could get spiritually off-track.

Years earlier, a brother in our congregation, Eric, had succumbed to a curious mind and—even though we were discouraged from doing so—started reading other religious material, including heretical pieces that spoke out against the Witnesses. I made a point of avoiding any knowledge even of the titles of these books, but I knew they were written by former Witnesses we branded "apostates." The things Eric read were so disturbing, he started questioning everything and stopped coming to the meetings, and eventually dropped out of sight. Ross said he "flipped out"—his pet term for anyone who became inactive.

In the beginning, many of Eric's friends reached out to him, but he rebuffed them all. He wanted to be left alone. No one saw him for months. When his name came up, we all shook our heads and prayed he'd find his way back from the questions, to certainty, to The Truth. Several months later, he wrote a letter to the elders, asking to be officially removed from the membership.

Disassociating oneself was considered a very serious action. Once that happens, active Witnesses are not allowed to talk to you or have anything to do with you. You are considered worse than a person without faith; there really isn't much anyone can do to save you. You have to initiate that on your own.

For a while, Eric's wife, Rachel, continued to come to the meetings, but it was difficult for her to attend alone. She was utterly devoted to her husband, even if she didn't share his doubts. Social invitations from the community came to a screeching halt. I once saw them dining at the local Red Robin, as Ross and I waited for a table. Because of Eric's status in the congregation, we avoided them both. It felt boorish to be so evasive, our eyes darting to the floor and then to the other side of the room, pretending not to notice them. As we lumbered past their table, following the hostess to our own, I noticed their downward glances and took it as a small sign of contrition. Eric's once-innocent doubts had come to this.

As Vince cited another Scripture, I wondered how Eric's questions had started. Had he heard his words anew on the doorstep of a coworker? And where was he now? It was impossible to picture him living a happy life. I'd spent a lifetime absorbing Bible stories like Dinah's and naturally assumed that anyone who discarded The Truth was doomed to isolation, to slog through time, aimless and miserable.

Over the years, the Watchtower Society had discussed religious doubts in the literature, acknowledging that they were natural and should be tended to with diligent prayer and study. Maybe it was my time to go through a minor doubting phase. On my thirtieth birthday, I had found myself in the company of Virginia Ellis, a gray-haired woman of faith and distinction. She got a winsome look in her eyes and said, "I remember turning thirty. It was then I noticed—for the first time in my life—I had my own unique, original thoughts. It was a lovely time." Perhaps that was what these new internal rumblings were—evidence of my maturity, an emerging ability to have my own credible and unique thoughts; thoughts that broadened me, thoughts that could transform my view of God and life and expand my horizons. The clutch in my belly loosened. After a lifetime of faithful service, I decided, a little bit of questioning was normal. Clearly, I was sitting at a spiritual plateau. Once I transcended it, I could reach new heights of spiritual conviction and awareness.

In retrospect, I know that is exactly what happened, but not the way I imagined it that day.

Vince concluded his sermon and left the stage. The clapping of the congregation rattled me out of my reverie. We were halfway through the two-hour meeting.

Next would come a question-and-answer discussion of *The Watchtower*, led by another elder, Jerry Mendez. As I turned to the last page of that day's *Watchtower* lesson, I felt something else nagging at me, another memory sprouting up. These memories stirred a sentimental loyalty. My encounter with Nick was not the first time I'd bristled at the prospect of destruction at God's hand.

I was four or five years old, wide-eyed and trusting. "Hurry and get dressed," my mother said, as she placed my dress on the bed, next to Woody Woodpecker and a tattered coloring book. Usually she let me choose my own clothes, but circuit assemblies were special. We would spend all day Saturday and Sunday inside the Lincoln High School gymnasium. Members of ten congregations would be there, totaling close to one thousand people. In between prayers, sermons, and singing the kingdom songs, we would be reunited with old friends we hadn't seen since the previous assembly, three months earlier.

I followed instructions. She had selected my favorite dress, made of light green seersucker. I slipped on my white patent leather shoes and pulled a scratchy white wool cardigan from the dresser. From the bookcase I retrieved my Bible and songbook and a half-used spiral tablet and put them into my straw purse. A tube of cherry-flavored lip gloss and a fountain pen rattled against the plastic lining. With my purse in one hand, sweater in the other, I left in search of Randy.

I found him in my parents' room, standing in front of the dressing mirror, struggling to tie his tie. I sat down on my parents' neatly made bed, just to the left of my brother. The closet door was open, and he had taken a tie from my father's small collection.

"I'll buckle your shoes in a minute," he said, his eyes fixed on the mirror.

"Did Dad say you could wear his tie?" I asked.

"Shut up and mind your own business," he said.

I watched and waited. This was the type of answer I was used to hearing from him.

"Maybe Dad will come with us today, or tomorrow," I mused.

Randy sat down on the bed next to me and pulled my legs up across his knees.

"You're such a dreamer," he said, shaking his head as he buckled my shoes. "Dad doesn't care about this stuff. He'd rather die at Armageddon than spend a weekend wearing a coat and tie."

"Don't say terrible things like that!" I pulled my legs up to my chest and wrapped my arms around them. In their lighter moments, Mom would joke about Dad's being a "heathen," and from her tone I surmised this was not a compliment. However, it had never occurred to me until that moment that he could die. This horrific possibility wrapped around me like a weighty shawl. A hollow crater formed in my chest as I visualized the foretold army of winged black horses, their eyes filled with fire, ridden by faceless hooded riders, descending from heaven in droves. That was how I always imagined the Great Battle would begin. These fierce, righteous avengers had x-ray vision into everyone's heart. They knew whom to strike and whom to spare, even if you were sitting in tidy rows at school or in line at the grocery store. Dad didn't stand a chance, even reading the morning paper at our kitchen table.

Randy grabbed both my ankles and yanked them back to his lap.

"Don't be such a baby," he said, continuing to buckle my shoes.

"Do you really, really believe that, Randy? Really?"

"Sure." He was nonchalant, having somehow already worked this reality out for himself.

The bathroom door flew open and Lory emerged in the hallway wearing a bright pink dress. It was the first time we had seen her in high heels and panty hose. She twirled in feminine triumph, then disappeared down the hall, toward the living room. Mom clapped her hands briskly as she rushed into her room.

"Okay, kids. It's my turn to get dressed. Randy, put that tie away and go get one of your clip-ons. Have your father help you, and then ask him to get out the camera."

He hung his head but obeyed.

"You, young lady, come here so I can comb your hair." She sat down next to me, in the spot Randy had left warm. "Why the long face?"

"Randy said Dad is going to die at Armageddon."

She froze in place for a split second, then pulled a hairbrush and band from the dresser and sat down on the bed.

"He did, did he?"

I came to stand with my back to her, facing the mirror. I watched the reflection of her face, expecting to see some hint of outrage at my brother's damning suggestion.

"How could he say something so terrible?" I said.

Her face held matter-of-fact restraint as she looped my long hair through the rubber band, right, then left, like a jockey gently whipping a horse.

"Lindy, that is completely up to your father. He is a wonderful dad and a good provider, but until he becomes a true Witness for Jehovah, there are no guarantees." She paused and looked me in the eye. "You know that." She pulled a ribbon from the dresser drawer and started tying it around my ponytail. "We don't know when Armageddon will strike, but it could happen any day, any moment. We must 'keep in expectation of it.' [She loved this quote from the minor prophets.] All you and I can do is be a good example for your dad, behave, and let him see how happy The Truth makes us."

Like my brother, her banal tone revealed not one iota of dread or panic. Images of the black-caped, faceless hooded riders filled my mind. At any moment, they might come to strike down my father, and no one seemed to care. I felt a sudden, overpowering compulsion to locate him. I feared what could happen if we left him alone in the house. She brushed my ponytail one last time as I pulled away and ran down the hall.

Dad was next to my brother on the living room couch. He was pulling the Kodak Instamatic from the case, his muscles rippling near the sleeve line of his T-shirt. Randy opened a pack of flash bulbs the shape and size of ice cubes. Dropping my purse and sweater, I ran to Dad's side and threw my arms around his neck, taking in his familiar scent of Aqua Velva.

"Randy says you're going to die at Armageddon," I blurted out.

Startled at first, he peeled me off his shoulder and sat me

down firmly on the couch. He wore a huge grin, but that vanished as he registered the depths of my despair.

"He did, did he?" He stole a quick glance at Randy, then back at me. His eyes were dancing, but his face was serious. He was barefoot, wearing blue jeans.

"It's not funny." I was wiping the tears from my eyes. "Can't you come with us? You'll be safe there. I'll introduce you to all of our friends. Everyone will like you. I promise, promise, promise."

I couldn't stop myself from panting and pleading. He put his arm around me and waited until I caught my breath. My sister, Lory, sat watching from the corner, her long legs stretched out in front of her, her arms dangling between them. She resembled a colt at rest.

"Now, you listen to me, young lady." His eyes possessed a steely hardness that rattled me into submission.

"Armageddon doesn't have anything to do with me. That's just some self-righteous assholes' way of scaring people into action. I'm not interested in sitting around all day, listening to somebody else tell me what's right and what's wrong. I have enough sense in my head to figure that out myself. You can believe that if you want to. Everyone needs something to believe."

I imagined one of the faceless riders—maybe even Jehovah God himself—watching from heaven, shaking his head and jotting down a few notes.

"I would love to spend the day with you kids," he said in a softer voice, "but your mother gets her way when it comes to these assemblies. Next weekend will be different. Don't worry, Lindy. I'm not going anywhere. What could be safer than being here at home?"

He toggled my chin with genuine affection, then resumed loading film into the camera. He was as clear and resolute as my mother had been moments earlier.

Mom rushed into the room, a flurry of black-and-white-checked chiffon, holding her Bible and songbook.

"Okay, everyone, let's hurry, or we'll be late. Dad's going to take a picture of you outside, in front of the rhododendron. It's in full bloom, and everyone looks wonderful."

I felt light-headed and woozy. No one else sensed the danger at hand, but the only choice laid out for me was to fall in line.

Preparing for our pose on the lawn, Lory clutched her hands behind her, leaning slightly forward in her new heels. The massive purple blooms of the rhododendron fanned out behind us in all directions. Randy smiled pensively, pulling each side of his bow tie. Dad came at me with a spidery hand to tickle my belly.

"Come on, I know there's a smile in there somewhere," he said. My forced laughter released some of the pressure. I managed a smile, aware of my mother's advice.

After Dad snapped a few photos, Lory, Randy, and I jumped into the Impala. Dad walked Mom to her side of the car and kissed her on the cheek before she got in.

"We'll be home around five o'clock and have something easy, like fish sticks, for dinner," she said.

Dad stood in the driveway and watched us pull back into the street. Mom honked the horn as she put the car in gear and accelerated forward. We all waved to Dad, but he didn't see us. He'd already turned to walk up the front porch.

C⌒ᴐ

I felt Ross's arm lift off my shoulder where it had been resting at the back of the seat. He opened his Bible and raised his hand to comment. We waited for an attendant to walk up the aisle to bring him the microphone. We were on the last paragraph of that day's *Watchtower.* I had reminisced through the whole lesson.

"We must never forget that Satan wants to use the futility of life in this world to discourage us and make us give up," Ross said. Then he picked up the open Bible resting on his knee to read the verse supporting his point.

I resolved that from that point on that I would diligently attend all of the weekly meetings—Tuesday nights, Thursday nights, and Sunday mornings—no matter how tired I was or

‌‌‌‍‌‌‌‍‍‍

‌‌‍‍‍‌‍‍‌‍‌‌‌‌‍‍‍‌

---

how early my flight left the next morning. I would also keep up a minimum of two hours per week in the door-to-door ministry, which meant getting up every Saturday morning and allowing enough time to think through what I might share, then knocking on those doors. When I got home from the Kingdom Hall that day, I didn't waste any time putting the latest issues of the *The Watchtower* and *Awake!* in my briefcase, to read on the plane or during the bus ride to work.

Chapter 2

ᯒ

Let the mind be a thoroughfare for all thoughts, not a select few.
—John Keats

Six months before that fateful doorstep meeting with Nick Marshall, my boss, John Sullivan, called me into his office.

"I have a onetime favor to ask, and it's big," he said, and took an unusually deep breath. "Can you travel down to Los Angeles with Nancy and help her conduct the Coast Federal Bank training?"

That was when my corporate career started to take off. I'd worked at US Bank—then the biggest bank in the Pacific Northwest—for about eight years. Until then, I had performed a wide range of traditional secretarial jobs, though it was politically correct to call me an administrative assistant. The title made little difference to me. Either way, various bosses over those eight years would ask me to organize a strategy meeting and I would call my fellow secretaries to coordinate six people in the same conference room the following Tuesday at ten o'clock. Then I photocopied all the handouts needed for the meeting— which usually required detours to answer the phone and tend to a temperamental Xerox machine. After I'd compiled, bound, and laid out all the materials in tidy rows in the conference room, I'd brew the coffee and arrange for pastries.

If a fellow secretary called in sick or went on vacation, I was the person trusted to cover for them. Over those years, I developed a reputation for being unflappable, a lighthearted and efficient multitasker. When John secured a promotion and transferred to lead the sales efforts of a newly formed department, he asked me to join him as that group's assistant. Ross and I were about to buy our first house, so the increase in salary was appealing. Intrigued by a change in scenery, I was delighted to follow him to greener pastures. Within four months, John was asking me for help beyond the scope of my administrative role.

"What do you mean, conduct the training?" I asked. Of course I knew what "conduct" meant, but I was hanging on his every word, alert to grasp the meaning he ascribed to it.

"I mean lead one of the training sessions," he answered. "Coast is pulling together two hundred fifty of their staff for two days, and Nancy can do only one day at a time. You'll watch her do the training one day, you'll take good notes, and the next day both of you will be running the training simultaneously in meeting rooms right across the hall from each other. They simply don't have a meeting room that is large enough to accommodate everyone that day, so we need two trainers."

Nancy was the training manager who traveled to other bank headquarters to instruct their staff in how to sell our services and fill out the legal forms.

I just sat there looking at John, trying to absorb the request and his confidence in me to help him through a desperate situation.

"Linda, Coast Federal is our biggest account, and you probably know this program better than anyone. You've seen every element of the training from beginning to end. You handle yourself well. I know you can do this, and you'd be helping the whole team out. We can't blow this program launch."

Our department had been formed to introduce an innovative program to sell our loan services to other banks across the country. There were thousands of smaller community banks that chose not to staff their own departments, so they sold our loans as if they were their own, for a fee.

One month later, I was boarding a plane to Los Angeles on my first official business trip. Later that day, wearing a new Nordstrom suit, I was being introduced to a room full of bankers. John was right: I knew the material and was innately equipped to articulate the finer points with ease. Talking to a crowd felt very natural. I'd had a lot of practice.

At the age of nine, when I started knocking on doors with a prepared sermon, I also enrolled in the Theocratic Ministry School, which was run weekly out of the Kingdom Hall. Every Thursday night, six preassigned members of the congregation delivered five-minute talks on various Bible topics and were then publicly evaluated by one of the elders on specific speech competencies. The Ministry School wasn't a program you graduated from, per se, and it was never meant to replace our primary school education. Over the years, I delivered hundreds of talks and demonstrations of door-to-door talking techniques and along the way became adept at speaking in front of a group.

My very first talk was on the obscure subject of Gehenna, which Jesus mentions in several parables. His listeners would have known he was referring to the local garbage dump, set just outside the city walls of Jerusalem, where a fire burned nonstop, ready to claim all things unsavory, including the bodies of criminals viewed unworthy of burial. Because I was a girl and the biblical principle of headship prohibits females from speaking directly to the congregation, I was asked to sit on the stage with my brother, Randy, and relay the information to him in a pre-prepared dialogue. There we sat, nine and fourteen years old, respectively, talking to each other about the symbolic interpretation of burning flesh in never-ending flames. Several hours of research, writing, and rehearsing went into that five-minute presentation, supported by Mom's guiding hand.

At the conclusion, before Randy and I could rise from our chairs to leave the stage, the congregation clapped and cheered, as was the tradition for all first-timers. The presiding elder, who years later would officiate my wedding, rose to the podium and started his feedback with praise: "Wow, young lady, you sure know how to talk," which brought a wave of laughter from the crowd.

He had me there. It was no secret I'd inherited my father's gift for gab. Then along came the Ministry School, which taught me how to organize and articulate my thoughts clearly. From my years of door-to-door work, I had learned how to think on my feet and had mastered the art of persuasion at a young age. According to my mother, I came into this world somehow knowing how to remain calm and centered in charged situations. Inside I got crazy jitters like anyone else, but I intuitively knew how to hold it together.

At the end of those first Coach Federal training sessions, all of the participant evaluations came back very positive, describing me as "animated," "engaging," "clear," and "understandable." But I didn't need that to tell me something special had occurred. I had felt completely alive and connected to that audience. That day, a lifetime of expertise and cultivated talents was successfully unleashed outside the realm of proselytizing, and a nascent ambition was ignited. It was remarkable to see how transferable and marketable these skills were. I was energized and ready for more. Nancy and I celebrated with martinis while we waited to board our flight home.

As the program expanded, I was asked to fill in again and again. Nancy got pregnant and appreciated a helping hand on the road. When it was no longer healthy for her to travel, I became the sole trainer. As John's sales staff brought in more clients, I was hiring my own contract trainers to help me keep up.

One year after John's initial request for temporary training help, I had my own office with a mahogany desk, an expense account, and an assistant who arranged for my meetings. I knew the names of all the flight attendants on Alaska Airlines flight #141 to Burbank. I purchased Travelpro luggage with wheels.

It had been six months since my unsettling encounter on Nick Marshall's doorstep, when I'd renewed my commitment to healthy spiritual habits. I continued to grapple with key tenets of my faith, especially the concept of mass destruction of the wicked, but interesting work and upward mobility allowed me to push those uncomfortable thoughts aside. Ross and I shared the joy of purchasing our first home. There was furniture to buy and a kitchen to remodel. Life pulled me forward.

One afternoon, just before five o'clock, John called me into his office and asked me to shut the door. Under his leadership, the group had done so well that we had moved to a higher floor of the forty-story pink Italian marble Bank Tower. His corner office had a view of the Willamette River, reflecting a bright blue sky, Mount Hood jagged and white in the east.

"Linda, I have some great news for you."

He was leaning on the front of his desk, no tie, his shirt-sleeves rolled up to his elbows. In his early forties, John always came across as energetic and upbeat. He motioned for me to take a seat. He was holding his oak-and-bronze name plaque in his hands. I'd never seen him do that before. These plaques were quite luxurious and given only to officers of the bank. The rest of us had plastic name plaques held upright in plastic stands. John had a big grin on his face and was having a hard time keeping still.

"Congratulations. The board has approved your promotion to assistant vice president."

My eyes widened as he handed me the plaque; then I realized it had my name on it. It felt dense and significant, the letters of my name deeply engraved, then dipped in bronze. It was like being given the keys to some secret club.

I blurted out my news to Ross the minute I walked in the front door. Together we did a dance of joy in the living room. He grabbed me with both arms by the waist and twirled me around so fast, my hand swatted a lamp off the side table. My salary had increased twofold since I'd joined the department. I was making more money than I'd ever dreamed of, more money than Ross made as a garage-door salesman. We agreed to pay off the credit card we'd used to fund our kitchen remodel and buy a new car.

Because it was Thursday, and I'd committed to be more regular attending meetings, we deferred a celebration and went to the Kingdom Hall, something I outwardly agreed to but secretly resented, attending in body only, to please my husband. Throughout the meeting, my mind wandered again, reveling in my promotion. I imagined the members of the Board sitting around a large oval table, each dressed in a navy pin-striped suit, hearing a lengthy reading of my accomplishments, then nodding their heads in approval and one by one using their Montblanc pens to sign on the dotted line. I didn't tell anyone at the Kingdom Hall that night about my promotion because I didn't know how to bring it up without sounding like a braggart. Truer still, I didn't want to spark worry among the friends who had already expressed concerns when I traveled on business and missed meetings.

The next day, Nick Marshall made a point of stopping by my office to congratulate me. "Well deserved," he said. He had never mentioned our doorstep conversation. I'd found myself in the occasional meeting with him and his staff and continued to feel an appreciation for who he was as a person, how he handled complex matters with fairness and integrity. It was impossible to think of him as doomed, which made me a complacent Witness—but I preferred this new, compassionate acceptance I was developing for so-called worldly people, and the growing sense of belonging I felt among my coworkers.

In spite of my new resolve, as the months slipped by, the headiness and new demands of my job made it hard to focus on the *Watchtower* and *Awake!* magazines I slipped into my briefcase each week. On a flight to Chicago, I tried to muster interest in an article titled "Is There Only One True Church?" then cast a glance across the airplane aisle, failing to see the harm in these people of varying beliefs. The flight attendants began the cabin service. Most of the passengers were quiet or engrossed in their own reading. It was difficult to imagine the faceless hooded riders on black-winged stallions coming to take them out. I struggled to reconcile those images with the compassionate Jehovah I'd grown up with. Life no longer seemed so black and white. Perhaps our differences could teach us something besides condemnation. I put *The Watchtower* away and reached for my two more compelling options—*The Seven Habits of Highly Effective People* or *Do I Have to Give Up Me to Be Loved by You?*—which had begged to be purchased from the airport bookstore. I chose the latter. The extra earnings from my promotion had not diminished the arguments Ross and I had over our finances. I knew something bigger than money issues was playing out between us, but I didn't know what to do about it. Ross had watched as I'd packed my suitcase for this trip, and had asked if I wanted to spend our summer vacation volunteering for the Watchtower Society, either by preaching in an area where smaller congregations needed help or by supporting the construction of a new Kingdom Hall downstate. It was something we'd discussed many times. Perhaps this was finally the year to do it. But the desire now felt foreign, antiquated. I had no interest in going but expressed that as concern about our ability to afford it. Ross rolled his eyes at my rebuffs and left for work without saying goodbye.

The first two paragraphs of the book spoke of the human hunger for love and intimacy that allow for individual fulfillment. Shifting my gaze to the blue horizon beyond the airplane window, I had to admit that Ross was always supportive of my choices. He was never repressive or dogmatic with me. So why did I feel so choked off from happiness, confined to a preset ideal?

I first met Ross at the home of our mutual friend Bill Keller. We were twenty years old, and Bill had somehow saved enough money to buy a house. To celebrate this milestone, he threw a housewarming party to which I was invited.

Nearing the front porch of Bill's modest two-bedroom bungalow, I saw familiar, smiling faces through the picture window and heard the muted suggestion of laughter and music.

The screen door creaked as I opened it. Bill stood up from the plaid couch and placed his beer can down on an overturned milk crate.

"Linda," he shouted over the music, moving his tall, lanky body toward me.

"Congratulations, Bill," I said, giving him a hug, and my housewarming gift, a large tub of peanut butter.

"And who do we have here?" a voice came from the kitchen entry behind Bill. "Could it be the famous Linda Tucker?"

"Yes," said Bill. A tall guy with short red hair came out of the kitchen and stood next to Bill. "Linda, this is Ross, one of my new roommates."

Ross put his hand out to shake mine. His freckled face held laughing eyes and a sheepish grin.

"I didn't realize I was famous," I said. "You must have received a briefing."

"You're famous in these parts," said Ross. "I've been looking forward to meeting you."

"Ross, can you give Linda a tour of the house while I find the perfect place for this beautiful gift?" said Bill.

Even though it felt set up and Ross seemed overeager, I was amused by the attention and trusted Bill's sense of people. To be polite, I agreed to wander through the house with Ross. In each of the rooms there were other people I knew, and we stopped to say hello and make introductions as needed. Those who knew Ross greeted him as Rossman. He had an easy, uncontrived way about him.

He led the way to the unfinished basement. I admired his athletic build as he galloped down the wooden stairs, faded Levi's hugging well-developed hamstrings. Standing at the foot of the stairs, I found myself in one cavernous room that followed the footprint of the entire house. In the middle of the room was a group of people standing around Bill, listening intently as he pointed to some overhead pipes. At one end of the room were a washer and dryer, and at the other was a wide strip of brown carpet set atop the cold gray floor, a waterbed at its center.

"This is my room," Ross said. "Please pardon the bareness. I know it's not much, but it's freedom," he said.

I could empathize. At the time, I was living with another pioneer in a one-bedroom house that we rented from a Witness family for one hundred dollars per month. It lacked a solid foundation, but the kitchen, bath, and woodstove were in good working order. It provided my first step toward independence from my parents' home, and the low rent—offered exclusively to pioneers—was manageable on a part-time wage.

Bill had finished discussing whatever intrigued the group about the pipes and electrical wiring, and we followed them all back up the stairs, spilling en masse into the yellow kitchen. Large boxes of fresh pizza were just arriving via delivery. As the group scattered around the dining and living rooms to eat, I stood off to the side of the kitchen sink, and Ross joined me.

"Ross, how long have you known Bill?"

"About two years," he said. "The Kytes introduced me to him a few months before I got baptized."

He went on to describe his experience in high school, when he fell in love from a distance with the Kyte sisters, Emily and Paige, both of whom were Witnesses. Besides being beautiful young women, he was drawn to their wholesomeness. One day, he showed up on their doorstep for a friendly, unannounced visit. Michael, the girls' father, greeted him. Michael was not a Witness but shared Ross's interest in watching football and tennis on TV. The two became fast friends in a household dominated by women.

Soon Ross was a dinner guest prior to all Monday-night football games. After the season ended, he remained a regular fixture at the table. All along, when she found an opening, Ellen the girl's mother, witnessed to Ross.

"Ellen told me later that she expected The Truth might turn me off and I'd run for the hills," Ross said. "Instead, as I listened, she recognized my longing for something real to hold on to and freely offered what she had."

Over dinner dishes, Ellen told Ross the most amazing Bible

stories. The stories turned into a weekly Bible study. Next he bought a suit, trimmed his bushy hair, and started showing up at the Kingdom Hall. By his senior year in high school, Ross was presenting himself for baptism, the outward expression of complete dedication to God. Because it is a symbolic gesture of a lifetime commitment, Witnesses do not baptize young children.

"That was two years ago," Ross continued, handing me a beer he'd retrieved from the fridge. "I'm the only member of my family who's a Witness. Through Emily and Paige, I've made all kinds of new friends, including Bill. I always wanted brothers and sisters, and now I have them."

Listening to Ross's story, I got a sense of how Michael and Ellen first experienced him. I saw how his unrelenting friendliness could win over the entire family. Here was a person who did nothing to hide his flaws or embellish a story to appear the hero. He seemed comfortable and unaware of this innocence. Part of me thought him simple and unsophisticated, but I admired the courage and commitment he showed to change his life so completely. I spent the majority of my time in the door-to-door ministry, looking for people willing to make this type of dramatic conversion. It disarmed me to meet someone so sincere and open at first meeting. Something fluttered inside my chest and then relaxed. I knew intuitively this person would not judge me or look down upon me. I wanted to believe his openness was caused by something he saw in me, something that put him at ease in the same way.

"From what I hear," Ross said, "your story is quite different from mine."

And then he paused to focus his gaze on me, the way a TV reporter might do as he shifts his microphone and awaits a reply. I noticed the soft skin of his lips and wondered what it would be like to kiss them.

"What have you heard?" I was in a coy mood and jumped down off the counter, standing about a foot away from him. "You seem to already know a few things about me, and I wouldn't want to bore you by repeating anything."

He smiled like someone who had been caught stealing a glimpse of another's poker hand. "At my insistence, Bill has told me a thing or two about you—all of it good, of course. Ed Torres and I work together, and he's been talking you up for months now. Ever since you moved in to his congregation, he's been telling me about this wonderful woman I should meet. He keeps encouraging me to come over and visit your congregation's Sunday meeting."

A wave of heat radiated through my chest and cheeks as I imagined having unknowingly been the central topic of several conversations. In Witness circles, visiting someone's congregation was a classic courtship move.

"Please go on," Ross said. "Bill said you were raised in The Truth, just like he was. But I understand your dad isn't a Witness, which means your mom took the lead teaching you, just like Ellen did with Emily and Paige. Is that right?"

His genuine curiosity summoned my story into focus. I told him that my mom's immediate family were all Witnesses and had raised her with those principles. They lived in the small town of Dundee in the Willamette Valley, decades before it became a denizen of world-renowned pinot noirs. Dad was a dashing football player at Newberg High School. Mom was a cheerleader. They became sweethearts. A better athlete than student, Dad enlisted in the navy when he was barely nineteen. After basic training, he shipped off to Korea. Mom got a job as an operator at the phone company and waited. When he returned, my parents got married and the newlyweds settled near the navy base in San Diego. All three of their children were born there. During those years, Mom took the path of least resistance and became an inactive Witness, though she never forgot The Truth. By all accounts, they had a good life and were happy.

One day, when they were just about school age, my brother and sister came home and asked Mom for permission to go to church. The kids they were playing with had invited them along to Mass. This would prove to be a turning point in our family's destiny. Mother cringed at even a whisper of her children entering a Catholic church—or any church—and through that aversion, a spiritual commitment awakened in her.

"That evening," I said, "my parents had a heart-to-heart conversation. Mom declared her intention to dedicate her life to Jehovah and formalize it through baptism, and her wish that their children be raised as Witnesses. Dad agreed, on two conditions. The first was that each be free as adults to choose the religion anew. The second was that none of his children ever peddle religion on any street corner."

Ross and I both burst out laughing. He grabbed a paper towel to cover his mouth. We were both shaking our heads, completely at ease with each other. I was giggling at him as much as I was the irony of this story. My siblings and I all grew up and pioneered; every one of us had "peddled religion."

I took a minute to catch my breath. "I didn't learn of this agreement until just a few years ago."

"From what I hear, your dad is a really great guy, very supportive, even though he isn't a Witness," Ross said.

"That's true. And I don't think he has regrets about making that agreement. He's proud of the way we've all turned out. He knows we're happy. The Truth keeps us safe from so many evils in the world."

By this time, everyone else had gradually gone into the living room, leaving us alone in the kitchen. I took a seat at the table. I was enjoying the conversation and decided to lob a challenge.

"So, Ross, what else has Bill told you about me?"

He looked down and started gathering used paper plates and crumpled napkins and tossing them into the trash. Next he turned on the faucet and washed his hands. Picking up the towel to dry his hands, he answered, "He said you're an official member of the Triple A Club."

A smile came to me immediately. In Witness parlance, "Triple A" stood for *Available After Armageddon.* Claiming membership in the Triple A Club was a lighthearted way of saying you intended to remain single until after Armageddon.

We continued to believe in the imminent arrival of the Great Battle, when the faceless hooded riders would come to cleanse the earth of all nonbelievers, evil people, governments, and structures that did not hail Jehovah. We were not clear exactly *how* all of that would shake out—whether there would be literal fire and brimstone–like destruction—but the Scriptures were clear in predicting it. Ask any god-fearing Witness—it was right there in the book of Revelation. Every war, earthquake, and political scandal was evidence of how far we were into the Last Days.

It was an axiom from my childhood. As I was growing up, I remember Mom's heavy sighs with each passing year. Near Labor Day, as we purchased new school supplies and mourned the end of summer, she would say, "It's hard to believe another year has passed in this old system." Through the years, the milestones changed, but never the sentiment. When Lory received her high school diploma, Mom became reflective and said, "I never thought my oldest would graduate in this system." Six years later, the lament became "I never thought Lindy, my baby, would graduate in this system." At each new year, she'd wonder aloud, "Will *this* be the year we see Armageddon?"

A natural outcome of this belief is a willingness to postpone the normal activities of life, such as marriage and having children, until the promised New System. That New System was the be-all and end-all, when all the Armageddon dust would settle and God would restore the earth to a literal paradise. The Triple A Club was an inside joke, yes, but also a statement of faith. Jesus and the Apostle Paul had both spoken of singleness as a gift, leaving anyone who chose it free to concentrate on Jehovah God's interests, like preaching and teaching, without the distractions of matrimony. If you declared yourself a Triple A Club member, you also chose to forgo dating, since Witnesses believe that dating should be done only with a view toward marriage. Recreational dating was frowned upon, as it could lead to premarital sex, which was, as you can imagine, a big no-no.

"I will neither confirm nor deny membership," I said to Ross, unable to resist a little flirting. At that time in my life, I felt marriage was several years away. I often dreamed about the possibility of applying to live and work at Bethel, the world headquarters of Jehovah's Witnesses in New York, or going on a missionary assignment, evangelizing amid exotic adventures in faraway lands. Settling down in Portland, Oregon, was not my long-term plan, and pioneering was my first step in a career that would allow me to serve others while seeing the world. I'd imagined that, somewhere along the way, years down the road, I would meet an equally adventurous and dedicated brother who would sweep me off my feet and marry me.

"What about you, Ross? Are you a member of Triple A?"

"No way." He shook his head. "I've always been the sort to have a special girl in my life—though you happen to be catching me between girlfriends. Let me make that perfectly clear. I know myself well enough to know *not* having someone would be way more of a distraction than having one. The right one, that is. Not even my religious conversion will change that."

He'd as much as said he was looking for a wife.

By the end of the evening, I, too, was calling him Rossman. He got my phone number from Bill and called me two days later. We started spending time together, either with groups of friends, or "alone" in public places, like restaurants. The Watchtower Society discouraged single people of the opposite sex from spending time truly alone, which could lead to temptation and the sin of premarital sex.

As I found myself falling in love with Ross, I appreciated the wisdom of chaperones. I had every intention of being a virgin when I married, and the sexual attraction I felt on first meeting Ross only grew as we spent time together. Thankfully, we had many friends in common, so group activities, such as skiing and going to movies, were not difficult to organize.

My actions soon made it clear that I was not a tried-and-true member of the Triple A Club. Ross was working full-time for a maintenance-and-construction company while I kept busy pioneering, conducting Bible studies with interested people in the community, and working to cover modest expenses. When we spoke about the future, we included the possibility of pioneering or applying to Bethel as a couple. That made it easier for me to set aside my plans to go solo, dismissing them as distant and unlikely.

Within four months we were engaged, and in another four months we were married. During our engagement, I experienced bouts of restlessness, sensing how far I was drifting from my dreams in which I ventured out as a single young woman; learned a new language; and traveled the world, preaching, teaching, and serving others while having grand adventures: ministering to children under tropical palms or reading soothing Bible verses to the destitute victims of heartless warlords in faraway lands.

As I got to know Ross, I realized the emotional accessibility I originally found so attractive masked mood swings and self-doubt. I lacked the maturity to help him through those rough patches and often resented the need to. I contemplated breaking the engagement or postponing the wedding. We were both twenty-one years old. When I allowed myself to think about our inexperience, I got scared, sometimes waking in the middle of the night to full-throttle panic. We had very few financial resources between us, as we were both living paycheck to paycheck, and I didn't believe the myth that two can live as inexpensively as one.

One month before the wedding, I shared my doubts with one of the elders who knew us both. He listened and, while assuring me it was not too late to back out, reminded me that doing so would break a sacred vow, a promise. Hadn't Jesus taught us to let our yes mean yes?

To this day, I believe the wedding would never have happened if only I'd had the courage to postpone it. But I was young and the entire affair had gathered a momentum that felt bigger than I was. I couldn't face the responsibility of humiliating Ross or disappointing my mother, who was fully absorbed in wedding plans. Our sexual urges were also peaking, and marriage was the only acceptable way to satisfy them. Whenever we were together, that longing to connect overshadowed all good sense. So I tamped down any disquiet, passing it off to myself and others as common nerves experienced by all brides-to-be.

Mom and Dad gave us a beautiful formal wedding and evening reception. People started to arrive at the Kingdom Hall one hour before the ceremony, to be assured of a seat. The usher left off counting attendance at 536. People were lined up along the back wall and side aisles. Earl, the elder who married us, had been a friend of my family for years. People often referred to him as Earl the Pearl because of his kind and tireless work on behalf of the congregation. He was proud, he said, to have known me since I was three years old and to have experienced the joy of watching me grow into a "fine Christian woman." Earl also had words of commendation for Ross. He wished us "every happiness in this system and beyond. May you both be among the survivors at Armageddon." Then he asked, "Who gives this woman in marriage to this man?"

Dad rose from the first row, dashing in his rented tux, and said, "I do," then sat back down. Ross stood proud in his coat and tails, while I wore the traditional high collar and white lace. Attended by three friends each, with Bill Keller as best man, we exchanged wedding vows written and approved by the Watchtower Society. Ross went first, promising to "take me as his wedded wife, to love and cherish according to the Divine Law as set forth in the Holy Scriptures for Christian husbands, for as long as we both shall live together on Earth, according to God's marital arrangement." My vows included all of that and the addition of a commitment not only to love and cherish my husband, but to show him "deep respect" as my spiritual head. We exchanged rings, kissed in front of the congregation, and smiled at the riotous applause when Earl introduced us as man and wife.

"Anything to drink, miss?" I was shaken from my reverie by the flight attendant, a beautiful blonde woman with long acrylic nails painted bright red. Ross would have called them "dragon nails." "We'll land in Chicago in about three hours."

I ordered a cup of black coffee and flipped through my book. The chapter that caught my eye was titled "Learning to Stay Open in the Face of Fear."

Chapter 3

༾

To thine own self be true.
—William Shakespeare

A few months later, on a Sunday afternoon, Mom and I met for lunch at McMennaman's, a restaurant that was equal distance from our homes. The warm sun and cloudless sky allowed us to dine on the outdoor patio.

We met like this every few months, just the two of us. Sometimes Mom came downtown to meet me at my office and we walked to the Bijou Café in Old Town, or, if we were in the mood for stained glass, mahogany, and hot turkey sandwiches, we headed to Huber's, one of the oldest restaurants in the city.

Given my increased travel schedule and Mom's indulgence of her grandchildren, our lunch dates had become less frequent. My brother and his wife had moved into a house two blocks from my parents, giving Mom and Dad frequent and joyful access to their children, Sheena and Tyler. To her credit, as much as Mom loved being a grandmother, she had never put pressure on my sister or me to have children. Thanks be to Randy for filling the void.

Since Ross and I had married so young, we had agreed to postpone children until we were in our late twenties and had bought our first house. Having children was never something I felt strongly about, but Ross wanted to create the idyllic nuclear family he yearned for and had never had. In our community,

postponing children was considered virtuous, an acknowledgment of where we were in the stream of time. But if Armageddon took longer than expected and you ended up pregnant,
well, who could blame you for succumbing to the natural order
of things?

The waiter brought our check just as Mom removed a plastic vitamin case from her purse. The action caught his eye,
but it was a routine I had grown accustomed to. Mom pulled
out her supplements and popped them into her mouth two at
a time, dousing each round with a gulp of water. Her hands
were soft and capable, whispers of dirt from the rose garden
under her nails. At least fifteen years earlier, she had frightened us all when she had discovered a grapefruit-size tumor in
her abdomen. That was when she stopped frying Sunday bacon
and started reading *Prevention* magazine. She was a proud and
determined ovarian cancer survivor.

"One day," my father would say, "she's going to choke on all
those vitamin pills. That's what's gonna kill her—just you wait."

Now she sat before me, a few weeks past her fifty-eighth
birthday, strong and vibrant. Neither of us thought to mention
this. Believing these celebrations had their roots in non-Christian,
pagan traditions, birthdays were absent any expectation of a party.

That isn't to say that my family never had cause for celebration. On the contrary, when my dad became an official, on-the-
books, 100 percent Jehovah's Witness at fifty-eight years of age,
with three grown children and two grandchildren, and then
was baptized as a Witness, his unlikely conversion caused a level
of unbridled joy in my family and throughout the community.

My family had waited over thirty years for that moment,
often doubtful it would ever come. Dad was turned off by religion at a tender age. His mom, my Grandma Emily, took him
to the Baptist church in Tulsa, where the minister had a policy
of saving the front rows for latecomers, in hopes that the humil-

iation of a late arrival would discourage that behavior. Grandpa Ward had passed away, and Grandma was a widow with two young children. They often found themselves next to the pulpit after enduring the walk of shame. The lack of warmth and hospitality, so pervasive in the South, made a huge dent on Dad's boyish memory. It frightened him to watch the minister flapping his arms, lathering at the mouth with a fire-and-brimstone message. Little wonder that he grew up to be an atheist and regularly debated the theory of evolution with my mother. As we kids got older and better "informed," we joined Mom in a formidable rally to support creation. We liked to remind Dad that evolution was "only a theory." It was a quarrel we never resolved.

Over the years, Dad leaned away from atheism and toward agnosticism, though I can't account for why. As an outdoor lover who enjoyed teaching my brother to hunt and fish, perhaps he acquiesced to Mom's insistence of intelligent design. Still, he resisted claiming allegiance to any deity. Over the years, we all learned to avoid dinner conversations about the merits of carbon testing, politics, or Jesus Christ. Doing so got the entire household riled up, Dad "taking the Lord's name in vain" and stomping off to watch TV, Mom collapsing in resentment, ordering the kids to clear the table and do our homework. The passing years mellowed us all, and a mutually respectful détente was achieved. We never lost hope that Dad would come around, but we accepted him as he was, and he never prevented us from following our well-worn path to the Kingdom Hall.

Then Phil Rivers came into Dad's life like a gift from heaven. For many years, Dad agreed to let us host the weekly Bible study at our home. Every Tuesday night, Dad greeted our guests at the front door and pointed them downstairs to our family room. He stayed upstairs to watch television, volume turned low out of respect. This continued through the years after Lory, Randy, and I had all married and moved away. A successful graphic designer by trade, Phil was the latest in a long succession of elders assigned to lead the study group. He and his wife, Grace, became Witnesses after their three children were born.

They were first contacted by other Witnesses in the door-to-door ministry, and both responded to the message out of concern over what kind of world their children might inherit.

Phil was well into his forties, but his well-toned, stocky build and jaunty personality gave him the air of a thirty-year-old. He kept fit by running five miles each day. Phil and Grace were two of the few Witnesses I knew with college degrees. They were well off, well traveled, and interesting, especially to my dad. There was a certain indescribable something about Phil that Dad couldn't dismiss, and the feeling was mutual. When Dad learned that Phil had a daily addiction to ice cream, he made a point of having a fresh gallon at the ready each Tuesday. After the Bible study, everyone was invited upstairs to linger for dessert. Phil and Grace were usually the last to leave; he and my dad sat together at the kitchen table while the women chatted on the couch. Phil was just as interested in getting to know my father as a person as he was in teaching him anything about God. I suspect my father was undone by the genuine personal interest Phil showed, minus any agenda to convert him. One day he said, "Frank, no matter what happens—whether you ever study the Bible or not—we'll always be friends."

And Dad knew that he meant it. "He's not a bullshitter," Dad said. Phil had come from the world and did not fear its influences the same way we Lifers did. Soon Mom and Dad were playing cards each weekend with Phil and Grace and dining out with them often. Throughout most of their marriage, my parents did not blend much of their social lives. Mom had rich friendships with women in the congregation, but relationships with other couples were rare because Dad was an unbeliever. I noticed a gentle felicity emerge between my parents as they basked in the joy of this new era.

Phil never mistook Dad's absence of scholarly accomplishments for a lack of intelligence. The two men shared a fascination with history and love of a well-told story. For the sheer joy and mental stimulation of it, they purchased a four-foot roll of white butcher-block paper and over many months mapped out a timeline of man's history on Earth. At the far end of the paper was a line for Year Zero, to mark the first of the seven "creative days" described in Genesis. Using a scale of one inch per hundred years, they unfurled all the major stories of the Bible, marked with notches across the advancing timeline, like seams on a football. Job came to life as the affluent Oriental, and once his era was on the page, it was clear that he had lived at the same time as Moses, though it was unknown whether the two ever met.

Dad was captivated by the political intrigue and forces of nature that divided the nation of Israel throughout millennia. They traced Jesus's maternal and paternal lineage back to Abraham, validating his arrival as the "promised seed." King Solomon and Cleopatra got up and walked right across the page in all their regal splendor. Phil and my father made their way through the Psalms and the Gospels, watching water turn to wine, then traveled with the Apostle Paul to ancient Corinth.

Each time I went to visit my parents, Dad unrolled the timeline like a scroll to show me his latest discovery. The project had become the talk of the Bible study group and then the congregation. Whether he could admit it or not, Dad had become a student of the Bible and was enthralled with what he was learning. Jehovah had become as real to him as Caesar or the Pharaohs.

Then he started attending Sunday services with Mom. His language and demeanor softened. Sunday meetings led to Tuesday-night Bible study, which led to Thursday night's Theocratic Ministry School. He enrolled as a student and started giving five-minute talks from the podium. Despite his shyness at approaching strangers, he even started knocking on doors. Over the span of five years, Dad embraced all the Witness activities except the ultimate one: symbolizing his dedication through baptism.

A few months after Dad started preaching, I was rinsing lettuce at my kitchen sink in preparation for dinner when he phoned with an announcement.

"I've got a secret, but you must promise *not* to tell your mother."

"What are you talking about?" I nestled the phone between my ear and shoulder and began to dry the lettuce.

"I plan to get baptized at the next assembly, and I want it to be a surprise for your mom."

I dropped the towel to the floor and grabbed the phone with my right hand. Unnamed stars in faraway galaxies seemed to pause in their orbits. I stared out the window, allowing his words to sink in.

"Hello? Lindy, did you hear what I said?"

"You said you plan to get baptized," I stammered. These were the words I'd yearned to hear since childhood, the black hooded riders awaiting dispatch to wage their righteous war. I cracked a joke to deflect the intensity of the moment. "Who are you, and what have you done with my dad?"

"Thought you'd never see the day, right?" he said. "But I figured, why not? I'm doing everything anyway. It's about time."

I never asked him directly, but I knew there was more to it. He'd always been deeply in love with my mother. Despite their arguments and bickering, the early passion of their teens had ripened to a symbiotic partnership. I think he grew weary of pushing against her and resisting The Truth. He discovered that letting go made him happy, and that everything in his life got a little easier and made more sense when he surrendered to Mom's program.

"Why don't you want Mom to know? She'll pee her pants when she finds out."

"She's been nagging me to do this for a while, and I told her months ago to drop it. After thirty-plus years of marriage, you'd think she'd know that doesn't work with me, but she can't help herself, so we've been avoiding the subject ever since. I just want to see her face when they call for the baptism candidates to come forward and I step on up. Won't that be fun?"

I pulled a chair from the kitchen table and sat down. "Amazing. Do you think you'll actually be able to pull it off? Mom has ways of finding things out, you know."

"I will if people like you keep quiet. I've already discussed this with Phil. He's arranged for me to begin the review process with the rest of the elders." A coterie of three elders meets one-on-one with all baptismal candidates to ensure the purity of their hearts and clarity of mind on church doctrine, using a review of eighty questions and answers.

"Who else have you told?" I was wiping tears from my cheeks. Dad wouldn't be investing this much time in details if he weren't fully committed.

"Randy and Marlene know. They'll come that morning with the kids but will stay in the back so your mother doesn't see them. I'll talk to Lory later today."

His voice danced across the phone line. I found a pen and jotted down the date on our calendar, two months away.

"Dad, I'm thrilled. I'll tell Ross the minute he walks in the door. And don't worry—your secret is safe with us."

We all derived morbid pleasure from successfully keeping this secret from Mom, especially one so big, taut with postponed expectations. As we shared the news with our friends, word spread throughout the entire city, to people we didn't even know. It's big news when an unbelieving spouse comes around, sparking hope in those in the same situation. Adding to the intrigue, Lory, Randy, and I kept our own secret from both parents: we planned a celebration dinner that evening, hosted by my sister, as a surprise for them both. Several families planned to come by for dessert and pay their respects.

Dad grew giddy with the unfolding success of his plan. Before the assembly started on the day of his baptism, as Mom sipped coffee and visited with friends in the dining area, Dad stood near the foyer, smiling and greeting friends passing by, shaking everyone's hand. He was like a politician working a crowd for reelection. When he insisted on sitting near the stage—to be close to the seating area roped off for baptismal candidates—Mom was oblivious to the significance. Dad saved seats for Lory, her husband Ove, Ross, and me just in front of him and Mom, on the aisle a few yards from the baptismal pool. Several close friends of the family, including Phil and Grace, were sitting nearby. They were all in on the ruse and wanting to see Mom's face when all was revealed. Randy, Marlene, and the kids attended a congregation assigned to gather on a different weekend, so they made a point of arriving just as the program started, to avoid raising Mom's suspicions.

The morning program opened with a call to song and prayer. Then we took our seats and fought our impatience through a series of fifteen-minute discourses. I could barely concentrate, squirming in my seat between Ross and my sister. As much as I'd yearned for this day my entire life, I'd mitigated future disappointment by refusing to think too far ahead, compartmentalizing my dad's prospects for eternal life into an opaque safe haven of my own imagination. Now I was confused and my heart burned. The five-year-old in me wanted to do cartwheels through the aisles, singing "Hallelujah!" while the emerging independent thinker shouted, *You don't believe this stuff anymore!* I resolved the tension by falling in line. This day was about Dad, not my crisis of faith.

Lory also appeared unsettled, organizing her purse, passing Lifesavers, feigning attention. Ove sat down halfway through the program and confirmed with a thumbs-up gesture that Randy and his family had arrived and were waiting in the foyer.

The protracted first hour finally passed. The elder facilitating the program took the podium and set the stage for the main event of the day.

"Brothers and sisters, the special part of our program has come, one many have spent years or months preparing for. Please stand and sing song number twenty-nine, "Jehovah's Happy People." While we sing, we invite all fourteen of the baptismal candidates to come to the front and take your seats in the area reserved for you. Please bring everything you need to go straight to the pool at the conclusion of the talk that Brother Anderson has prepared just for you."

With that, everyone stood to sing. Dad grabbed his Bible and songbook and stepped away from Mom, into the aisle. A few other men and women were passing him, headed to the special area. He walked several feet up to the area and joined his voice with the crowd's.

Great God, we've vowed to do your will;
In wisdom your work we'll fulfill.
For then we know we'll have a part
In making glad your loving heart.

Lory, Ove, Ross, and I all turned to observe my mother. Earlier, she had looked ravishing in her crimson dress, radiating vitality. Now she looked pale and confused, staring at my father, who looked straight ahead as he sang. Her gaze then turned to us and saw eight eyes filled with tears looking back at her, all of us smiling to reassure her. Mom dropped down to her seat, blinking and baffled. We all sat down with her, and I leaned my arm over the chair back, resting it on her lap.

"Dad wanted to surprise you," I said. The music was still swirling around us. Grace, seated to the right, put her arm around Mom as her eyes filled with tears, not saying a word.

"Oh, that rascal," she said, reaching for Kleenex in her purse, smiling, unable to see through the tears. Lory handed her several tissues, and Mom dabbed her eyes until she could see us clearly.

"You all knew about this?" she asked, her disbelief compounding as she gradually understood all that had been hidden from her.

"What about reviewing the eighty questions with the elders?" she asked.

"All done," Grace said. "Phil handled that quietly, per Frank's wishes."

Her mouth curled into a smile, and then we were giggling with her, nodding to assure her this was real. Suddenly, a grave look struck her. "Randy," she said. "Randy shouldn't miss this."

"He's here," I said, squeezing her knee. "He, Marlene, and the kids are in the back. Dad's been working on this for months. He thought of everything."

She collapsed into the back of the chair, her defenses down, surrendering to the moment, looking at my dad, shaking her head, blowing her nose. As the song came to a close, he glanced back at her, and I imagined I saw the victorious grin of the young man she'd fallen in love with. We settled back in our seats with the rest of the crowd as the elder leading the discourse reviewed the wisdom and significance of this step. "Immersion is a symbol of a lifelong commitment, a vow, to dedicate one's life to serve Jehovah." He spoke of the joy but also the gravity of this action, reminding us that Jesus did not present himself to John the Baptist until he was thirty years old—of age, responsible, and aware. In keeping with Christ's example, all candidates would be fully immersed in the pool.

The talk ended, and all the candidates were invited to stand and publicly affirm their dedication with a loud "yes." I could hear my dad's singular voice, apart from the rest. There was a prayer, muffled by my own tears, and the sighs of those near me. We were invited to sing one last song as the candidates filed into a line and walked to the changing rooms behind the stage. Then the meeting adjourned for a two-hour lunch break. Those who wished could stand by and observe the immersion. A crowd gathered near the front with my family. Randy came forward and hugged my mother. Sheena and Tyler were adorable in their Sunday finest. Marlene was elegant, wearing a creamy chiffon dress with a diamond brooch she kept for special occasions.

In short order Dad came out, the first to be immersed. He was wearing swim trunks and a white T-shirt. He approached the pool, handed his towel to an attendant, and walked down four steps into the water. I was struck by how assured and content he appeared. The water came just below his waist. An elder was waiting at the center and reached out his hand, maneuvering my father to stand at an angle in front of him. Dad crossed his arms over his heart and pinched his nose with one hand. The elder wrapped one arm around him, placed his hand at his chest, and dunked him backward, quickly, adroitly. Those of us standing near, a crowd of about fifty people, clapped in bliss. Part of me wanted to whistle and holler. My childhood dream was coming true. Yes, I was happy. After so many years of wanting something, I could not help but get caught up in the joy surrounding me. But my heart was a tangle of unresolved doubts and family loyalty.

Dad emerged, soaking wet and smiling. He got his bearings, wiped his face and hair, thanked the elder, and slowly walked up and out of the pool back to the changing room. We lingered with the crowd, watching the other candidates while Dad got dressed.

"Excuse me." A tall blonde woman approached my sister and me as we were waiting. "Are you the girls whose father just got baptized?"

"Yes," Lory said.

"I should have known by your tears," she said. She pulled a little girl in to her side. "How long did you wait?"

"Over thirty years," Lory said. "It was a long haul."

"Everyone here is talking about it, and I just had to see for myself," she said. "I came into The Truth a few years ago, but my husband isn't interested. You give me hope."

"Never give up," I said. "Someday he may surprise you."

I heard a loud cry and turned to see my mother running to hug my dad as he came out to greet us. Their embrace lasted a long time. I'd never seen them so happy, so in sync. Seeing them that way eased my upset and confusion. Lory and I moved back toward our family and waited our turn as Mom and Dad spoke quietly. A crowd had gathered around my father, people who'd known him and my family for years, who'd watched his transformation and wanted to congratulate him. It was then that I noticed Randy sitting in the first row of seats, sobbing uncontrollably beside my five-year-old nephew, Tyler, whose small hands rested tenderly on his father's knee, his clip-on tie askew. Randy wept for several minutes, and it seemed his young son understood they were tears of joy. Everyone was hugging everyone else—friends of our family, people who'd babysat us, mentored us, watched us grow, married us. Then Ove invited only the immediate family to stand for a photo near the stage.

I grabbed Dad's hand and stood to his left, Mom at his right. Randy had gained his equilibrium and placed his arm around Mom, his hand resting on Dad's shoulder. Lory stood close to Randy, wearing the fragile smile of the bemused.

That day was to be the beginning of a bright future for our family. As the black hooded riders receded, we turned a page to the next chapter, one that began with all of us united in The Truth. No one would have predicted the plot twist I would introduce later that same year.

⟳

"It's five miles beyond this lookout," Ross said, as he folded the cycling map and stuck it back in his rear pocket.

"You mean five miles to lunch," I replied.

We were on the last leg of a bike ride around Haag Lake, in the western foothills of our county, between Portland and the Pacific Ocean. It was a warm, cloudless Saturday afternoon in February, and I had convinced Ross to play hooky from field service and have a play day. We'd packed the picnic basket with turkey sandwiches, chips, and beer and wrestled our bikes onto the sport rack of the new Honda that I had purchased with funds from my recent promotion.

The workweek had been mentally demanding and the physical exertion of the bike ride had squeezed the stress out of my body. I was feeling alive and optimistic. From the lookout, we could see the lake below, clear blue and new. The warm, woody musk of fir trees floated around us.

"Why don't we do this more often?" I said. "It feels so good."

Ross didn't answer, but he nodded as he shrugged his shoulders. He was wearing a cheap Styrofoam helmet, the band tight under his chin, bits of his red hair curling up around the rim.

"Maybe we can take the whole weekend off." This was my way of suggesting that we not attend the meeting on Sunday. "We could sleep in, have sex, read the paper in bed, maybe go out for breakfast. What do you say?"

"Sounds tempting," Ross said. "Are you sure you want to miss a whole week's worth of meetings?" Two days earlier, I had worked late and Ross had gone to the Kingdom Hall without me.

After a few more gulps of water, we started cycling along the level grade overlooking the shimmering lake, empty of boats so early in the season. Other cyclists were passing us now, but we rode in tandem so we could talk.

"Ross, don't you ever get tired? I mean, of pushing, studying, always going to the meetings, go-go-go. We work hard all week, and then we go hard all weekend. The rest of the world doesn't live like this. They actually do fun, interesting activities as a lifestyle, not just for special occasions."

"Sure, I get tired, but then we take a break like today, and, bam, I'm ready to go again. I'm actually looking forward to the meeting tomorrow. Brian Halvorson is coming to give the talk, remember? Maybe we can take him and Joanie to lunch afterward."

"Okay," I said. Our friendship with Brian and Joanie went back more than ten years, before any of us was married. They were always easy and fun to be with, but a lethargy came over me at the thought of getting up to an alarm clock.

"You know, Lindy, sometimes I worry about you."

"Really? Why?"

"Well, you just aren't the same old Linda. You work a lot and you're tired all the time. You're missing a lot of meetings. When you do go, you haven't previewed the lessons. You rarely raise your hand to participate. That's not the enthusiastic Linda I married. Remember that twenty-year-old pioneer who was putting in ninety hours per month in the service while she held down a part-time job?"

"Give me a break, I haven't changed *that* much."

By this time, we had reached a stretch of road that ran right along the edge of the lake. A breeze came up and challenged our pace. "Sure you have. Last Thursday you got home from work just as I was leaving for the Hall, and decided to stay home. The old Linda would have just hopped in the car and joined me."

"I was tired."

"Tired? When has that ever stopped you? You have more energy than most people I know. If your heart is into something, you can go and go."

"You exaggerate."

"Do I?" Ross continued. "Remember the old days when we started street work in downtown Portland at seven o'clock in the morning? We would stay out in field service all day, stop for dinner, then make a few return visits. Heck, sometimes we'd even go see a late movie."

"Ross, that was over eight years ago—we were in our early twenties."

Everything he said was true. I was struck by a depressing realization, not necessarily the one he intended. I'd spent my life in honorable mediocrity, a grind, a landscape where service and routine dominated. Yes, I'd enjoyed many fun moments, but they were just thin strips of clay eking out space between the boulders of obligation and seeking to please others. Where was the bliss, the pleasure, of living?

"No, Linda, there has been a change in you, and it has nothing to do with age. One thing I know about you: when you set your mind and heart on something, there isn't anything that stands in your way, including older bones. No, there's something else on your mind. I've seen you, looking off dreamily as we drive down the road. You were doing it this morning on the way here. When are you going to clue me in?"

We were back at our car by now. Ross leaned his bike up against a nearby tree, removed his helmet and gloves, leaned against the side of the car, and, crossing his hands at his lap, watched and waited while I did the same. We'd been married nine years. The first year was a tangle of tears and tantrums as two kids gutted it out. We'd grown up together, in the shadow of theocratic routines and the moral support of our families and our congregation.

"Well? Are you going to tell me what's going on in that pretty little head of yours?" he asked. He looked big bear—

friendly, open, and accepting, ready to hear whatever I needed to say.

I was debating how much to reveal. He continued to look at me.

"My mind has been working a million miles an hour these days," I started.

"Yes, I see that. What's going on?"

Ross opened the car trunk, and together we lifted the cooler to the ground. He pulled out two beers while I removed my biking shoes and slipped on flip-flops. Ross twisted the top off a Full Sail Ale and handed it to me. I was mildly dehydrated from the ride, so the beer went straight to my head. I felt the endorphin high from the exercise, the hops hitting me between the eyes. It made me want to open up and trust my husband.

"The strangest thing happened to me while I was out in field service."

"Go on. I'm listening." Holding a beer in his left hand, he pulled out two lawn chairs with his right, opening each with a quick snap of the wrist and setting them down on either side of the cooler, facing the lake. "Have a seat."

"I ran into Nick Marshall, from work," I said as I sat. "I've talked about him before, haven't I? He works on the credit side of our business."

"His name sounds vaguely familiar." Ross sat down.

"I was with Hannah Thomas, and it was my turn to talk, and Nick came to the door. I wasn't especially nervous—he knows I'm a Witness. So I did my usual routine, but it was so strange . . ."

"Strange how?"

"Well, he was perfectly hospitable and engaging. But once the small talk was over and I got into the message, I sorta morphed into some *Twilight Zone*–type reality. There I was, talking, just like normal, saying all the right things, but it was someone else speaking. It wasn't really . . . me."

"I'm not tracking with you here," said Ross, a puzzled look on his face. "Say more."

That was all the encouragement I needed. For months I'd felt like a beach ball held underwater, the pressure building, needing to pop to the surface. Full Sail Ale, fresh air, and Ross's soft, freckled face were all the coaxing I needed.

"Well, it was like I became Nick and heard myself through his ears. I was hearing the message for the first time, not from my point of view, but from Nick's. And here's the thing, Ross, the really big thing: I wasn't buying it. You know how people look at us sometimes with pity, sometimes with disdain?"

He squinted as he nodded his head.

"Well, I didn't feel any of that from Nick, per se, but I was completely detached, out of my body, and not sure of the truth of what I was saying. None of it. It just didn't seem necessary."

"What do you mean, necessary?"

Neither of us was making any moves to set up the picnic. We sat looking at the lake and each other. I paused to take myself back to the moment I had been standing on Nick Marshall's porch. It was important to me that Ross understand my dilemma.

"The turning point was when I started talking about how Jehovah would destroy the wicked at Armageddon. "Destroy"— it's a pretty strong word, don't you think?"

"I suppose," he said.

"Nick is really a decent man. You would love him—funny, hardworking, a family man, a bit of a rascal, a golfer. Your kind of guy. He's worked hard and done well for himself. Anyway, it felt inappropriate to basically say, 'Jehovah is going to destroy you if you don't play by his rules.' I mean, who am I to deliver that kind of news?"

"But you didn't come right out and say Jehovah would destroy Nick and his family."

"Not in so many words. But isn't that our underlying message?" I adjusted to my radio-announcer voice. "And in this corner are the people who did things Jehovah's way. They get to live forever in paradise on Earth. In the other corner, boo-hoo, are all the pour souls who didn't play by the right set of rules." What I'm trying to say is, I suddenly heard myself for the first time, saying, 'You, Nick Marshall, will personally be destroyed unless you do this and that.' Ouch! Who am I to be saying that? It struck me like a lightning bolt. I've always believed, until now, anyway, that our message had the potential to save someone's life, and that preaching was an act of compassion toward my neighbors. But how helpful or loving is it to create even more divisions and separations than already exist in the world?"

"When did this happen?" Ross asked, the outside corners of his eyes drooping down.

"A while ago, maybe even a year."

"One *year*? Why didn't you tell me sooner?" he asked, standing up to remove the picnic basket from the backseat. He was moving more slowly now.

"I guess I needed to sort it out on my own first. Everyone has doubts, right? Haven't you ever had doubts?"

"No. Not really."

"But you converted when you were nineteen, Ross. I've been a Witness all my life. I think it's normal for someone like me to have doubts."

"Yes, I think it probably is."

"So I decided I was just going through a phase."

"A crisis of faith," he said.

"Yes! Exactly." It was a relief to have a term for it. "A crisis of faith."

"I've heard other people talk about this," he said. "How you go through times when you need to reaffirm your faith. Take it to a higher level."

"That's exactly what I thought—I thought it might have something to do with being in my early thirties. We've entered a new stage of life as responsible homeowners, and then I've been getting all these great opportunities at work. Swirling through those transitions, I concluded it's normal to have these thoughts."

The beach ball was on the top of the water now, released, bouncing around freely.

"My first reaction was to study more, pray more, carry *The Watchtower* with me, read it on my flights."

Ross watched me and listened, sitting in his chair, holding his beer but not drinking.

"But, Ross, here's the part that frightens me." I took a deep breath and spoke the truth: "My heart's just not in it. I'm just not that interested anymore."

"You mean in studying? In praying?"

"In the whole thing," I said. The phrase caught in my throat; the implications were too big to pass through this opening.

"You mean The Truth?" Ross asked.

"I'm just not sure what I believe anymore," I answered. My voice dropped.

"Wow." Ross was blank-faced, his shoulders slumped.

"It makes it hard to go out in service. I feel like such a hypocrite, and then I don't go, which ends up making me feel guilty." I stopped short of telling him how disingenuous I'd felt the day of Dad's baptism, of the split I'd felt between joy and impending doom.

"I had no idea all of this was going on. I thought you were just preoccupied with work."

He took a sip of his beer, then started peeling the label with his thumbs.

"Sounds to me like you're still sorting this out for yourself. When are you going to talk to the elders?"

My stomach tensed at the suggestion, and my hands tightened around my cold beer bottle.

"Never, that's when!" I said, my voice returning. "Why in the world would I do that?"

"Because it's their job, that's why. To lend spiritual support to those who are ailing."

"And you think I'm ailing? Spiritually weak? Is that what you think?"

"Now, don't get defensive. You just said yourself, you've been through a lot of life changes in the last year, working, buying our house, and remodeling the kitchen. Who can blame you for getting tired and distracted?"

"Ross, I've been tired before. This feeling isn't about being run down. Weren't you just telling me how much energy I have when my heart's engaged? Just a minute ago you were calling this a 'crisis of faith.'"

"Which is exactly why you should go to the elders. That's what they're there for."

We continued sipping our beers, feigning interest in the gnats swarming around the cattails. My relief turned to disappointment. I'd put off this conversation because I'd never really believed Ross had the capacity to help me sort this out. All he could offer were trite solutions. On the one hand, I was grateful that he hadn't overreacted to my confession. On the other hand, he didn't seem to grasp the magnitude of my anguish. To be fair, I'd done a good job of hiding it.

It was then I knew I would not share the final part of my confession. I had already sought help—not from the elders, but from a psychologist. I had seen her four times and planned to continue. My inner conflict had been so intense—and its potential ramifications so life-altering—I wanted the impartial reality check of a mental-health professional. My closest confidants were all Witnesses whom I couldn't possibly count on for unbiased listening. I'd kept my therapy a secret, making weekly visits on my lunch hour, no one the wiser. If anyone in the Witness community knew I was seeing a therapist, it would raise a red flag. Therapists could not be relied upon to give me the "proper" spiritual perspective. I'd considered a meeting with the elders but dismissed it early on. As my new, fuller self emerged, I sensed I could trust it to explore answers unfettered by the elders' influence. I'd swapped Bible study and prayer for the private sanctuary of my therapist's office and found it an ideal place to chip away the carapace around my doubts. There I dared to utter my skepticism, safe in the knowledge I would not be judged as "ailing."

"Are you ready to eat?" I asked Ross.

"Starved," he said. "Let's move closer to the water."

As we stood to relocate, I felt vulnerable and weak, like my knees might give out.

"Rossman, please don't worry about me. I'll figure this out."

He gave me a big bear hug.

"I know. You've always been strong. It will all work out."

He seemed to be reassuring himself. It gave me little comfort.

We enjoyed our lakefront picnic, and later that night we went to the movies, captivated by Harrison Ford as *The Fugitive*. My troubles seemed minor in comparison with grappling with murder, prison shackles, and betrayal. And I took consolation from the ending: after weeks of relentless struggle, the lead character proved his innocence, made peace with his captors, and secured his freedom. Maybe I could do the same.

Chapter 4

❧

You will not be punished for your anger. You will be punished by your anger.

—Mahatma Gandhi

In the months after I confessed my crisis of faith to Ross, we continued drifting further apart. Or, to be more accurate, I started pulling away, guarding my words, shifting any reliance on him. Whenever he tried to talk about the growing distance between us, I put him off, sinking into a chair, heavy and lethargic, blanking out, refusing to engage. My therapist offered an explanation for this. It takes a lot of emotional energy to shut oneself down, she said. That is why I felt so sleepy when it occurred. She suggested this was a pattern I'd adopted as a child to deal with the many occasions when I'd had to suppress my true feelings in order to fit in. She invited me to reflect upon all the ways I fell in line with what others said was acceptable, ignoring my own intuition or desires.

Until I sorted out my feelings and what I wanted to do about them, I was afraid to speak openly with Ross. Hiding was easier than tackling these problems with him.

I spent hours journaling, fantasizing about a different life, one that freed me from the roles and rules that had once seemed so wise and ordinary. To boost my career, I had started taking golf lessons so I could play with clients, who were mostly middle-aged bankers. In these fantasies, I imagined leisurely mornings reading the paper, followed by nine holes of golf in the afternoon, my handicap improving with each round. Other times I pictured riding my bicycle through the French countryside, stopping in tiny villages to meet the local townspeople and play a round of boules. That got me wondering whether I should take French lessons, my true love, or the more practical Spanish. "To hell with practical!" I wrote, emphatically dotting multiple exclamation marks.

Returning from a business trip on a long plane ride from Chicago, I'd confessed my spiritual questioning across the aisle to my coworker Robyn. She gave me an open invitation to join her for services at her ecumenical church. I was surprised by my openness to accept her offer, picturing myself next to her in the pew, curious and open. Any self-respecting Witness would have declined such invitations immediately. Acts of interfaith were discouraged. Up until that point in my life, I'd been inside other churches of Christendom only a few times, to attend the occasional wedding of a relative or pay my respects at a funeral. Decisions even to attend those events were approached with wary thoughtfulness.

Robyn was active in a Catholic charity, so I asked her how her priest felt about her attending other nondenominational services. "Oh," she replied, batting my question aside with her hand like a fly at a picnic, "he's a very liberal priest. Besides, I don't have people in my life who get hung up on things like that." She was so matter-of-fact. I envied her.

I also started fantasizing about some of the men I was working with. I imagined sophisticated dinner conversations about business, art, or world events. I wondered what it would feel like to flirt, to express sensual longing and be coveted. These visions of romance became so frequent and intense, I feared I'd "committed adultery in my heart."

These dreamy episodes always felt plausible, if only . . .

If only I didn't have to go to all these meetings. If only I had more time. If only I earned more money. If only I belonged to a community that encouraged spiritual exploration. If only I didn't have so many people counting on me to be good. If only the definition of "good" could be expanded to include detours. If only I could explore without being judged and worried over by all the most important people in my life. If only I were single. There—I said it. *If only I were single.*

One common theme in all my fantasies was that Ross was not in them.

The most disturbing fantasy came as I searched for a way out. I started daydreaming about receiving a phone call from the police. "Your husband," the official, monotonic voice would say, "has been killed in a car accident. I assure you, ma'am, he suffered no pain. From the angle of the wreckage, we are absolutely sure he was killed instantly." In these imagined episodes, I would experience intense sadness and months of grief and upheaval. But time heals all wounds, and then I'd be free.

These fantasies generated a lot of guilt in me. One day, I mustered the nerve to share this twisted daydream with my therapist, seeing it as evidence of my cold, cold heart. She smiled softly and informed me this was a common and normal fantasy among people wishing for a divorce.

Divorce. In the Witness community, it just wasn't done. Marriage was considered so sacred, the only scriptural grounds for ending it were infidelity or death. No wonder I sought resolution in daydreams. Church policy did not recognize irreconcilable differences or growing apart as acceptable reasons to split up; these issues were often taken for spiritual weakness and evidence of a breach in the spiritual practices of study and prayer.

One night Ross and I joined our good friends Erik and Marie for dinner and a movie. I was quiet and detached throughout the evening. Erik and Marie held each other's hands; we did not. Marie laughed at Erik's jokes; I stared off when Ross spoke. The conversation seemed bathetic and trivial. At my suggestion, we saw *The Fugitive* for a second time. It was my one guarantee of enjoying the outing. I was grateful for the dark respite of the theater, the familiar torpor setting in. I sat with arms crossed, declining offers of popcorn and M&M'S.

"What is the matter with you?" Ross asked, as we got in the car to drive home. "You were so . . . so bitchy."

"Give me a break," I said, as we both closed our doors. "Do we really need to hear the long version of the story about how you landed the 'big sale' for the Overhead Door Company?"

I realized this was a very condescending thing to say but said it anyway, like the bitch he had accused me of being.

"Erik and Marie loved that story, especially the punch line," he said, leaning back, both hands resting on the steering wheel. "Linda, you are not allowed to make fun of my work. I don't make light of what you do, running all around the country, thinking you're better than me. That's not okay. Especially in front of our good friends."

His eyes were watery. I took a few deep breaths but couldn't ignore the miasma of frustration and sadness hanging between us. I wiped a tear from my cheek. Ross was looking straight ahead. We were headed in a direction I wasn't ready to go in, and I wanted to slow things down, to escape.

"I'm sorry," I said, my voice lower. "You're right. I acted like a child."

"Linda," Ross said, turning in his seat to face me, "do you still love me?"

His directness startled me. He was looking right at me, holding my gaze.

"Of course I love you, Ross," I said, putting my hand on his. "Of course."

But I had paused too long, giving him time to read the truth behind my eyes.

It was a perfect day for a barbecue. We had been asked to bring a blueberry cheesecake, a bottle of wine, and a six-pack of 7UP to Jerry and Julia Mendez's for a going-away party. Scott Chapman had realized his boyhood dream of being accepted into Bethel, the worldwide headquarters of Jehovah's Witnesses in Brooklyn, New York. The entire congregation was very proud of him, especially those who had watched him mature from a snot-nosed punk into a handsome, articulate young man of nineteen.

It was difficult to find a parking space. The streets were filled with the cars of Scott's well-wishers.

"We should have come earlier," Ross said, wedging the car into a narrow space four blocks from the party.

"Excuse me," I replied, "but I don't recall you offering to help make this dessert."

It was Sunday, so our morning had been consumed attending the two-hour service at the Kingdom Hall. After we'd shopped for ingredients and arrived home, we'd had just enough time to assemble the cheesecake and allow it to set in the fridge. Ross used that time to watch sports on TV; I pulled out my laptop and composed a letter to an important client. During that day's sermon, my mind had drifted to a complex business proposal I'd been formulating with my boss, and the perfect words to describe it had come to me. I'd written it down on the back cover of my *Watchtower* and was happy to have captured it in a typed document.

"Excuse me," Ross said, jolting the emergency brake, "I don't recall anyone forcing you to work on a Sunday."

It was a conversation we'd been having with greater frequency. My work at the bank had evolved into more than just a job. The inner workings of business—at least the consumer side of finance—had been revealed to me, and I found it fascinating. I sat in on marketing meetings, where promotional storyboards were presented and ad campaigns were analyzed. I was regularly asked to weigh in on the message of these campaigns, and my clients' feedback indicated that I had solid input to offer. There were pricing models to consider, which factored in the current cost of funds and reserves for loan loss, and I was beginning to see the bigger picture of how the ebb and flow of politics and world events impacted the economy and our profits. The term 'prime lending rate' on the six o'clock news held a whole new meaning. I was beginning to understand why people cared about it. Observing how my efforts made direct impact on our group's bottom line had a visceral effect on me. Being part of a winning team was fun. Every day held something new and engaging. Our start-up initiatives were seeing impressive wins and received the adulation of the bank president. One day, John even took me along to meet the president in his marble office at the top of the bank tower. Spending ten minutes on a Sunday to write a business letter did not feel like an inconvenience to me.

"Let's drop this argument and go enjoy our friends, okay?" I said to Ross. We got out of the car and started walking in silence toward Jerry and Julia's house.

Scott was playing basketball in the driveway with eight other brothers. Standing at the foul line, he slowly bounced the ball, preparing to take a free throw. As we approached the sidewalk, Ross yelled out, "Brick!" His concentration interrupted, Scott turned and smiled. Ross handed me his car keys and wallet. "I'll be in soon," he said. He was off to join the game.

I opened the screen door from Julia's kitchen and stepped onto the back deck, where Jerry was presiding over the grill. He was wearing an apron that said KISS THE COOK. The tangy smoke from the marinade floated through the yard and whetted my appetite.

"It's hard to say who'll be the star today," I said, standing next to Jerry, watching him slather each piece with sauce. "Scott or your famous chicken."

"Your flattery entitles you to an extra piece," Jerry said, smiling as he closed the lid on the grill.

Wandering into the backyard, I found Ross surrounded by an entourage of eager children, waiting their turn for a piggyback ride. Jerry asked everyone to gather around the food tables. A hush came over the crowd as he bowed his head and led us in a prayer. Ross and I were part of the first wave of people through the dinner line. We filled our plates with grilled chicken, potato salad, and corn on the cob, then sat out of the way on a step on the deck, balancing our plates on our knees.

"I told Todd about your experience in service," Ross said, looking straight ahead.

"What experience?" My hours in the service were dwindling. I couldn't think of any recent encounters worth mentioning.

"You know—the one from several months ago."

Scanning my memory banks, I wasn't registering anything.

"The one that upset you so much—the one where you met that guy from work."

My face flushed, and I imagined myself a spectacle, as if my whereabouts had just been exposed by a high beam climbing the wall of Cell Block C.

"Are you kidding me?" I felt heat rising in my cheeks.

"No," Ross said, and then took a bite of potato salad, his eyes following someone across the yard.

"When?" I tried to remember a time when Todd and Ross had been together. Ross said nothing.

"When were you with Todd?" I repeated.

"This morning, after the meeting. He walked me out to the car. We were trying to schedule a golf time, but he also wanted to know if you were all right."

"*All right*? What does that mean, *all right*?" I asked. My back stiffened as I crammed my plastic fork into my food. "I was at the meeting, wasn't I? I'm here now, aren't I? How could I not be all right?"

I bit my lip as Ross took another bite of chicken. "Ross, I told you that in confidence." My voice was lower now. "It was between *us*."

"Calm down," he said. "Todd was just expressing concern. He's noticed you're not the same old enthusiastic Linda." He flashed a forced smile at one of the passing children.

Jerry sat down within earshot, and more people came to occupy the open seats around us. Ross gave me a look that said, *We can talk about this later.* I gave him a look back that said, *You better believe we will.*

Todd was standing in the far corner of the yard, leaning against the fence, laughing as he talked to another brother. He was one of the first people I had passed as I'd entered the house. We had exchanged pleasantries as he'd walked out to join the basketball game. I struggled to manage my breathing and keep up appearances while simultaneously sending invisible daggers at my husband. How many people in this group were also wondering if I was "all right"? Were they talking about me behind my back?

A knot in my stomach replaced my appetite. The jovial environment was wearing thin and wasn't conducive to either a screaming match or a river of tears. I stood up, thinking I would go to the restroom and pull myself together. Then something visceral happened and I sat back down. I leaned toward Ross, tilted my head, and whispered, "I'm so angry, I can't even see straight. I'm going to leave."

I refused to look him in the eye, but I knew he'd stopped chewing, frozen in place.

"I'm sure you won't have any trouble getting a ride home," I continued. "Don't worry. I'm going quietly. When people notice I'm gone, you can tell them whatever you please. Don't forget to bring our cheesecake platter home."

Without waiting for an answer, I slipped through the back screen door, past the living room, and out the front door. I'd never done anything like that before. I felt exhilarated, enlivened by actions true to my emotions. As soon as I reached my car, the tears began, quick and clean, a mix of righteous indignation and relief. I cried all the way home.

Chapter 5

❧

And the day came when the risk it took to remain tight in
the bud was more painful than the risk it took to blossom.

—Anaïs Nin

My first stop inside our front door was the liquor cabinet, where I looked for a way to dull my senses. Weeping over the barware, I mixed myself a tall Seagram's and 7UP.

I tried to imagine the conversation Todd and Ross had had about me earlier that day. I pictured them standing in the Kingdom Hall parking lot, Ross's forthcoming, naive mind not seeing that this was more than idle chitchat, unaware of Todd's agenda. How would the questioning have started? *Linda sure is spending a lot of time in LA.* Or *Linda seems distracted. Is everything okay on the home front?*

At whom was I most angry: Ross or Todd? I resented Todd's prying. Ross was an easy target, always saying just a little too much. I, on the other hand, was consistently the picture of discretion, careful and deliberate about what I revealed. Todd knew this, and Ross had taken the bait.

About an hour later, Ross walked through the front door, pausing when he saw me. I must have been quite a sight, wearing a matted terry bathrobe, face puffy from tears, fixing my second drink.

"I'll have what you're having." He walked past the kitchen bar, shoulders slumped.

"Fix it yourself," I said, taking a seat at the dining room

table. "Your arms aren't broken, and we already know your mouth is working fine." The whiskey had seeped into my anger and liquefied it.

"Linda, I don't understand why you're so worked up."

"You go running your mouth, and I have to draw pictures for you?"

"Calm down," he said.

"I will not calm down." I slammed my hand on the table. "That is the second time you've said that to me today. Don't you get it? You betrayed my confidence."

"How do you figure?" asked Ross, pouring himself a shot of whiskey.

"How about you tell me exactly what you and Todd talked about? And I mean *exactly*. If you two are going to talk about me, I have a right to know everything that was said."

"Fine." Ross sat down at the table. "I have nothing to hide."

He took a drink and continued. "It was a very brief, well-meaning conversation."

"Well-meaning—I'll bet. I want word for word," I said, wiping my nose with a soggy Kleenex I pulled from my robe pocket. "How did it start?"

"Like I said, Todd walked me out to the car so we could arrange a tee time for Tuesday. Then he asked about you."

"And . . . ?" I spun my drink around, rattling the ice.

"Todd commented that you had lost some of your light-heartedness, your sparkle. I couldn't disagree with him. I told him you were just working too hard."

"And then what?" I asked.

"He'd also noticed your service hours were slipping and you weren't commenting as much at the meetings. He asked me if we were regular with our family Bible study."

"That is none of his business." Telling Todd the truth would only invite scrutiny.

"It *is* his business. Todd cares about us. Besides, Linda, it felt good to be honest, to not pretend everything is fine. Because everything is not fine. Things haven't been fine for a long time."

69

"How did you answer?" I asked, leaning forward, dreading his response.

"I told him the simple truth—and he empathized, by the way: that by the time we work and sleep and eat, attend meetings, and go in service, there's no time left."

"Ross, what did you tell him about my encounter with Nick Marshall, that guy from my work?"

"Oh," he said, as if this piece were an afterthought. "I didn't say much about the encounter, because I wasn't there. But I did share with him how it made you feel."

"How's that?"

"That it had stirred up doubts and that sometimes you question the teachings."

I stood up. "Did you actually use the word 'doubt'?"

Ross rolled his eyes to the ceiling, scanning his memory. "Yes. Yes, I'm sure I did."

I started pacing between the dining table and the sofa.

"Great, just great. You didn't have permission to discuss that with anyone. Not even someone with good intentions."

"Linda, this isn't just about you. If anything, Todd had stern words for me."

"Really?" I sat across from him at the table. "Like what?"

Ross was pouring himself a second drink. "He wanted to know what I had done, as the spiritual head of this family, to help you work through your doubts. And I had to admit I'd let it slide. I figured you would work it out on your own, and that's what I told Todd. He told me I was a fool not to pay more attention to this."

"Yes, you are a fool, but not for the reasons Todd thinks," I said.

We sat in silence for several minutes, only my staccato inhalations interrupting the hush. Ross had the hollow look of someone at loose ends. Like a cowboy in a saloon, he swigged his last drops of whiskey and stood up.

"It's not too late," he said. "Todd has suggested that he and Jerry come by soon for a shepherding call. I think it's a great idea."

"No, that's *not* a great idea." My equilibrium returned. I stood up and leaned in on both arms, looking Ross straight in the eye. "It's intrusive. It's unwelcome."

Turning around, I walked into the kitchen for a glass of water, my bare feet slapping against the cool linoleum. Though I was riven with disgust, my level of belligerence was a surprise even to me. "I won't do it, Ross!" I shouted over my shoulder.

"But I already told Todd it was a go." He followed me into the kitchen.

"Then by all means, enjoy your meeting with him." I turned from the sink, gulping my water. "I won't be there."

"What's the matter with you?" His voice was gaining strength. "You've become so blatantly disrespectful. Todd is just trying to help, and we both need help."

"I don't recall asking for Todd's help."

"What is that supposed to mean?"

"It means I don't appreciate people going behind my back. If Todd is such a good friend, if he's so worried about me, then why didn't he come straight to me?"

"I'm the spiritual head of the family. It's appropriate for him to come to me first. You know that."

"Bullshit." Weary of self-censorship, I thought swearing seemed an emphatic way to express my disdain. "That system doesn't work for me anymore."

"What system?" Ross asked, his voice suddenly thin. There were tears in his eyes. We had stumbled onto a land mine. Sudden moves were risky. An implacable resolve came over me.

"Headship, for one. It's so dated and patriarchal. To think another person is responsible for me and my spiritual well-being is ridiculous. Don't you see that, Ross?"

He blanched. Behind his eyes, I could just make out an unwanted realization breaking through the surface of his mind.

"Theocratic hierarchy, for another. And I don't like putting on a happy face as we go door-to-door, condemning other people and their religions. The whole thing is veiled in kindness— just like Todd's offer—but it's divisive."

The more I said, the more we realized the latitude and longitude of my drift.

"I feel so out of place," I said. I blinked a tear. My eyelids were too heavy to hold up.

"That settles it," Ross said. "I'm more convinced then ever. We have to meet with Todd and Jerry."

"I don't have to do anything."

Stumbling down the hall to our room, I slammed the door behind me and fell into bed. I heard the rattle of car keys, followed shortly by the sound of the front door creaking open.

Engulfed in the comfort of darkness and cool sheets, I set my muddled mind free to float around the words just spoken. I mentally replayed the conversation, embellishing with flip imaginary comments, dumbfounded Ross couldn't see how he had violated my trust. The whiskey had loosened my tongue, exposing realizations I'd been shaping for months. The avalanche of true feelings was an exhausting relief to express.

Suddenly, out of my stupor rose an essential truth I couldn't believe I had forgotten. *This is what Witnesses do when someone is "ailing."* Just like loyal geese who temporarily abort migration to nurse and beseech a member of the flock who has fallen behind, they will blab and squawk to each other, deliberately assigning roles, a communal effort to protect and nurture. Ross was following Witness protocol, offering help that trumped all marital confidences.

Who needs it? My head was filled with ideas and voices— worldly voices—Ross would never be able to hear. Perhaps it was I who had betrayed Ross. He still didn't know I was seeing a therapist. There, in my personal sacristy, I'd been gathering the clarity and will to speak up. Ross's action was equivalent to calling in the cavalry. I wondered how I might summon the courage to stand in my questions for however long it took to land on my own ground. Inside me, a hysterical angst was building. I was now facing a series of conversations I wasn't sure I was ready for.

I wallowed in the peculiar sort of loneliness reserved for

married couples engulfed in conflict. Deeply connected by the ups and downs that come from nine years of shared living, we now stood at separate ends of a vast chasm, and I couldn't fathom how to make things right without short-changing my process. A sense of belonging was very important to both of us. These new developments would bring an end to our blending in. Ross had married me thinking I would be his ideal Christian mate. We moved around a community that valued together-ness and idealized conformity. These thoughts plagued me as I drifted to sleep.

The next thing I knew, I was being jostled awake as some-one sat down at the foot of the bed. Lifting my head from the pillow, I saw Ross, still wearing the same clothes from the night before. Dawn slipped through the blinds. His side of the bed was undisturbed. It was just a few minutes before my alarm was set to go off.

"Linda, wake up. I have something to tell you." His shirt was untucked and wrinkled.

"What is it? What's going on?" I asked, sitting up in bed. My head began to pound, an aggressive reminder of too much whiskey. I switched on the lamp and winced.

"First, promise not to kill me; then I'll tell you," Ross said. His face was drained of color.

"I promise. Now, can we get on with it? What's going on?"

"Last night I was in a car wreck."

The words sliced through my hangover. I imagined shat-tered glass and spilt blood on gray concrete, red lights flashing in the distance.

"What? Are you all right? Did anyone else get hurt? How did you get home?"

The synapses in my brain fired up instantly. The previous night's acrimony evaporated. Ross's mouth twitched as he gazed down, gathering the will to say more.

"Don't worry about me—I wasn't hurt at all, just shaken. And humiliated."

My heart softened with relief.

"What happened?" I asked gently.

"It was really stupid. Right after our argument, I decided to go for a drive to chill out."

"After all you had to drink?" I shook my head, barely remembering the rattling sound of the keys from the night before. I couldn't fathom being so angry as to abandon good sense and drive drunk.

He paused for a moment. "I took your car," he said, looking at me out of the corner of his eye, "so I could blast the stereo."

"You what?" I wasn't sure I had heard him right. "You took my car? My brand-new car?"

He nodded.

"And who did you crash into?" I asked, as I got out of bed and put on my bathrobe.

"That's the humiliating part. I'd had so much to drink, I ran right into the guardrail on Butner Road."

I rushed through the house and out the front door. There in the driveway sat my brand-new Honda, the front passenger side folded in, scuffed with white paint, headlight shattered. The now-familiar heaviness pressed down on my chest and shoulders. Turning back into the house, I found Ross sitting on the living room couch, next to a bed pillow and blanket.

"You slept out here last night?" I asked.

"Yeah. I figured we could both use the space," he said.

I walked over and sat down on the opposite end of the couch, pulling the blanket up over my legs.

"Did anyone see you crash?"

"Nope. Not a car or cop in sight."

"Talk about dumb luck," I said, shaking my head. "Barely a mile away from home, and no witnesses."

"Aren't you going to get angry?" Ross asked. "Go ahead. Don't hold back. I deserve it."

Try as I might, I couldn't muster any rage. It seemed pointless. In that moment, any respect I held for Ross dropped away, like overripe apples hitting the ground with a thud, then left to rot. For several months, I had wanted him to be valiant and strong so I could relax in my confusion. Instead, he had proven himself inept at keeping a secret and lacking the sense to stay home when he was drunk. There was no sense relying on him. I was on my own.

"No more yelling," I said. "I'm too tired to fight."

I put both arms around my knees and started rocking back and forth.

"But when you have that meeting with the elders, I think you should start by telling them about this," I said, then formed a mock smile and blinked both eyes.

He nodded his head in agreement. "Guess I deserved that one."

I stood up to leave.

"Stop," he said, and grabbed my hand. "Please sit down for a minute. I have something important to say."

He kept hold of my hand, steering me to sit next to him. The tangy smell of alcohol and warm skin floated through his crumpled shirt. My instinct was to pull away, but intuition told me to take a breath and sit tight.

"Linda, I've been up all night. Yes, I acted like an idiot, and not just last night." He took a deep breath. "I know you've been going through a lot of soul searching lately. And I know that you have doubts about our faith. What you don't know is that ever since you brought it up, I, too, have been soul searching, checking the teachings, reviewing where I stand."

"I didn't know that." I was genuinely surprised, touched, even.

"I can honestly say, unlike you, I don't have any doubts. None at all."

He continued to hold my hand as he spoke, and his palms were getting hot.

"You've never said it out loud, but I suspect you've thought about becoming completely inactive. That's the direction you're headed, anyway."

"Yes," I said.

"I love you so much, I even thought about whether or not I could become inactive, too. But I know in my heart that this is The Truth, and I'm sticking with it. I empathize with your predicament. I really do. And I know that putting up with me hasn't made it any easier. And I want you to know"—he paused and took a deep breath—"that I have struggled a lot with how to help you. And it seems to me that you don't really want my help, or anyone else's, for that matter. That fierce, independent streak of yours has gotten the better of you."

For the first time in months, I felt as if he acknowledged the depths of my desperation, even if he didn't fully understand it. As he faced his limits and admitted them aloud for the first time, his demeanor was one of surrender, shoulders rolled down, head hanging. And for several moments we sat together in the muck of it all.

"And I'm wondering," he continued, "if you wouldn't be better off, happier, with some space between us."

I pulled my hand away. "What are you suggesting?"

"Divorce."

Saying the word out loud opened up a black hole we would never emerge from.

"Are you serious?"

"You tell me," Ross answered. "We're going in two different directions. I hate it. If we carry on this way, we're just going to make each other miserable."

His frankness was mystifying. Witnesses sanction divorce only if one party has committed adultery. Since unfaithfulness was not the issue, Ross's suggestion was completely out of the blue, particularly coming from someone who had just declared his commitment to the teachings.

The radio alarm clicked on in the bedroom, my six o'clock wake-up call. I couldn't think of a more absurd way to start the day.

"It's been a tough night, and I need to go to work," I said, cupping his face in both of my hands. "We can talk about this later."

One hour later, dressed for work, I bolted through heavy rain toward my wrecked car. The driver's door opened after a stiff tug on the handle. The car was drivable but lacked its previous luster. As I backed out of the driveway, the tire rubbed the wheel well at the sharpest part of the turn.

Joining the queue of traffic on Skyline Boulevard, I welcomed the light of day and the solitude of my half-hour commute.

Just three days earlier, sitting in the safe enclave of my therapist's office, she had asked me to imagine my "dream life."

"What do you want more of?" she asked.

My first answer came without hesitation. "The exhilaration of expanding my skills through my work."

Each new client or project allowed me to discover new things about myself. It was a joyride for me, and I definitely wanted more.

"What do you want less of?" was my therapist's next question.

That answer also came clearly and without hesitation. "Freedom from the rigid JW routine. I don't want my spiritual value tied to how many hours I spend in field service, or whether or not I show up at the Kingdom Hall."

In that small room, where it was okay to utter the most blasphemous words, I then said, "Basically, I want to be left alone, to sort out what I believe, about God, spirituality, the world." My voice trailed off there. Then I added, "Without interference or having to explain or justify it to anyone, including my husband. And if I want to work late, so be it. If I want to rest, so be it."

As I passed the first billboards at the city limit, my windshield wipers kept a pounding rhythm. Next came a moment of lucid precision as I realized Ross's words were a gift. He had proposed one choice—divorce—that would grant me that freedom.

It all seemed so clear and benevolent. He deserved a nice, subservient, "Christian" wife who would join him, as I once had, in the intricate lifestyle of a true believer. If I stuck around as I was, his relationships with the community would be impacted, as would our marriage.

For me, divorce was a free pass to avoid the hassles of rebuilding a union addled by different dreams. Instead I could use my energies elsewhere and turn my inquisitive mind to grand explorations of the world at large. I'd spent my life a bit afraid of the world and how its influences might lead me astray, but that distrust or fear no longer gripped me. The appeal of a divorce was as much about curiosity and participation as it was about securing the mental and emotional space to sort through religious doubts. Instead of condemning the world with my doorstep sermons, perhaps I could open up to its offerings and find an expanded version of truth I could live with.

A smile came across my face as I made the final turn toward the US Bank Tower. My car exterior was ravaged, but the stereo worked fine. It still held the CD Ross had apparently been playing the night before. As if by magic, Gloria Estefan serenaded me:

Get on your feet
Stand up and take some action

As I veered into the parking garage, I started singing along. In the days that followed, this melody became my personal anthem.

Two weeks later, I sat Ross down in the living room and informed him of my plans. After months of fretting and deliberation, I had turned a corner and set my course toward freedom. My first step was to retain a divorce attorney. Next, I signed a lease for a one-bedroom apartment. I scheduled the movers and planned to leave in just two weeks more. There was no turning back.

"My attorney suggested we take a shot at dividing up our assets and liabilities together," I said. I felt worldly and brash, hearing myself say "my attorney" out loud for the first time and enjoying the new feeling of power it brought me.

Ross just looked at me, blinked, then stood up, walked down the hall to his office, and returned with a legal pad.

"Okay," he said, sitting back down on the couch, removing the top from the pen. "What do you want to keep? Or, should I say, what do you want to take?"

Aside from the verbal jab, he showed no emotion. I sat still for several moments, marveling at his composure. Inside I felt buoyant and carefree, relieved to have unveiled my stealthy plans. It reminded me of those scenes from *National Geographic* where a once captive and sedated zebra is released back into the wild, open plains. You watch a few long seconds while it stumbles, takes a breath, gets its bearings, and runs for its life. Then you hope for the best.

"I'd like to keep the stereo," he said. "And I'm not giving up this house."

The house represented my past, the place where I had endured the most distressing period of my life to date. I saw only weeds in the backyard, the list of projects we'd not yet gotten around to. *Good riddance*, I thought. Walking away from it was easy, like taking off a coat that's grown tight around the shoulders.

It didn't take long to sort things out. There was no quibbling over who got what table or painting or loan to pay off; I'd already given thought to the list, and it seemed like Ross had, too. When it was done, Ross mixed us both a drink and we ordered a pizza. It was Saturday night, and neither of us had anything else to do but hang out with each other. Curled up in sweatpants on separate ends of the couch, we sipped our drinks and stared holes in the carpet.

"I'll call Jerry and request a meeting tomorrow," Ross said, getting up from the couch. "It's important to me that the elders hear this from us first."

I agreed. It felt like the honorable thing to do, and I had nothing to lose. Ross would finally get me to meet with the elders, but now the terms were acceptable. I'd made my decision and had no fears of being dissuaded.

The next day, Ross got behind the wheel of the repaired Honda without saying a word. I took the passenger seat, and we rode in silence toward the Kingdom Hall, taking the usual route down Butner Road. As we waited at the stop sign, my eyes came to rest on the guardrail he'd crashed into a few weeks earlier. It was stable and steady, peppered with the black rubber marks of many close calls. I squeezed the door handle a little more tightly. *This is the last time we'll ever go the Hall together*—a sobering thought that beckoned an unexpected melancholy. So many parts of my life were about to end.

Ross turned the Honda toward the Kingdom Hall and parked next to Jerry's Taurus. I wasn't expecting to see the second car, which I recognized as Vince Lloyd's. Jerry must have asked him to join us. Ross hadn't been expecting anyone else, or, if he had, he hadn't mentioned it. The door was unlocked, but the Hall was dark and hollow, except for light emanating from a smaller meeting room in the rear of the building. There, we found both men. Jerry was setting four chairs in a circle. Diminutive in height and round in girth, he bounced around like a ball. Every part of him was round: his head, his cheeks, eyes like coins behind round wire glasses, waist spilling over either side of his belt. This gave him a jolly persona, rolling along with no sharp edges to harm whatever or whomever he came in contact with. Vince was plugging in a space heater to take the chill off. He was long-limbed and frail, pushing his wire-frame glasses up the rim of his nose as he stood.

It was midafternoon, and they were still wearing suits and ties from the morning services. Ross had gone to the morning meeting without me and still had on his suit pants and dress shirt, jacket and tie now discarded. I'd spent the morning browsing the local furniture stores, excitedly filling my mind with decorating ideas for my new apartment—and, later, collecting my thoughts for this meeting. The fact that Jerry had invited a second elder added a level of formality and seriousness. We were close to both men and their families. Vince's fifteen-year-old daughter, Lucy, had always looked up to me. In her teen innocence, she had declared she wanted to grow up to be just like me, "smart and nice." Now I cringed at the trite description. Having always been the good girl on the right side of the law, I was entering uncharted territory with this conversation.

The mood was solemn. There were no warm welcomes or handshakes. No one smiled. Jerry sat down and motioned for us to take our seats. His eyes scanned my face and movements as I sat. His gaze lingered for a long moment on my blue jeans. It was a deliberate departure for me to be dressed casually. Did he read it as disrespect or defiance? Vince sat down next to me and raised his shoulders briefly to unbutton his gabardine jacket, one I recognized as an anniversary gift from his wife.

"Ross tells us you've decided to end your marriage," Jerry said.

"Yes," I said. "I've hired an attorney." There was that phrase again—"an attorney." It was getting easier to say.

"And what, may I ask, are the grounds of the petition?" Vince asked.

I wondered why it was any of his business but answered anyway.

"Irreconcilable differences," I said. Ross was sitting next to me, elbows resting on each knee, head bowed, looking down at the floor.

"And how long have you been married?" Jerry asked.

"Coming up on ten years," I said.

"And what does that mean, exactly, 'irreconcilable differences'?" asked Vince.

The tension in his voice triggered my defenses. This was a time to speak the truth if ever there was one.

"It means I'm not happy with my marriage. I haven't been happy for a long time. I'm tired of feeling mismatched. I want to be free, to live my life as I please. I know that may sound selfish, but that is what I want."

Saying this out loud felt liberating. Declaring my plans gave them substance.

"Is there anything else we should know about?" asked Jerry. "Or any*one* else?"

It was the one question Ross had failed to ask me. I understood the intent behind Jerry's question. He wanted to determine if I had broken any biblical laws. Was I an adulteress? That would have turned this from a family squabble into a judicial matter.

"There is no one else," I said. "Truly." The vulnerability of my situation hit me with a fresh awareness. I was leaving the safe haven of my known world, and I had no committed companions. While I'd been sincerely enjoying my time with coworkers and cultivating new friendships, much of that provided a convenient distraction from being alone. None of those new relationships had withstood the test of time. To my horror, a coil of pressure released in my chest, and I broke down and started to cry. It was difficult to let them—or anyone—see how upset and afraid I was. Grappling with loneliness was something that would come much later; at this moment, I was struck only by the fear that there was a slim chance I was making a grave mistake, one that I would regret for the rest of my life.

My sobs were the only sound in the room. Jerry reached in his jacket and passed me a handkerchief with his short, round fingers. He looked perplexed, his forehead rippled with worry. I accepted the cloth and slowed my breathing as I unfolded it. It seemed an eternity before I was composed enough to speak.

"I've been very despondent and believe my best chance for happiness is to move on," I said, then blew my nose.

"And what are your plans?" he asked me.

"To live," I said. "To enjoy life. To have free time and the space to ponder the meaning of it all. I don't know if Ross has already told you this, but I've found an apartment close to the city and plan to move in a few weeks."

"Have you completely forgotten Jehovah?" asked Vince.

"If Jehovah is the loving God we talk about, I think he'll cut me some slack. I plan to take a break from meetings, service, everything. I've been questioning many things I believe, not taking anything for granted, and am looking for the space to sort it all out. You can't imagine how much I've thought about this."

All three men were looking at me in a stunned stupor. The tearful crack in my armor may have given them hope of reaching me, but I already had enough sense to trust the small voice inside me that said, *Trust it, you got this, keep going.*

"You won't be seeing me around here for a while," I said. "If at all."

"You're playing with fire, my dear," said Jerry. "Your husband can't be expected to wait around and put his life on hold while you follow the whims of your heart."

That comment tripped a wire inside me, and suddenly my sadness flared into anger. The space heater had done its job, and I was feeling hot and light-headed, in need of electrolytes.

"No one's asking him to wait around," I said. "That's why I'm getting a divorce. I hold no hope for this marriage to continue and no interest in working through our differences." In Witness lingo, this was about as bad an attitude as you could display.

"You are both young and vibrant people," Jerry said. "No matter what the law of the land says, you are still bound by your wedding vows in Jehovah's eyes. You well know there are only two ways to scripturally sever those ties."

Death or adultery. Yes, we all knew about the double bind. It didn't even need to be said aloud.

"It's only a matter of time before one or both of you steps outside the bounds of marriage," Jerry continued. "If you persist in doing this, you open yourself and Ross up to a lot of heartache."

Angry tears rolled down my cheeks. I was being cast as the villain. Ross was looking down. We were separate units now, expected to answer separate questions. Why wasn't anyone interrogating him?

"There has already been a lot of heartache. You can't imagine how unhappy I've been—*we've* been," I said. It was not a loud, biting unhappiness, but a subtle knowing that I was no longer in the right place, no longer willing to overlook some obvious truths for a life and a marriage that were "good enough," characterized by the slow burn of resignation that makes you numb to joy and pleasure.

Jerry's shoulders slumped. "This is very sad," he said, shaking his head. "I sensed you two were struggling, but I only get involved if people ask. If you'd come to me sooner, maybe I could have helped you."

"This will disappoint a lot of people," Vince said, looking owlish with his wire rims and puffy frown. Perhaps he was thinking of his wife, Sarah, a good friend of mine, and Lucy.

"So many have looked up to you, and not just in our congregation, but throughout the city."

"I've disappointed very *few* people in my short life, Vince," I said. "I've wasted so much time. Guess what? There could be advantages to disappointing others. It's not always a bad thing. These people you speak of don't have to live in my skin day after day." There was a growing edge in my voice. "They'll think whatever they think about me, feel whatever they will feel. But then they'll go on with their day. Meanwhile, I'm the one who suffers. Trust me, gentlemen, I've thought about this six ways to Sunday, for weeks and months, and am very clear that this is the right path for me."

I was implacable, and both men saw my calm determination.

Vince reached into his briefcase, pulled out his Bible, and flipped its pages to a specific verse.

"Linda," he said in a stern monotone, "this conversation reminds me of Paul's prophecy in 2 Timothy, chapter 3."

Then he read directly from the Bible:

"But know this, that in the last days critical times hard to deal with will be here. For men will be lovers of themselves, lovers of money, self assuming, haughty, blasphemers, disobedient to parents, unthankful, disloyal, having no natural affection, not open to any agreement, slanderers, without self-control, fierce, without love of goodness, betrayers, headstrong, puffed up with pride, lovers of pleasure rather than lovers of God, having a form of godly devotion but proving false to its power, and from these turn away."

He paused and placed the Bible in his lap, moving in slow motion to let the words sink in. He looked me in the eye and said, "By your actions, you fulfill this Scripture."

The words landed like knuckles in my belly, steeling my breath. In the myriad times I'd heard that verse, I had always imagined groups of baleful, wretched people, worldly people, *other* people. Vince was now applying it to *me*. I'd made the transition from being one of the humble sheep to being a stiff-necked, stubborn goat and empathized with the latter. How smug I had been. Was this an official reproving? I hadn't broken any biblical laws, so there was nothing they could do but shake their heads. I was voluntarily taking a break, which was my prerogative. An unwise one in their eyes, yes, and potentially scandalous. I knew the elders would not talk outside their ranks, but people would wonder all kinds of things and there would be talk. However, I was unofficially removing myself, so there was no more for them to do but shame and scare me.

"Is there anything else?" I asked, defiant, eyes clear. I folded the handkerchief and returned it to Jerry.

"May we visit you after you settle in to your new apartment?" Jerry inquired. "We care about you and would like to check in from time to time to see how you are."

His kindness was a sharp contrast with Vince's denunciation, and it caught me off guard. I noticed my inclination to say yes, to please and appease him, and then thought better of it.

"Jerry," I said, "I appreciate that, but I know where to find you."

I had deliberately chosen an apartment complex that had a locked security gate. No one could reach my front door unannounced.

"As for you," Jerry said, looking at Ross for the first time, "we will meet with you again later. This situation is a reflection on you as the spiritual head of the house, and you have failed to 'preside over your household in a fine manner.' We will review your ministerial privileges in the congregation and get back to you."

Ross nodded, passive and accepting whatever discipline might come. I wanted to stand up in his defense and remind them he was not responsible for me. I'd made these choices of my own free will with eyes wide open. Ross shouldn't be punished for that. But I stopped myself from speaking. Things were changing. We both needed to stand on our own two feet.

"Shall we close our meeting with a prayer?" Jerry asked.

I couldn't imagine sitting still for more.

"Thank you, no." And I turned to Ross, who looked at me like I'd gone mad. "I'll wait for you outside."

It was a shocking change for me to decline their alms, but I was finally freed from their opinions. It was the first time any of us had seen this side of me. I was opening myself to new standards of spirituality. For the first time in my life, I was doing exactly what I wanted, without concern for pleasing others. It was exhilarating. I felt larger than life. And I was terrified. *Perhaps I'm getting too full of myself. Please don't let them be right.* But I had to get out of the room, and so I left, retracing my steps through the dark and vacant foyer, welcoming the fresh air and light of the outdoors.

Chapter 6

That a marriage ends is less than ideal; but all things end under heaven, and if temporality is held to be invalidation, then nothing real succeeds.

—John Updike

"News will travel fast," Ross said, as he drove us home. "We should tell your parents as soon as possible."

His face was drawn, and his hands gripped the steering wheel.

I'd been thinking the same thing. Our conversation with the elders was just the first in a long line of confessions and announcements.

"I'll call them when I get home and see if I can't stop by later today or tomorrow after work," I said.

I could hardly believe this was happening. In the past twenty-four hours, I had unleashed a plan and was headed downstream, moving fast, bouncing between the rapids.

"I think we should tell your parents together," said Ross. He looked straight ahead as he drove.

"Whatever for?" I asked. "I'd think you'd want to avoid that conversation."

"Don't get me wrong, I dread this whole damn thing. But it feels like the right thing to do. I might as well face the firing squad and get it over with."

"Fine," I said. There was a long pause. I had no problem with Ross joining me. I wasn't going to say anything to them that he couldn't hear or didn't already know. It somehow felt right to go together, and he was entitled to manage his relationship with my parents however he wished.

"If it's okay with you," I said, "I'd rather not be there when you tell your mom."

"Fine," he said.

"I'm going to have my hands full with the rest of my family."

"I said it was fine."

We walked in the front door of the house. Ross headed to his office and closed the door. I dialed my parents.

Dad answered the phone.

"You sound out of breath," I said.

"Hey, Lindy," Dad said. "We're just leaving for the Rivers'. They're having a bunch of people over for dinner. We were getting in the car when I heard the phone ring."

"Okay, then, Dad," I said, speaking more quickly, relieved that he'd answered the phone instead of Mom, "I'll let you go, but are you and Mom going to be around tomorrow after work?"

Whenever we found ourselves in their neighborhood, we popped in unannounced to see my parents. They welcomed spontaneous visits. We would raid the refrigerator, open a beer or make some tea, tear open a bag of chips, and sit down with them at the kitchen table. But we never did that on a weeknight and I wanted to be sure they'd be home. I did my best to sound nonchalant. Calling ahead added a level of formality none of us was used to.

"Yeah, sure," he said.

"Ross and I are going to be over that way, and we thought we'd stop by."

He did not question me the way Mom would. The less said, the better. I didn't want curious minds set in motion. If I said we had news to share, they might think we were coming to announce a pregnancy, and no good could come from that.

"Okay. Have fun, and say hi to Mom for us," I said.

"For us." I'd have to get used to not saying that anymore.

That night I lay awake into the wee hours, unable to sleep in anticipation of the talk with my parents. My request for a divorce would astonish them, but that was the least of my worries. That news would pale in comparison with my plans for a break from The Truth. Exhausted by these worries, I fluffed my pillows and slipped more deeply between my cool sheets, pulling the covers to my chin.

The next day, Ross and I carpooled to work. At quitting time, he left his office on the northeast side and parked the Honda at an open meter on the corner near my office. For some unspoken reason, as I approached the car, he got out from behind the wheel and sat in the passenger seat. Perhaps he wanted to emphasize it was I who was driving this process. This was my car—the car that I had bought and we had agreed I would keep. I got in and drove south in silence down the I-5 corridor to Tigard, where my parents lived.

Following the serpentine taillights through the Terwilliger curves, my hands were slippery from perspiration and ice cold around the steering wheel. I'd spent the day distracted, mentally rehearsing what I would say, anticipating my parents' shock and disappointment. They would implore me to come to my senses, especially when I told them I was not only leaving my marriage but also questioning my religion. One was bad enough, but the two together would be hard for them to grasp. In some ways, it was hard for me to grasp. Throughout that day, I had slipped into a recurring fantasy in which they embraced me and accepted my plan, no questions asked, and consoled me as only parents can, nodding their heads and frowning as I poured out my heart and told them how unhappy I'd become. In this imagined scenario, I started to cry, Mom rocked me gently and told me to shush, and Dad said, "Everything will be all right." They saw my despair and didn't try to dissuade me. They encouraged any change that would bring me relief.

My car tires crunched onto the gravel of my parents' driveway. The garage door was open, and Dad was inside, car hood up, pouring Pennzoil into the Ford.

"Hello, Lindy," he said, as Ross and I walked past him, toward the back door of the house. "Hey, Ross."

"Hi, Dad," we replied in unison. He was casual and happy, wiping his hands on a shop rag, not suspecting a thing. At that moment, I wanted to abort the whole mission, just forget it all and talk about the weather or our plans for the summer, anything but what was really going on. Ross and I had agreed I would take the lead.

"I'm right behind you," Dad said. "Your mom's just inside."

Ross opened the back door and stepped into the dining room.

"Hello, Ruth," he shouted to announce our presence. I entered behind him and walked to the fridge. He immediately took a seat at the dining table, his usual spot, the place to the left of my dad's.

"Hi, kids," Mom called up from the basement. "Make yourselves at home. I'm hanging clothes from the dryer."

Out of habit, I stood gazing into the open fridge, wanting something to do besides wait. But I wasn't hungry. I felt neither full nor empty, and oddly disconnected, as if I'd never need to eat again, floating through life, nourishment unnecessary.

"Do you want anything?" I asked Ross.

"Nope," he said. He was even-tempered, but I could tell he was nervous by the quick way he sat down. He was ready to call the meeting to order, deliver the news, and get out of there. Who could blame him? I felt the same way. There was a consoling camaraderie in being there together. We were both facing the firing squad.

Mom emerged from the basement through the door at the top of the stairs, near one end of the kitchen. She was still in the clothes she'd worn to work—a wool navy skirt, blouse, and button-down vest—but had traded her high heels for house slippers.

"Such a nice surprise to see you," she said. "Dad didn't say what was bringing you this way on a Monday night."

"Oh, this and that," I said, turning to look at her as she walked to the sink and washed her hands. I closed the fridge.

Dad came in from the garage, washed his hands, and stood next to Mom.

I joined Ross at the table. We looked at each other and then at them. As their familial repartee wound down, there was a pause. They realized we were quietly observing them. I could feel my pulse in my throat.

"Do you guys want something to snack on," asked Mom, "or some tea?"

Ross was long-faced and forlorn. His lethargy and my pensiveness were beginning to register with them.

"No, Mom," Ross said. Mom and Dad glanced at each other.

"We have something to tell you," I said. "Please sit down."

They both took their usual places at the table. The only sound was the furnace pushing heat through the vent near my feet. I just sat there. I'd rehearsed about five different lead-ins to my news, but everything I'd practiced felt like dust on my tongue. Could I open my mouth and blow it out like a whistle?

"What is it, dear?" Mom asked. She reached out and put her warm hand around my wrist. Dad was leaning into the table, looking at me.

"Two days ago, I asked him"—I pointed at Ross while looking at Mom—"for a divorce."

Mom pulled her hand away. Dad scowled, and his eyes drooped down at the corners. Ross sat in resignation.

"I've hired an attorney." I stanched the fear and went on, though I felt as if someone else were talking. "The papers are being drawn up. The grounds are irreconcilable differences. In the state of Oregon, as long as the petition is not contested— and Ross assures me it won't be—the divorce will be final within three months of the judge's favorable ruling."

Dad looked at Ross. Ross looked back, shook his head, and shrugged. Mom sat in stunned silence, looking at me, then at Ross, then at my dad.

"Yesterday we told the elders," Ross said. "Linda has found an apartment near Skyline and will be moving out at the end of this month."

"But why?" Mom asked in disbelief. Dad's eyes were soft and curious as he looked at me.

"Oh, Mom, there are so many reasons. I don't want to get into it all now. But I haven't been happy for a long time. And there's more." I was on a roll and needed to get this last part out, the hardest admission of all.

"I can't imagine," said Mom.

"I've been having doubts about The Truth." The words barely squeezed through my tight throat.

"The Truth?" Mom said. Dad—the one person who might have defended me a few months earlier—looked puzzled. I was feeling light-headed and woozy, hoping I wouldn't have to explain further but knowing I would.

"Yes, Mom, The Truth." I took a deep breath. Unlike at our meeting with the elders, I felt no urge to cry. I was having difficulty connecting to the sadness and confusion I was about to report on. It all felt very distant and exhausting, like a sound coming from another room that you can't quite make out.

"Months ago I started taking a second look at everything I believe, not taking anything for granted. I'm unclear and unsettled about many things, but what I do know is that I'm tired of the way The Truth condemns people—good people. People I know. It separates me from them in a way that doesn't feel good."

"*Doesn't feel good?*" she echoed. "Part of being a true Christian means we often won't *feel* good. You know that." She shook her head. "This highfalutin job of yours has put you in *way* too much contact with worldly people." She turned away from me and spoke to Dad. "This is what happens when you let your guard down."

"No, Mom." I collected myself as she turned back to me. "It's much deeper than that. I've noticed a deep spiritual questioning of everything I've been taught and a yearning for something more in life. I want some room to move around, the space to explore other beliefs."

"What does that mean? I don't even know what you're saying." She looked baffled. Dad was focusing his gaze on the center of the table.

"Yesterday I told the elders I was taking a break."

"A break?"

"Yes, Mom, a break. From everything—meetings, service, study. Everything."

Dad closed his eyes and shook his head. Mom's brown eyes darted across my face and eyes, searching in wonder. Then she turned to Ross.

"What do you think of all this, Ross?" she asked.

He frowned and shook his head. "I think it's terrible. A great tragedy. Things haven't been great between us for a while, but I never expected this. And she's got it all figured out: an attorney, an apartment, all the answers."

Mom nodded. "That's Lindy. Ever since she was little, she's always been way ahead of us."

"And," Dad added, "when she gets her mind made up about something, you'd best get out of her way."

Mom turned back to me. "This is a good man you have here, and you're going to let him go?"

I didn't answer. It made no sense to stay in a marriage that tethered me to a religion I doubted, a religion that demanded allegiance to another person even after I'd outgrown both.

"Lindy, honey, this makes you both so vulnerable to trouble." I knew she was saying this because she cared, but the more she talked, the more I ratcheted down. "Before you take such extreme measures, perhaps you can let the elders help you."

"It's past that, Mom," I said.

"Is there someone else?" she asked.

"No," I said. "When will this community realize that boredom and unhappiness can be enough of a reason to end a marriage?" They could also be worthy signals to leave a religion.

The furnace clicked off. We all sat there. Mom looked at Dad.

"Do you have anything you want to ask her?" she said to him.

"I'm sorry you've been so unhappy," he said.

"Before you go too far with this," Mom continued, "I want

you to talk to your sister. Lory will tell you how hard it is to go through a divorce. Don't you remember what a terrible time that was for her?"

"Yes," I said. My sister married her first husband when she was nineteen, and by her late twenties she'd grown very unhappy. As the marriage lost its luster, she had an affair with her boss. When the marriage ended, the congregation elders officially reproved Lory for her sin. She was very sorry for what she'd done, ended the affair, quit her job, and moved back to my parents' home until she could get back on her feet emotionally and financially, but especially spiritually. That had all happened about ten years earlier, but her story continued to fuel and validate all fears that working full-time in the world exposed a person to real dangers.

"This is a bit different, Mom," I said. Lory had never expressed doubts about The Truth; she'd merely become distracted by life.

"Of course everyone always thinks their own situation is different," Mom said.

"For starters," I said, "there is no one else. I have not been unfaithful."

"Okay," Mom said, and her tone softened. She shifted to a different tack. "I understand if you're unhappy in your marriage. Your father and I have had our unhappy periods, so we understand how difficult that can be. But, Lindy, honey, don't give up on your relationship with Jehovah."

I could feel my entire body tightening, my defenses building, and my voice was rigid and controlled when I responded, "When did I say I'd given up on my relationship with Jehovah? I only said I was taking a break from the meetings. Those are two separate things. Getting some space from an unhappy marriage and the relentless routine of meetings feels like a smart and healthy thing to do. It's an act of self-preservation."

"Self-preservation or selfishness?" Mom said. "Getting space is going to hurt a lot of people and will only take you further away from Jehovah. You'll only get more caught up in your job and being with worldly coworkers. It's bound to take its toll. It already has. Yes, you must promise me you will talk to your sister, and soon."

To appease her, I said I would.

"And, Lindy, you've gotta be careful out there in the big, bad world. You are going to find out that your only true friends are in The Truth. You can't count on worldly people for lasting friendship. They'll let you down every single time. It's just the way it is."

Dad was twitching his lips. He turned to Ross. "Ross, what are your plans?"

Ross half laughed and shook his head. "I don't know, Frank. Survive. Get a roommate so I can afford the mortgage. See what happens."

"Well, you're always welcome here," Dad said.

"Yes," Mom said. "You've been a good son-in-law. Have you told your mom yet?"

"That will happen tomorrow," Ross said. "I'm taking her out for lunch."

"I'm sure she'll be shocked," Mom said, then turned back to me. "Lindy, that's another horrible thing about this: it's a scourge on Jehovah's name and reflects poorly on our family. What will Elaine think when she finds out about this?"

"I think she'll be sad and feel protective of Ross and jump at the chance to support him," I said. "I doubt she'll give a second thought to Jehovah." I was growing impatient with her predictable line of thinking. "It's time for us to go," I added.

Everyone stood and hugged goodbye. It was difficult for me to read my father's emotions, to tell if he was sad *for* me or disappointed *in* me, but when we embraced, he held on for a few extra moments.

"Call your sister" were my mother's parting words.

⌒⌒

The next day, Lory called with an invitation. "Come over," she said. "We'll sit in the sunroom and you can tell me what's going on." I sensed her capacity to empathize with my unhappiness. My aching heart was drawn to her warmth and support. But there was only so much I could take in one week, and I told her I wouldn't come until Saturday. That would give me time to recuperate from the polemic of the previous week.

Ross and I found new ways to move around each other in the house. We were both considerate yet clumsy, experimenting with our independence, trying not to get in each other's way. He started sleeping on a futon in his office. We stopped our occasional carpooling to work, and I left off calling to tell him when I'd be home or to discuss dinner plans. Tuesday night, I made a point of arriving home after he'd left for the Kingdom Hall. He'd left a note in the kitchen, encouraging me to eat the leftover chicken. I started a fire with a Presto log, and then I sat for a while, sipping a glass of wine, staring at the flames, my mind uncoiling with each flicker of light. After eating, I put Gloria Estefan on the stereo and danced in the living room to "Get on Your Feet," replaying it several times until my clothes were damp with perspiration. I relished the huge release of energy and felt just as spiritual as—and much happier than—I would have felt sitting through another Bible lesson. By the time Ross came home, I was fast asleep in bed.

Chapter 7

❦

I'm not intolerant. I just know what it says in the Scriptures.
—Jesse Helms

My sister's home was tucked behind another house on Oak Street, just a few blocks from my parents'. I walked down the short paved sidewalk and entered through the back door.

I found Lory in the bathroom. Two pieces of the white floor tiling were displaced, and tubes of grout and caulking were open and resting on a folded newspaper. She was wearing rubber gloves.

"Just give me a minute," she said. "These tiles came loose, and I want to let them set while we visit."

I was grateful for the distraction, which allowed me to settle in. I wasn't sure what would happen here between us, but I knew she would have some choice words for me about getting a divorce and taking a sabbatical from The Truth. Lory's role in this drama was to talk some sense into me.

I looked up to Lory and was proud she was my sister, and I never doubted her love for me. But growing up, six years apart in age, we always seemed to be moving to a slightly different beat. We never sat for hours in our pajamas, brushing each other's hair, talking about boys, giggling, sharing our darkest fears and shimmering hopes. I always sensed she had drawn an unspoken emotional line that I didn't dare breach, so I never felt a sustained closeness to her.

Regardless, Lory was one of the most intelligent people I

knew, the kind of person you could see becoming a revolutionary brain surgeon or physicist. Instead, when she got out of high
school in the early '70s, she immediately started pioneering and
supported herself with part-time housekeeping jobs. After all,
Armageddon was coming and all prophecies pointed to these
being the Last Days of the worldly system. Her mental acuity
became focused on the Scriptures, and she spent hours studying
theocratic literature and researching topics in the encyclopedic
Aid to Bible Understanding and other Watchtower Society tomes.

Now, as my sister and I walked into her kitchen, I saw that
she'd set out two sets of teacups and shot glasses, and a full
bottle of Crown Royal Black. Steam was languishing over a
teakettle on the stove. A small plate held tea biscuits and my
favorite chocolate-covered toffee.

"It looks like you've prepared for all contingencies," I said.
"Booze, caffeine, chocolate, and sugar."

"That's right," Lory said.

She wasn't the sort to fuss over me, and I was surprised
and touched that she would have taken the time to make these
preparations. It lessened the knot I felt in my belly. *No. That
is exactly what she wants—for you to relax. You're dealing with a
smart cookie here. Keep your wits about you.* I took a deep breath.

She surprised me by pouring whiskey into both shot glasses.
My sister had never had a taste or physical tolerance for alcohol.

"Would you like some tea?" she asked, and I said I would.
She pulled a tray from the cupboard, lined it with a cloth napkin, and started placing the cups, glasses, and treats on it.

"I thought we'd talk in the sunroom," she said, pouring hot
water over tea bags.

"Fine," I said, complying with her plans, a sense of both
dread and guilt coming over me. She was going to a lot of trouble to receive me hospitably, and I knew in my heart she would
be unsuccessful at dissuading me. It would take a long time for
my family to accept that. Just the thought of it made me tired. I
grabbed the bottle of Crown Royal and followed my sister past
the dining room and into the beaming sunroom at the front of

the house. She set the tray down on the coffee table, and we both sat down on the couch.

"We've never done this before," I said.

"Sit in this room?" Lory said.

"That too," I said. "But I don't think I've ever had tea and whiskey at the same time, and I can't say I'd ever have imagined you'd be the one offering it to me."

I took my first sip from the shot glass, and Lory did the same.

"Okay," I said. "Go ahead and say what you have to say. I'm listening."

"I'm not sure I know what to say," she said, exchanging her shot glass for the cup of tea. "I can't say I was surprised when Mom told me about you and Ross. You two got married so young, and I know what a drag it can be to be married to an immature, overly emotional person."

Lory had never thought much of Ross and always kept her distance from him. Losing him as a brother-in-law would be no great loss for her. I think he reminded her of her first husband. They had similar carefree traits and just happened to have become friends during the time of her divorce. That made Ross suspect to Lory, and he never outgrew her bias.

"Ever since you bought your house, you've been under a lot of pressure," she said. "And renovating the kitchen so quickly was a mistake. Borrowing the money to make that happen only caused you more financial pressure." She took another sip of tea. "A new house, new car, new kitchen—no wonder you had to work so much."

She didn't say any of this with harshness, but more as a resigned observation. I had to admit, there was a thread of truth in what she said. We'd spent a lot of money in the previous two years, and how to manage our finances was a source of strain for Ross and me. Still, I resented her conclusion that money was at the heart of my woes.

"It would be easy to compare our failed marriages, but you may wish to remember that you don't have all the information," I said, pleased by my boldness. She was falling into the easy trap of comparing my situation to what she'd gone through almost ten years earlier, making judgments and assumptions along the way. "I'm not doing my job to keep the wolves at bay, Lory. I enjoy what I do for a living. My work is more than just a paycheck to me."

She shook her head. "Which is exactly what I'm afraid of," she said. "This whole work scene has gone to your head. I'm sure you're good at what you do, but is it worth risking your life?"

Her eyes got all watery, and she looked at me with a combination of warmth and fear that I had never seen before.

"Lindy," she continued, her voice soft and sibilant, "you've never done anything wrong in your whole life. Ever. You've always been a good girl. You've got a great reputation. Everyone looks up to you." Her voice trailed off, and a tear rolled down her face. She reached for a napkin from the tray and wiped her cheeks. Seeing her this openly emotional was unsettling. I froze for a moment, not knowing what to do, wondering if I should reach out and try to comfort her. My throat ached as I took another sip of whiskey and noticed I was also getting teary-eyed. It was disarming to see my sister express such explicit and genuine emotion and care for me. We'd never talked this frankly before.

"You need to understand," she said, "that the community will never forget this. Even when you straighten yourself out, you'll always be the person who strayed. It changes the way people look at you."

That was the moment I realized how much my sister had suffered during her own spiritual crisis. I was embarrassed to remember how I'd been one of the people who'd judged her. I was in my early twenties and every inch the Christian soldier, zealous and pioneering. When our family learned of her affair, we all lined up to meet with her one-on-one. Shortly after her indiscretions were revealed, she did what we all considered the honorable thing by ending the relationship, repenting for her sins, and turning her life around. She was single for several years, then found a loving relationship with Ove and was now an elder's wife. I had assumed her troubles were old news and long forgotten. Still, she seemed to be carrying that burden from the past. In small ways, I had helped her through that rough time, and now she was attempting to return the favor.

"Why didn't you just leave The Truth?" I asked. "Did you ever question it through all of this?"

"Not for one minute," she said. "I see now I just let my spiritual side whither, and that opened me up to a bunch of foolishness. I just wasn't myself. I wasn't thinking clearly. I failed a big test."

A cloud passed overhead, casting the room in gray for a few moments. I sipped some more from my shot glass. I hadn't thought about it in years, but I realized how much courage my sister had shown in admitting the "error" of her ways and returning to the meetings, filled with people who were judging her, even as they supported her spiritual recovery. I knew I would need that kind of courage, too, but for my own reasons. It struck me how much we had in common, my sister and I, raised in the same house, living in parallel, sharing religious and family traditions. And yet here we were, equally passionate and headed in completely different directions.

"What you went through took a lot of guts, Lory. I gotta hand it to you."

She was holding her teacup in her lap. Tears filled her eyes again. "But I *had* to." She covered her mouth with the napkin and composed herself. "I didn't want to die." She was referring to Armageddon. "This is what terrifies me when I listen to you talk," she said. "You're fooling around with *your life*, and all for some temporary relief from Ross and the ego gratification of a job."

I put the teacup back down. She'd hit a nerve. I'd spent my whole life in anticipation of Armageddon, and if it came the next day, I didn't know if I'd be saved or not. But my fear had diminished in contrast with my heart's longing. I now realized there were voices in my head shouting out old ways of believing that I had to suspend or ignore. I was making the radical choice to stop believing everything I thought. When I managed to do that, I experienced emotional relief and mental space. Still, there was always the slightest chance those black hooded riders could come get me—in which case, I was surely doomed. That was the risk hanging over me.

"Our situations are very different," I said. "For one thing, there is no one else."

"It's only a matter of time," she said. And I knew that much was true. For the first time in my life, I felt as if I'd graduated to some new place: we were speaking woman to woman, as adults. Our age difference did not matter.

"Chalking this up to relief and ego minimizes what's going on inside me. Besides, Lory, I think ego gets a bad rap sometimes. It has its place, doesn't it? It gets us out of bed in the morning, presses us forward in life, and encourages us to ask important questions. I'm wanting to explore the world and feel a part of it," I said.

"Then explore," she said, pleading now. "You can still have adventures and be a Witness. I don't understand why you want to leave The Truth. I don't buy it. I think that's all just an excuse."

"An excuse for what?" I asked. I'd spent months exploring my motivations in therapy and bristled at the idea of discussing them here.

"I don't know," she said, squinting as she scanned my face. "I haven't figured that out yet."

We were at an impasse. When I was little, I once asked Lory how she knew we had The Truth. I was a dreamy six-year-old who enjoyed childlike musings. Even then, I enjoyed mulling over big questions and wanted the opinion of someone older who had it all together. She replied at the time, "I just do. It makes so much sense." Lory was a True Believer, and she wasn't able to grasp the possibility I had doubts. She couldn't hear it. It was easier for her to project her own experience onto me and trust I'd eventually come out on the right side, as she had.

We both sat there, looking off into space. My whiskey was gone. She had barely touched hers.

"Can I have a glass of water?" I asked.

"Yeah, sure," she said, and left the room. I wasn't sure what we'd accomplished, and pondered how to make a graceful exit. I was glad I'd come, believing that just by showing up I'd fulfilled some kind of family expectation among all the others I was failing. Lory returned to the room, handed me the water, and sat back down on the couch, this time pulling her feet up and crossing her legs. I sensed the interrogation was over.

"Where is your new apartment?" she asked, and I described my place and plans to move.

"Have you and Ross finalized how you'll split everything up?" I told her how easy that had been for us.

"Just be careful you don't concede things because of guilt," she said. "Just because you're the one leaving doesn't mean you should let go of things you feel strong and sentimental about." Then she told me about an oil painting she'd relinquished in her divorce and always regretted. *My sister is giving me divorce advice. How strange.*

"Will you be talking to Randy soon?" she asked.

"Soon," I said. That would be my next hurdle: facing my big brother.

"Good," she said, grabbing a tea biscuit. "We're all really worried about you, Lindy."

"I know," I said. "But I'm actually feeling very strong. Last night I slept like a baby. I haven't done that in weeks."

"You can't fool me," she said. "You're going to look back on this as one of the hardest times in your life. One day I predict you will wake up and realize how stupid you're being. When that sorry day arrives, your family will be here for you, just like they were for me. I never would have made it without your help. And we'll all be here when you come to your senses, too."

I took a sip of water and avoided replying, thinking it would be better to conserve my strength and use my energy to walk the road ahead of me.

$\backsim$

It was a warm spring Saturday afternoon. The vibrant blue of the sky made my eyes sting, so I slipped on a pair of dark sunglasses. I turned the Honda into the mall parking lot and headed toward JCPenney. My brother's car was easy to spot, off by itself at the farthest end. As I parked my car next to his, I noticed his slumped shoulders and bowed head behind the wheel. *He's probably praying for me.* He glanced up and, upon seeing me, got out of his car and into my passenger seat. I turned off the ignition. Randy was wearing Levi's and a starched cotton shirt. There was a taut air and seriousness around him. His jaw was clenched as he settled into the seat, pushed the sun visor down, and leaned back in the shade it created. I pushed my seat all the way back and turned toward him.

Randy didn't want me coming to his house. We were both free to meet only at times when his two children were home, and it would have been difficult to speak in private. I also suspected he didn't want my niece, Sheena, to know we were talking or overhear our conversation. She looked up to me, and we often fawned over each other. I had invited him to come over to my apartment, but he had refused. I dismissed his reluctance by telling myself he was not ready to confront the full reality of my new life. When I had suggested meeting for coffee at a restaurant, he'd rejected the idea of being surrounded by strangers. Finally, he'd suggested this space for our rendezvous: a mall parking lot. I wondered if security would think a drug deal was going down. The whole scene felt covert and absurd.

I had just moved into my new apartment and was tired from the intensity of the week. I'd taken a few days off work, and Lory had surprised me by coming over to help me pack my belongings. It was the first time I'd had to hire professional movers. I no longer had a community to rally around the chore, no one to call about borrowing a truck. The contrast was a bit lonely, but another part of me enjoyed the independence and simplicity of taking action without having other people in my business. Lory and I watched as the burly pair of movers loaded my few bulky possessions—bed, dresser, piano, and assorted boxes—into the moving van. She then returned home, leaving me to direct them at the other end.

I'd spent the morning unpacking and hanging pictures, making a list of things to buy: bath towels, pots and pans, laundry detergent. These preoccupations kept me from preparing for this conversation, and by the time I met Randy, I was too physically spent to fret and was happily caught up in the overwhelming exhilaration of my newfound freedom. Interrupting my weekend for yet another grave and serious conversation about my "foolish" choices was annoying. I just wanted to get it over with.

And yet I loved my brother and felt it was only fair that he get a chance to speak his mind. He was the one who'd requested the meeting, so I thought he'd be the one to start the conversation. And so I sat there, saying nothing, looking at him look out the window. His bent knees were even with the dashboard. The muscles rippled under his cheeks with each clench of his jaw.

"I've been rehearsing what I was going to say to you," he began, still looking out the window. "I had all these sensible things to say, but then I realized"—he turned to look me in the eye—"I doubt you'd hear any of it. You were always so level-headed, but nothing about what you're doing makes any sense to me."

Good. Then this will be a short conversation.

"I can see why you'd think that," I said.

"Can you?" he asked. "Because from what I hear, you're being very irrational these days."

"Well, it doesn't feel irrational to me," I said. I could feel my whole body tighten up, my own jaw clenching.

Intimate conversations between Randy and me were rare. He wasn't someone I'd ever consulted before making a big decision. It wasn't that his opinions didn't matter, but I never felt that he added an original voice to the insights already available. He'd always lived by the book and had recently been appointed to serve as an elder in his congregation. He possessed an innate and quiet goodness, and I'd be hard-pressed to find a soul with a bad word to say about him. Except for playing basketball and going steady with a worldly girl in junior high school, he'd never done a single contrary thing in his life.

Five years my senior, Randy had always felt a bit distant. Growing up, I envied his ability to escape to a room of his own, filled at one time with the model airplanes he assembled, and later with canvas and brushes, stained color palettes, squeezed tubes of paints curled inward like toothpaste, turpentine—all the tools of an oil painter. Randy never took much to book learning, but he was good with his hands. He was an artist at heart. In particular, he was influenced by the Western art of Charles Russell, which captured his own experience in the wide-open spaces of central and eastern Oregon, where he went backpacking with friends or flyfishing and deer hunting with my father.

When we were little, he would quietly pass me Lifesavers during long-winded sermons at the Kingdom Hall, and I would never forget his assistance on my very first talk in the Theocratic Ministry School. It was Randy who taught me how to ride a bike. ("You're thinking too hard," he said in my ear, bracing me in a vertical position as I sat looking straight down our driveway. "Feel your way, and the balance will come naturally. Don't be scared. I'll be right behind you.") Despite my protests, he'd once forced me to help him dissect a frog in the garage and released me only after I threw up next to his surgical center. When he started dating, I was often the designated chaperone, which fostered an understandable disdain for my company, as he'd have to pay for three movie tickets and three dinners. But I always grew fond of his girlfriends and they of me, and I could always be bribed to look the other way when they kissed.

Still, any interest Randy took in my life always seemed an aside. He'd never expressed any explicit approval or disapproval in what I was doing—as long as I was doing well in The Truth, which, until now, had been a given.

"Randy, can you just accept that you don't understand but support me anyway?" I knew it was a long shot, but I had to pose the question. "Is that too much to ask?"

The words hadn't left my mouth when Randy let out a huge, chest-caving gasp. He bent over and set his face in both hands. It startled me to see such an intense physical response from my brother, and it rattled my defenses loose. He sobbed a few more times and then sat up, tears rolling down his red, flushed face. The last time I'd seen him cry like this had been at Dad's baptism. I removed my sunglasses. A titanic pool of emotion filled the car, slapping us both. I realized I was crying, too.

"There is no way in the world I can support what you're doing," he said. "Linda, you're leaving your husband. You're breaking up a family. And for what?"

"For what?" I repeated the question. Would he be able to hear my answer? If I spoke about doubts and yearning, it would sound like gibberish. Everything I was doing was fresh and scary. I'd vacillated enough and had now switched to action mode. I was willing to trust that my path would get clearer as I moved forward. But I was talking to someone who was not used to living with big questions. A teardrop dangled from Randy's chin. I reached into the backseat and pulled out a small box of Kleenex. We both dabbed our faces, and Randy blew his nose.

"Don't you remember how terrible it was, Lindy, when we were little and Dad wasn't in The Truth? Maybe you were too little to remember. Mom and Dad would argue over what we were and weren't allowed to do with the holidays and school activities. And all those arguments about the existence of God and evolution around the dinner table. It was terrible. Don't you remember?"

"Yes, I remember." But it was clear Randy's memories carried a vivid pain unique to his own experiences. Months of therapy had guided me into some of these painful memories, and I was just beginning to comprehend how our family dynamics and religious rigor had gotten all mixed up and created a stranglehold on me.

"And do you remember what a relief it was when he got baptized?"

"Yes," I said, and remembered how Randy wept as Dad was dipped briefly under the baptismal waters. At the time, his sensitive display made me appreciate the deep impact that growing up without a Witness father had had on him. I'd never seen such fragility from him. He seemed now to be filled with the same overwhelming emotions. Years had passed, and I'd assumed he'd released these feelings. I felt sick to my stomach, seeing how my actions resurrected old fears and familiar pain in him, as they had done with my sister.

"Now we have to worry about you," he said. "No one ever thought you'd become an unbeliever. You've always been one of the sane ones."

"I wouldn't say I'm an 'unbeliever,' per se, just not a 'believer.'" It sounded much better in my head than out loud.

Randy rolled his eyes and shook his head.

I decided to mount one last plea, because he was my big brother and I just wanted to be understood. "But, Randy, can't you please just *try* to understand what I'm going through? Odd as it may seem, I've never felt more sane in my life. Haven't you ever had a time in your life when you *just knew* you were doing the right thing, when you could *feel* it?"

"Marriage and The Truth are not things to be so easily discarded," he said, and a wave of heavy breaths started to overtake him a second time. He pushed the tissues to his eyes and managed to pull himself together. I was a catalyst for something bigger going on inside him. It seemed the only way I could make him feel better was to tell him what he wanted to hear. I was completely thrown off by his lack of compassion or attempt at understanding. I wanted him out of my car. The guilt of breaking up a family had been dumped in my lap, and it was clear Randy was speaking not just about Ross and me but about all of us—"the whole-fam-damily," as my father would say.

"Then we're done here," I said in a firm voice. "Really, I can't take any more of this, at least not today." I pulled one last Kleenex from the box on the dashboard and adjusted the rearview mirror so I could see my face. My eyes were beady and bloodshot. "Are you guys going to be able to come to dinner at my new place next weekend?" I asked, looking for some neutral conversation. I'd invited everyone in the immediate family over for a casual housewarming dinner. Everyone had said they would come. Randy and Marlene were the only holdouts.

"No," Randy said, and looked me straight in the eye. "That's not something we're going to do." A seed of cognition hit me, and my entire body registered the full meaning of his words. The intensity of his emotional outburst suddenly made more sense. I was stalling this conversation for another day, but Randy wasn't leaving any doors open. I'd failed his test. When he said he couldn't support me, he meant that he and his family, including my niece and nephew, wouldn't come to my house or help me in any way. My stand for freedom was more than he could tolerate, and he was taking immediate steps, exceeding even the judicial requirements of the church. He got out of the car without saying another word. My face and chest grew numb from the sense of finality. He returned to his car, fired the ignition, and drove away without even a glance toward me.

The shunning had begun.

Chapter 8

⌒

What you are looking for is what is looking.
—St. Francis of Assisi

The next weekend I reveled in two languorous mornings, sipping coffee and reading the paper in bed. With no call to evangelize and no one else to please or answer to, time took on a charitable expansiveness. I felt like I was on vacation. I was thirty-one years old and living alone for the first time. A quiet pride bubbled inside my newfound self-sufficiency. I don't recall feeling lonely, only liberated and grateful for this new peace and freedom.

Mom and Lory called to check in or invite me over, but with increasing frequency I already had plans and declined. I sensed through the long pauses that this disturbed them. All my fraternizing with worldly people lessened my chances of returning to the fold.

"I feel like I don't know you anymore," Mom said. I'd purchased new living room furniture and was thrilled when it was delivered. It was Saturday morning, and Mom was the first person I called to come over and see the ensemble. She dropped by my apartment on her way home from field service. She made passing comments about my "temporary insanity" and her expectation that I would "come to my senses" and return to my religion and even my marriage. As she sat down and ran her hand over the fabric of the couch, she made all the necessary compliments, but there was no enthusiasm behind her words. I'd spent the morning at home, and my bed was still unmade. She was wearing a skirt; I had on shorts for bike riding. "Really, Lindy, who is this person who does whatever she wants?" I sensed by the way she blew on her tea before sipping it that she thought I was selfish. Whenever we break away from long-established habits others create for us, those others must label us as selfish to preserve their sense of order. In this way, they assure themselves it's not the system that's flawed—it's you!

I didn't know the answer to her question and shrugged it aside. I had no idea who I was or who I was becoming. I felt like I was living someone else's life, floating through a dream. The only thing I knew for sure was that I had everything I needed to live well that day, and that had to be enough. Out of the courtesy she ingrained in me, I offered to make her a sandwich. To my relief, she declined, hugged me goodbye, and left.

Word of my defection traveled through the community, and as it did, people called Mom or Lory. They passed along my new home number and encouraged people to express their concern to me directly. After a full day at the office, I'd return home every night to many phone messages, all from people I shared a history of service with and considered my friends. Most were well intended and supportive.

"Linda, my heart goes out to you, and I hope you will call me if there is anything I can do," said one sister I'd pioneered with a decade earlier.

"Don't forget Jehovah," said another.

The elder who'd said the opening prayer at our wedding called to say he and his wife were heartbroken to hear Ross and I had split. "We're here if you need us."

As I listened to each message, I wrote the name and number of the caller down on a tablet by the phone. One night there were eight messages from concerned Witnesses. Soon there were pages filled with names and phone numbers. There were too many calls to return. Just the idea of it made me feel bone-tired and defeated.

It was a good time to focus my energy on my career, especially since it was funding my new adventures and was my only source of income. In just two years, our work team had grown to ten people. A familial bond, born of mutual respect and shared success, had developed among us. As my job shifted to include more business development, I started making joint sales calls with Geoff Singer, a man from another division of the bank. Our services were complementary, so we agreed to leverage our connections by forming an alliance and calling on prospective banking clients together. There was a kinship between us from the very beginning.

Our first challenge was to travel to Los Angeles, where I would introduce him to one of my best clients and convince her to promote his credit card products alongside the consumer loans my group provided. Geoff and I walked out of the meeting with her verbal commitment and celebrated with lunch at my favorite restaurant in Pasadena.

"I hope you don't mind my asking," Geoff said, "but what formal sales training have you had?"

"None."

"None whatsoever?" He squinted and cocked his head. I considered telling him my Witness story but thought better of it.

"Well, if you want my advice," he said, "don't ever get any. You're a natural salesperson, very articulate and trustworthy. Formal training would spoil you."

He was eighteen years my senior. His experience and opinions meant something to me. He looked at me with limpid eyes, and I knew I could trust him. I learned he'd been divorced for several years and had two children. He told me fascinating stories about his time in the military, with two-year rotations in Moscow, Paris, and Vienna, working on "secret stuff." This made me laugh, but he was quite serious.

Our sales efforts required regular strategy meetings back in Portland. Gradually, meetings that could be handled by phone were taking place in person, followed by lunch or a quick drink after work. We became a resource for each other, sharing news from the grapevine about the potential reorganization and adding our own interpretations to what we heard. I could feel myself being drawn to Geoff, flirting with him, looking forward to our meetings, paying extra attention to what I wore on those days. He walked into the office with a leonine grace that exuded confidence but fell short of the arrogance and aloofness common among successful executives.

One day, an after-work drink turned into a spontaneous dinner. Neither of us had anyone waiting at home, and we weren't ready for the conversation to end. We had given each other unspoken permission to make even more personal inquiries, and so we started sharing what had failed about our marriages. That was the day it first occurred to me that maybe my marriage had been a success. Ross and I had grown up together and learned a lot along the way. "Can't success be knowing when it's time to move on, taking the best of what you learned?" I asked.

"That's a very enlightened view, especially for someone still going through the process," Geoff said. "And what does your family think about it? Are they supportive?"

There was no way to answer that question fully without telling him the scope of my situation, that I'd left not only an unhappy marriage but also a religion where divorce is rare and looked upon as a sign of spiritual weakness. I explained how devout my family was, how I'd disappointed them all, how my brother wasn't talking to me. I'd wanted to share this with Geoff for some time. I could see by the way his eyes darkened that something protective was rising in him.

"I've lost my appetite," he said, and stopped eating, setting his fork down. He removed his wire-frame glasses and rubbed his eyes. He reached out and placed his hand on mine. "I had no idea all this was going on. You always seem so happy, so positive."

His warm touch resonated through my whole being. There was an intimacy and safety there that soothed the raw, vulnerable parts of me that felt guilty for all the pain I was causing and wondered where I might find redemption.

"When I'm with you, I'm happy," I said. Geoff smiled and continued holding my hand. "In the past, I've watched other Witnesses leave and thought they had flipped out. From a distance, it looks like a form of insanity. But I feel like I've flipped *in*, like I'm getting closer to who I really am. My heart and my gut feelings tell me I'm on the right track. So I keep going."

"If it feels good, do it," Geoff said. "That's my motto."

"I was taught that kind of thinking is dangerous and selfish," I said. "My mom likes to quote a Scripture: 'The heart is treacherous. Who can know it?' But I'm following my heart now, learning to trust it, and it's a huge relief."

The next day, Geoff had a bouquet of flowers delivered to my office, along with a handwritten note expressing his care for me. He invited me to dinner that Saturday night. Ah, romance! I sat at my desk and reread his note. I was going on my first date in eleven years, with a man I was attracted to and felt completely at home with.

We had dinner at Papa Hayden on Twenty-First Street. Geoff had remembered my saying it was my favorite restaurant. He'd come by my apartment to pick me up, and I'd invited him to come early enough to have a glass of wine. I had never entertained a single man alone before and was surprised by how calm and composed I felt. I knew if my mother saw me, she'd freak out. I was walking dangerously close to the line of adultery. My divorce was in process, and I hadn't seen my soon-to-be-ex-husband in weeks. But in Jehovah's eyes, we were still married. I was playing with fire and enjoying it. Geoff and I had an unspoken understanding that our relationship was shifting. In the days and moments leading up to our first date, I felt excitement, desire, and longing. I knew there might be an opportunity for sex. If it didn't happen that night, it was coming soon.

"If it feels good, do it. That's my motto."

Our conversation over dinner delved further into the past.

We shared stories about how we'd been raised, poignant memories of how life had disappointed us, books we'd read, and places we'd seen. There was no talk of the office, no mention of the present or the future. Strolling hand in hand from the restaurant toward Geoff's car, my silk dress swaying over my bare legs, I felt sensual and content, filled up by the meal and the company.

"Where to now, Linda?" Geoff asked, as he opened my car door.

"Back to my place."

"Your wish is my command."

He drove back to my apartment complex and parked. We rode the elevator up to the fourth floor, holding hands in silence. As I turned the key to open my door, Geoff spoke.

"Are you sure you want me to come in?" he whispered. " I won't be offended if you shoo me away."

"I'm sure." I couldn't bear the thought of his leaving. "Let's say good night inside." I pushed the door open. "Would you like tea, or another glass of wine?" I was aware of an abiding calm and lusty anticipation.

We took our wine out to the balcony overlooking the fountain and illuminated flower garden. I shivered in the spring night, and Geoff took off his leather jacket and draped it over my shoulders. His body heat was still in the lining as it touched my neck and arms. As he squeezed my shoulders with both hands, I felt the potency of his body. I leaned over and kissed him. It was a long, provocative kiss. A feeling like champagne bubbles traveled through my body. His jacket fell to the floor. I didn't need it anymore anyway; I could feel heat swirling up my chest. His hand pressed on the small of my back as he kissed my neck. We stopped just long enough to put down our wineglasses. I slid open the glass door to my bedroom and walked inside. Geoff followed and watched as I lit a candle on the nightstand. We sat down on the bed and came together again. Everything moved faster then—our hands, our hearts, our breathing. It had been a long time for both of us, and we were hungry. His nude body was a welcome stranger. His chest released the scent of foreign cologne. As he ran his hands over the backs of my thighs, I felt powerful and attractive and worldly in the best way. We moved back and forth in a hypnotic rhythm. Eventually, we came to rest in each other's arms, the candle losing its flame to a pool of melted wax.

"Thank you," Geoff said, and kissed me on the forehead. We lay there in content silence for a long while.

"You can stay as long as you'd like," I said. "All night, or not." *Spoken like an old pro*, I thought, like I'd done this a million adulterous times.

Geoff left very early the next morning, before breakfast, saying he didn't want to overstay his welcome. I appreciated the space and time to reflect. As I floated through that Sunday, doing laundry, riding my bike, shopping for groceries, I searched my heart and found only joy. There was no guilt or regret. I was stunned at how easy it had been to fornicate, how liberating it was to engage with another human on that level, without promises or contracts. Geoff called that evening, and we spoke the lilting language of lovers, making plans for our next rendezvous. My mother also called, curious about my weekend. I told her the truth about going to Papa Hayden's but lied about who I'd gone with, changing names to protect the guilty.

The next week, I received a second bouquet of flowers at the office. This time, they were from Ross. He'd taken the time to buy a Hallmark card that said, "I think of you often, and you'll be in my prayers through the days to come!!!" In bright blue ink, his familiar hand wrote how much I meant to him. He closed with this: "I hope I can help restore your faith in me and in Jehovah. Xoxoxoxoxo! Rossman"

I was astonished that he was holding on to any hope of reconciliation and baffled by the ongoing delusion that he would have any role in restoring my relationship with God. I was also heart-struck to think of the shame Ross was enduring. While

I enjoyed my newfound freedom to the hilt, he was slogging to meetings alone, enduring the watchful eye of a community that blamed him for failures as the spiritual head of the family. I called his house at a time when I knew he would not be home and left a short message to thank him for the flowers.

Geoff and I continued to spend time together, though we were careful not to broadcast our romantic relationship around the office. Understanding the nuances of my situation, he never spoke of the long term and gave me plenty of space to do my own thing. Our time together was lighthearted and joyful, lacking any need for commitments beyond the moment. I had never had a relationship like it before. We went to the movies, golfed, and took long strolls along the waterfront. He was very curious about my family and my religion, and I spent hours telling him family stories or explaining different tenets of the faith. These conversations were a venue beyond journaling and my therapist's office to exercise the growing voice within me. I needed to talk freely, sometimes critically, other times with appreciation, always sorting.

One night over dinner at Jake's restaurant, our conversation drifted back to a fond childhood memory. To break the monotony of rainy winter afternoons, Lory would play Mom's Kingston Trio record on the stereo console in our living room. She and Randy and I would sing along to "Hangman" or "Tom Dooley" while she made popcorn and Kool-Aid.

"I love the Kingston Trio," Geoff said. "Let's go buy one of their CDs tonight. We can listen to it back at your place." We settled the bill and proceeded with our spontaneous plan.

We left Tower Records in triumph, having succeeded in finding its last Kingston Trio CD. My car was parked in the front row of the store, and we were both putting on our seat belts when I saw two familiar faces. My stomach did a somersault. About thirty feet away, walking in our direction along the storefront, were John and Maeve Maguire, a couple who were in the same congregation as Ross—the same one I used to be part of. They were engrossed in conversation and did not notice me.

"Shit," I said, pulling the sun visor down, stiffening into a position that hid my face from them. The store was emanating a bright, blue-tinged light.

"What's the matter?" Geoff asked, looking at me, then at John and Maeve, who were now passing the front of my car, oblivious to my presence. "Do you know those people?"

"Yes," I whispered. "Are they gone yet?"

"They're headed into Albertsons. What gives?"

On the drive back to my apartment, I attempted to explain my odd behavior.

"Remember how I told you that in my religion marriage is binding until death?"

"Yes."

"According to the Scriptures—at least Witnesses' interpretation—only two things can bring a marriage to an end: death or adultery."

"So?" Geoff was leaning against the passenger side window, watching me drive, his face scrunched and puzzled. "You've filed for divorce. You've moved on with your life. What am I missing?"

We were waiting at an intersection for the light to change.

"The laws of the land do not override Jehovah's law. In his eyes, I'm still married, until either Ross or I die or one of us goes outside the marriage for sex. If anyone sees me with you, news will travel and I'll be forced to answer questions about our relationship."

"How is it anyone's business but ours?"

The light had turned green, and the car behind us honked. I looked ahead and continued to drive the last few miles home.

"That's your point of view—one I agree with, by the way. But, Geoff, it's not that simple. The elders are required to keep the congregation clean of immoral activity. Technically speaking, we're immoral people. But I'm worse than you, because I'm a member of the congregation."

"But I still don't understand. You've left the religion, so what difference does any of this nonsense make?"

I parked the car in my assigned space and turned off the

ignition. My anxiety grew; I feared he would think my family and me gullible fools.

"I voluntarily stopped participating, which doesn't break any biblical laws, per se. But if they found out I'd committed adultery, I could get disfellowshipped."

"Disfellowshipped? What does that mean?"

I really wanted him to understand my dilemma. "It means I'd be excommunicated, completely shunned, by everyone I know—even the people closest to me, my mom and dad, Lory." Saying their names was painful. I saw each of their faces in my mind's eye and lost my breath, unable to speak for several moments. My shoulders trembled, and I started to cry. "My brother is already shunning me. He won't return my calls. He refuses to come to my home. It's terrible, just terrible." My voice trailed off. I put my hand over my mouth to keep from falling apart completely.

Geoff pulled a cotton handkerchief from his jean pocket. "Here you go," he said, unfolding it for me. I covered my whole face with it and started to cry so hard I got the hiccups. Geoff didn't try to stop me. He just sat there, gallant and waiting. After what seemed like an eternity, my breathing slowed and I wiped my eyes dry. We were both leaning against our door windows, looking at each other. Every few seconds, I hiccuped. Geoff's face was filled with compassion and bewilderment. "Take your time. But I want to hear the rest."

I nodded my head as more tears came. After several minutes, I was able to keep talking through intermittent tears.

"Witnesses have a judicial process they follow whenever a sin like adultery becomes known. If the sinner is repentant—I mean, if the sinner is sorry for their wrongdoing—they are usually reproved by the elders and then prescribed some course of Bible study to address their spiritual weakness." I paused for a moment, embarrassed to continue. "I know this probably sounds crazy."

"Yes, it does, but keep going."

"If the sinner isn't repentant, the elders may determine they are a threat to the spiritual well-being of the entire congregation and expel—disfellowship—them."

"Good grief," he said, rolling his eyes.

"Geoff, there's nothing about what we've done that I regret. Your company is a gift. But I just don't want to be put in a position where I have to answer any questions. I've been through so much already. I've been a huge disappointment to my parents. My whole family is mortified. I couldn't stand to embarrass them further."

"Would they really shun you? They're your parents!"

"Trust me." I nodded my head, my voice cracking as I spoke. "There's one thing I know as sure as I'm sitting here: they would shun me. They're devout. My own brother is already doing it, without any 'official' ruling. As much as it would hurt, they would comply."

Geoff looked off into the distance, twitching his jaw, then looked back at me. "As a father, I can't imagine anything my two children might do that would cause me to turn my back on them. It's gotta be the worst thing you could ask a parent to do."

I was folding the handkerchief and blotting my cheeks.

"I bet a lot of parents who go through this sneak around it and talk to their children anyway."

"My therapist said the same thing. But I don't want to test this anytime soon." Over the years, I had seen many Witness parents adhere to the church rules and shun their children. Their indelible sadness made it difficult to question their faithfulness.

"What is the purpose of it?"

"To protect the congregation and, hopefully, to create motivation for repentance down the road."

"Ah, I see. Guilt as the great motivator."

"Something like that."

Geoff took my hands in his and leaned toward me.

"I'm glad you shared this with me. Now I see why you were acting so weird back there. You can count on me to jump behind a store display at a moment's notice."

I was astonished by the emotional terrain I had covered in just a few hours: the joy we shared over dinner; delight at finding the CD; dread at seeing familiar faces; sorrow while explaining my fears; then relief, comfort, and exhaustion.

"Can I ask one more question before we go inside?" Geoff still held my hands but leaned back.

"Sure."

"Where does this leave Ross? Can he start dating again, too?"

"No," I said, frowning at the reminder. "As long as he sticks to the religion, he's bound by those rules. Until I die or commit adultery, he's not free. And until I admit to the adultery, he's stuck being single. Talk about guilt."

"Poor guy," Geoff said, reaching for the car door. "This is why I avoid religion: too many rules that mess with people's lives."

"Amen."

⌒⌒

While Geoff and I continued our breezy camaraderie and light-hearted romance, my former boss John, who had recently been transferred to another division, discreetly approached me about a job working for him in his new department, organizing a massive training initiative. I already missed working with him and was flattered. I decided I didn't have anything to lose by agreeing to have a few confidential, exploratory conversations with members of his new staff.

One day, as I drove west over the Burnside Bridge after lunching with two members of John's group, I had an epiphany. If I was going to investigate other jobs, why not expand the search even further, to include other companies and other cities? *Other cities?* Yes, why not? What would it be like to get a fresh start in Seattle, San Diego, or Chicago, all places I adored? Any job change would require an adjustment. Portland was beginning to feel small and stifling. Everywhere I went, I ran the risk of an awkward moment, bumping into someone from the community. Whether I was alone or with another person, such encounters were not welcome. Then there was the proximity of my family and their relentless watching and unfulfilled expectations. The thought of distance made me smile.

In for a penny, in for a pound. Why not move?

PART TWO

Chicago, 1994

Chapter 9

The world is conspiring in your favor.

—Anonymous

It was just past midnight as we walked our bikes out of the parking lot, toward the crowd gathering at Grant Park. Despite the late hour, a hot Lake Michigan breeze swirled around my bare arms and legs. Other cyclists were migrating with us, dressed in black cycling shorts, helmets and gloves hanging off handlebars or crooked elbows, bike shoes curled up at the toes with court-jester flair, clicking against the pavement as we walked. We followed the arrows on signs that read: WELCOME, FRIENDS OF THE PARK, TO THE FIFTH ANNUAL L.A.T.E. RIDE—REGISTRATION BOOTHS AHEAD.

I was one of five thousand cyclists who would soon overtake a core of Chicago's city streets following a twenty-five-mile loop through the western neighborhoods, heading north, then returning south along the lakefront bike path, ending where we now stood, near Buckingham Fountain.

"Can you hold my bike?" Steve asked. "I'll sign us in at Registration."

"Sure," I said. When he returned, we helped each other pin the numbers to our shirts, which allowed us entry to the preride party. Steve was a few inches taller than I, and as he stood near me, I sensed his lean, fit body. He had short brown hair and a neatly trimmed goatee he sometimes stroked with one hand while listening to me or formulating a thought.

We'd met on a blind date two months earlier, when I'd traveled to Chicago for a series of job interviews. I was stunned even to be there, with him, about to ride bikes in the middle of the night through the second-largest city in the country—a city I now lived in.

I'd just moved here one month earlier and was finding it robust and magical, my own New World. I was glad to stand and get my bearings, absorbing the stunning architecture and watching people gathering at such an unlikely hour.

So this is what life is like in a big city.

Once I had opened up to the idea that I could take a job anywhere, leaving Portland had become more than a necessity—it had taken on the pull of destiny. The logistics and specifics came together with dizzying speed and ease. I knew business development was my métier and set out to find a job in a new city—preferably Seattle or Chicago—selling financial services. I updated my résumé and discreetly told select colleagues about my goal. Within two weeks, I had three interviews lined up.

I'd expected it could take six months to one year to line up the right work situation. To spare my family further anguish, I kept my job hunt and desire to leave Portland secret until I knew exactly where I was going. But when this all came together—only three months after my first dramatic divorce announcement—I set out to reveal my plans in detail.

Unfortunately, the Witness grapevine beat me to the punch. I made the mistake of disclosing my plans to Ross during a midweek phone call to cover some mundane divorce details. In retrospect, it was a foolhardy disclosure. I hadn't broken the habit of sharing good news with him. I was going to tell my family that weekend and swore him to secrecy, trusting his discernment. The next day, my parents were attending a meeting at the Kingdom Hall when Todd Sterling approached and started lamenting my move to Chicago. Mom and Dad were stunned by the news and embarrassed to hear it this way. Befuddled, they left early and phoned Lory, who then phoned me in tears. They were angry with Ross and disappointed in me. They put two and two together, realizing my recent "business" trips to Chicago were part of a thoughtful exit strategy.

While Mom, Dad, and Lory were all sad to see me move, I made no effort to communicate with Randy, and the others avoided mentioning him. I'd given them a lot to process in a short period of time, throwing myself wholeheartedly into life-altering choices without seeking their advice or needing their help to make anything happen. A moving crew would arrive at my door and handle everything at my new employer's expense. This left them with only the task of preparing themselves emotionally, and I felt a heavy cloak of despair and resignation come over them. In every sense, I was moving farther away.

Brian reluctantly accepted my resignation. "You're biting off a lot of change at once," he said. "Divorce, a new job, a new city." His grave expression showed genuine concern for me. He didn't know to mention the fourth change: leaving the Witness fold. "If anything changes after you move, and you want to come back, just give me a call." I squirmed as he spoke, not wanting to think about all the extremes in my life.

⌒ↄ

As my family drove me to the airport, less than thirty-six hours before I'd report for my first day at my new job, my hope and longing were bigger than any sense of loss in leaving. While we waited together at the gate, I struggled to find a polite balance between excitement and sadness. When the time came to board the plane, I kissed and hugged everyone goodbye. Lory handed me a letter I was to read on the plane, and two homemade cassettes of all the Kingston Trio albums we'd ever listened to. "In case you get homesick," she said, then looked down and stepped aside. I took my seat on the plane and grabbed some Kleenex in case an avalanche of emotion struck me, but the tears never came.

And now here I was, just one month into my new life, when Steve got this idea for us to do the L.A.T.E. Ride. It wasn't a competitive race, but the excitement at the starting line was palpable. Columbus Drive and Congress were blocked off from traffic and filled with "gearheads," as Steve called them. Under the bright lights, riders synced up their pedals as Tom Petty sang out "Learning to Fly." The start gun blasted, and we were off, heading through the Loop, past street barricades and traffic cops. It seemed like the whole city had rolled out a red carpet welcome. It was enough to make me woozy. People sitting on their brownstone porches clapped and shouted encouragement as we rode by. The drivers of cars waiting to cross at large intersections honked their horns and waved as cyclists passed in clusters.

Steve was showing me the *real* Chicago. He knew his way around and favored restaurants and bars that were off the beaten track. On our first date, he took me to Rosa's on Armitage, a blues club he felt was much more authentic than the better-known "tourist" clubs on Halsted Street. He had a cynical edge about him and was a bit of a raconteur, which stimulated my own wit, igniting a snappy repartee. Part of my appeal to him, I think, was that I could give him a verbal run for his money. Sometimes his stories would turn into rants, but I found him handsome and engaging; his complaints showed he cared about things that mattered, and he offered me a window into the zeitgeist of my new city.

He also thought the hassles my family gave me over religion were preposterous. His reaction to my high-level summary was so over the top, laced with acrimony on my behalf, that I immediately understood it would not be a safe conversation topic for us. If, for example, I told him about my sister's going-away letter, how she'd lamented my selfishness, alluded to the Scripture about "pride coming before a crash," pronounced me a "worldly person," and reminded me that "Satan is a cruel master; he will cheat you out of life," no good would come of it. Under his mordant tone, I sensed a spiritual side, but I knew this was not a person to sort my doubts with. To my surprise, I found this refreshing. Here was someone to have fun with, pure and simple.

A few minutes into the start of the L.A.T.E. Ride, Steve and I found our cadence and settled in side by side. Occasionally I caught a glimpse inside bars and clubs as wobbly patrons came out to the streets to cheer us on. There was a whole world here that carried on while most of us slept—another part of the real Chicago, equal parts grit and glitter. Within a half hour, we reached the halfway point and a refreshment center for the riders. Steve didn't want to stop, but I didn't want the ride to end too quickly.

"Stick with me," Steve said, motioning me along. "The best is up ahead."

We continued through the parking lot and past our resting comrades and arrived on the lakefront bike path, just north of Montrose Harbor. It was darker here and quiet enough to hear the lake whisper. The sounds of the slip sails hitting the tops of their bobbing boat masts played a delicate music. The moonlight cast a mystical haze over everything. Steve was riding ahead, but he slowed the pace and looked back from time to time to observe my reverie.

"We're almost to the clock tower," Steve said. "It's next to the Waveland golf course, in case you ever want to play." He despised the game but knew I was trying to learn. He never missed a chance to point out different things in the city he thought might interest me. The week before, as we rode the L train south to see a movie in the Gold Coast, he stopped at the kiosk to point out the different routes. The diagram reminded me of the table of elements from high school science class, with all its circles and street names and colors weaving in and out. Knowing my new job would require me to travel, Steve pointed out where to transfer from the Brown Line to the Blue Line to access O'Hare.

A breeze whipped up from the lake as we rode beyond the golf course. To the right, separated by four lanes of traffic on Lake Shore Drive, a hospital and several high-rise apartment buildings pulsed with life. Even in these wee hours, there were plenty of lights on, and I felt the life of hundreds of thousands of people beating around me. I was delirious with the contrast of nature and city so close together, so tolerant of each other.

When we rolled under the bridge at Diversey Harbor, Steve said, "Let's stop here" and pulled off the path, down toward the breakers of the lake, stopping just at the water's edge. "Check out that view."

The water was endless. We might as well have been at the ocean, and the moon was so full and the sky so clear, it was impossible to escape into darkness.

"Isn't this better than a neon-bright sag stop?" Steve asked. I nodded and stared at the expanse. We got off our bikes and rested them on the ground. Steve put his hand on my shoulder, pulling me close. *How did I manage to land here, to be so lucky to find this urban paradise? To find a job here that I like? To find such a generous and handsome guide? I must be doing something right. There must be a god somewhere who is smiling on me.* My skin was dewy from the moist air. I turned to find Steve looking at me with soft eyes, and we kissed. It was a long, gentle kiss between two people captivated by the fullness of one moment. We sat awhile longer in silence then collected ourselves and carried on past the sandy beach at North Avenue, the volleyball courts a deserted playground. Other cyclists passed from time to time, and there was a constant stream of headlights leaving Michigan Avenue for the Drive. The sun was just starting to push dawn our way as we completed the ride at the corner edge of Buckingham Fountain, stopping between two of the bronze seahorses casting their waters outward. A fine mist sprinkled my face and arms. Mellow rock was thumping from the XRT stage, and sweaty riders were scattered throughout the gardens of the park, laughing, lying around. I watched over our bikes while Steve retrieved the orange juice and granola bars provided for all those who crossed the finish line. I moved closer to the fountain and pulled a quarter from my back pocket. *Better odds than a penny. In God we trust. Please let me find whatever it is I'm looking for. Please help me ask the right questions.* I tossed the coin into the sparkly waters just as the fountain's center spires surged. Then I grabbed our bikes and pushed them toward Steve, who was waving me over to a bench that overlooked Monroe Harbor and the rising sun.

Chapter 10

⤶

Take the first step in faith. You don't have to see the whole
staircase. Just take the first step.

—Martin Luther King, Jr.

Harris Bank was headquartered downtown in the Loop,
smack dab in the center of banking and commerce, a few
blocks from city hall and the Board of Trade. Unfortunately,
the division I worked in was housed in the northern suburbs,
one hour's drive from where I lived. I was committed to living
in the city and reluctantly joined the hordes of people who spent
hours each day in their cars.

My first apartment was on the fourteenth floor of a modern
high-rise on Clark Street. What it lacked in architectural character, it made up for with features I thought critical to ease my
transition: an assigned parking place in a covered garage, central
air-conditioning, a doorman, and a small outdoor patio with a
lake view. On summer mornings I would step into the muggy
breeze of that patio, my first cup of coffee in hand, bare feet
against cool concrete, and gaze at the lake, a quarter mile away,
glistening between other tall buildings in the neighborhood.
Looking down, I could see the green lawns of Lincoln Park
and the bike path behind Diversey Harbor. On the rooftops of
some of the brownstones were beautifully appointed patios with
seating areas and terraces shaded by large swaths of bougainvil-
lea. I pondered this human tendency to add grace and beauty

throughout Chicago, softening the edges, connecting us to the simple pleasures of the natural world. I purchased outdoor chairs and petunias and often spent evenings on that patio, watching the parade: apartments showing life, lights twinkling in the distance, people walking their dogs one last time before sleep.

The building had two doormen to watch over the lobby. Norman took the evening shift, and Demetri was there each morning, seven days a week, as sure as the sunrise. Norman was a round and jolly soul with skin as black as the darkest shadow. He lived on the South Side and insisted on calling me Miss Linda. He often read a crumpled copy of the King James Bible as he sat behind the marbled desk, wearing a black suit and tie.

Demetri liked to brag about his Sicilian heritage. His hair was sleek and shiny, like a raven, and the shaved skin of his neck bulged over the edge of his white collar. Straight-faced he looked imposing, but when he smiled, an unexpected humanity pushed through the lines on his face and he would light up, eager to break away from his *Tribune* and thermos of coffee to greet the residents passing through.

It was all so *urban*.

The first month of my new job, I devoted time to educating myself and getting the lay of the land. I reviewed the list of area banks and bank presidents and investigated their backgrounds. I was swimming in new waters and wanted to understand the customer experience of what I'd be selling. My days were filled with internal meetings, making the rounds to coworkers, seeing all the areas that would interact and support the client. There was a whole team of salespeople like me, and another group of managers and customer service people to handle the clients once our work was done. The other salespeople took me on calls, and the managers invited me to join them on client progress meetings. I rode along as a passenger throughout Chicagoland, further grounding myself in the territory inside and outside the city. The financial analyst helped me understand the complex pricing model, so that I'd be able to explain the revenue strategy on all proposals with an executive management committee and get their approval.

All the numbers and variables were intimidating, and my head seized with information overload as I sat through my first monthly staff meeting. About twenty people, gathered around a long, rectangular table, filled a large conference room. Our chief product officer was explaining the newest iteration of pricing interchange, followed by a long question-and-answer period. The bankcard industry is a very esoteric branch of financial services that has its own unique language. The acronyms were flying left and right.

"Will I ever learn all this?" I whispered to the person seated next to me.

"No," he said frankly. "I've been doing this for years, and trust me, it's impossible to know it all. And it keeps changing with updates in technology. Each deal will teach you something new, you'll see."

Despite my overwhelm, it was a very liberating time for me personally. New friends and coworkers knew only the "present" me—the single, thirty-three-year-old executive type—and whatever else I chose to reveal. Here there was no "past" of religious rules, unstudied *Watchtower* and *Awake!* magazines, or dejected family. I could walk the city streets and revel in fresh anonymity, free of concern about bumping into anyone who might inquire into my spiritual well-being. I had the emotional and spiritual space I'd yearned for. I was the auteur of a new life and a new persona.

Regular calls from home were my only connection to my former life. Once a week, usually on Sundays, Mom would call and we'd talk until finally, at the end, Dad would come on the line. Never much of a phone talker, he would ask, "How you doin', Lindy? Humidity melted you away yet?" When I asked about him, he'd reply, "Same old, same old." It was the routine we'd always had—short but sweet. Lory called in the middle of the week and less often. In the early months, I found these calls comforting. We discussed how the tomatoes were thriving in the garden, Randy's family camping trip to eastern Oregon, the deck Ove was building out back. Sometimes I admitted to being overwhelmed, experiencing brief periods of exhaustion and bouts of loneliness. But it was impossible to disguise my overriding enthusiasm when describing my latest adventures: scoring bleacher seats at Wrigley Field, watching Fourth of July fireworks with the masses at Grant Park, sitting three feet from Ahmad Jamal as he played piano at the Blackstone, and having tea with my next-door neighbor, a dancer with the Joffrey Ballet.

In every conversation, specific things were left unsaid. A steady and affectionate relationship had developed between Steve and me, and we were spending time together on the weekends and occasionally during the week. My family would have been aghast just to think I was romantically involved with anyone, let alone someone I'd met on a blind date. One time I mentioned him by name and hinted he was a coworker. As a rule, I was vague about whom I spent time with, guiding my family to deduce I was with new girlfriends from the office. And when I had been with girlfriends, I would go into detail about the meal we'd shared but avoided mentioning how much fun we'd had later, dancing to Bob Marley songs at a reggae bar with a variety of attractive men.

The calls left me conflicted. The joy of hearing mundane news was tempered by the need to hide much of the person I was becoming. I felt hollow and two-faced. These conversations lacked intimacy and were a steady reminder of the widening chasm between us. But I didn't think I had a choice. If I told the fuller truth, the campaign for my salvation would intensify. I'd be questioned for signs of "repentance" but couldn't locate any remorse. Then what? I wasn't strong enough to face it. So I mourned the widening gap and carried on enjoying my clandestine, worldly ways.

Chapter 11

✧

Sell your cleverness. Buy bewilderment.
—Rumi

From time to time, Ross phoned from Portland. Our divorce had been final for a few months, and though our house had been awarded to him, my name was still on the deed and mortgage. He kept me posted on his efforts to refinance without me, releasing me once and for all from that obligation. These conversations were cordial but never lasted long. I didn't have much to say to him and wasn't interested in hearing about everyone and everything I'd left behind.

"Before we hang up, I need to ask one more thing," said Ross. It was a Sunday afternoon, and I'd just settled in to read the paper and watch TV.

"Go ahead," I said. "Ask away."

"Are you seeing anyone?" he said, and my heart seized up.

"No," came my fast reply—maybe too fast, I thought. "No," I repeated. And I paused. Earlier that afternoon, I'd returned from a first date with a handsome Italian named Mario. He'd approached me in the grocery store and, after making charming observations about the similar contents in our carts, asked for my phone number. Mesmerized by his wit and deep blue eyes, I'd surrendered to the pickup. We'd met for pizza and had a promising good time. He'd gently kissed my hand good night and asked if he could see me again.

I couldn't tell Ross the truth. Not yet. There was too much at stake for me.

"Ross, I'm way too busy with this new job and acclimating to this big city to find time for romance."

"I see," he said, sounding ragged and worn. There was a long, awkward pause. I leaned against the kitchen wall and slowly slid down to the floor.

"Why do you ask me this?" I said.

"Because I'm tired," he said. I could feel his defeat. "I want my life back. I go to work, I keep up the house, go to meetings and out in service. But it's all drudgery."

I could see his sad blue eyes in my mind and felt the tears that must be welling there.

"Everyone's looking out for me, trying to keep me busy," he continued. "Socially, I mean." And he paused for a moment. The conversation became stilted. "Linda, I need to know, is there any hope of us getting back together? Are you ever going to come home?"

I shuddered. Could I believe my ears? Did he seriously hope for reconciliation? If he was, it could only be out of a sense of religious obligation, not love. Truer still, I knew he was longing for a physical connection. My insides were rattling with guilt. He was overriding natural desires, clinging to antiquated rules that demanded he live the life of a celibate, while I kicked up my heels.

"Ross, I love it here. I can't imagine I'll ever live in Portland again."

I sat there for a long while in the silence between us, a silence that contained our despair and anger, at different things for different reasons.

"Sorry," I continued, holding back tears. "But that is the truth of it."

After I hung up, I sat on the kitchen floor for a long while, feeling like a lying, conniving, hard-hearted bitch of an ex-wife. Of course he was free to do as he liked. But I knew he was suffering and would endure this unhappiness for a long time, rather than break "God's law." I, on the other hand, was no longer interested in appeasing a God that cared about what I did in my bedroom. Our divorce was final, and Ross's choices were no longer my business, but when he called me like this, it *felt* like my business.

I stood up and walked over to take in the view. Fall had turned to winter. Night was descending, and the lake looked placid, reflecting the gunmetal hue of the sky. It was too cold to sit on the balcony. I wrapped myself in a blanket, curled up on the couch, tears braiding down my cheeks.

How had it come to this? Niggling doubts, a crisis of faith, a desire to move freely in the world, and here I was, in a "moral" showdown with my former spouse. Whoever had sex first was the adulterer. For either of us, there would be shame and the invitation from on high—delivered via the elders—to repent. Seeking forgiveness was the gateway to good standing in the church. If Ross should succumb to his loneliness, he would surely regret it, confess his "sin," and be received with love. That same love would be extended to me, but I just couldn't muster any regret. To say I was sorry for the way I'd been living my life these past months would be a lie. To reveal my sin would cost me everything, because I was unrepentant. The Witness community would have no choice but to cast me out. If Ross slipped up, he'd still have his family, his community. I would not. I was surer than ever that my family would turn their backs on me—as Randy had done—and I wasn't strong enough to face being shunned by them.

The next thing I knew, I was awakened by pelting rain that sounded like someone from the floor above was beating a rug against the window. Raising my head from the arm of the couch, I felt a sharp crick in my neck. I was still in my jeans and blouse from earlier, eyes puffy, mouth dry, surrounded by wads of used Kleenex. It was two o'clock in the morning, and I needed to be up for work in four hours.

The first snows began to fall, and so did the temperatures. Lake winds gave new meaning to the phrase "wind chill," which until then had brought to my mind a slight breeze, perhaps the need to throw on a jacket. But no. I'd soon develop whole new distinctions for the term "cold." Temperatures dropped below freezing for days on end, joined by sharp and angry winds. At times I'd find myself huddled in a cluster of fellow pedestrians, struggling to stand upright at a crosswalk.

Meanwhile, pressures from work were mounting. I'd been there five months and, despite relentless effort, hadn't signed one bank to our services. I'd had greater expectations for myself, and so, it turned out, did Catherine's boss, Richard Wallace. Richard was the executive vice president overseeing our division, an old-school banker from the pin-striped-suit era, rumored to be just a few years away from retirement. Richard presided over the pricing committee and had seen me present regularly. He knew I was working, but where were those signed contracts? At my job interview he'd asked me why he should pay for my relocation from one state to another, when I lacked experience in the bankcard industry. "Because I *do* have experience in sales and banking," I'd replied. "And I'm a natural salesperson; my trustworthy nature puts bankers at ease." It sounded good at the time but now had the ring of overconfidence.

Every month Richard sat in his gilded corner office, reading the sales report. Every month he wandered back to the sales department, past my cubicle, into Catherine's office, closing the door behind him. He was distressed to see zeros by my name and needed regular assurance that I was working out okay. This I learned when Catherine took me out to lunch and told me as much. She'd come up through the ranks and had done my job for several years. Chicago's community bank network is fairly close knit, and she knew many of the people I was calling on and clearly understood all the dynamics that went into these bigger deals. Her support was unwavering. "If Richard ever talks to you directly about this, don't let him get to you," she said. "You're doing all the right things, so just keep at it."

My ego took a beating every time the monthly sales report came out. It listed the salespeople in order of most sales year-to-date, and my name had been at the bottom five months in a row. Several coworkers were new hires, just like me, and they were tallying up the wins, making my lack even more conspicuous. These coworkers had been hired to sell to a direct client base, and Catherine reminded me that always yields faster results. She was convinced that I should stay focused on the bank network, which she likened to hunting elephants: it may take a while, but when you get one down, it's big.

Despite her assurances, my confidence suffered. Banks are infamous for their hierarchical structure, which fosters an overemphasis on titles. I came in with the same assistant vice president title I'd earned in Portland. Besides Catherine and Dave, our longtime leading sales people, both vice presidents, I was the only person on the team with an officer designation. People work years to get that sort of recognition, and I'd walked in with it. Coworkers with "lesser" titles were outselling me, and I was sure Richard was not the only one to notice. I'd lie in bed at night, imagining month after long month passing, zeros swirling around my head. Had I bitten off more then I could chew? Was God punishing me for doubting? I'd imagine the day Richard would emerge from Catherine's office, point to the flat line next to my name, and fire me on the spot. What a disappointment I'd been, after all my hubris, all my big plans.

My freedom was tied up in this job, and I was petrified of failure. My base salary was enough to cover my expenses, but I'd counted on my commission checks to pay off debt, build savings, and eventually fund grand vacation adventures. These would now come later than I'd expected, if at all. But there was more at stake. In the wee hours of the morning, I played out mental scenarios where I lost my job, then became penniless and dependent upon my parents. I'd have no choice but to return to Portland in defeat, Mom shaking her head, lamenting how the world will always let you down. They'd invite me to sleep in my old room until I could get back on my feet. They'd welcome me back, of course, and drag me to the Kingdom Hall. Dreams vanquished, I'd acquiesce, receding once again into a dull, methodical life.

Chapter 12

⌒☋

The first cure for illusion is despair.
　　　　　　　　　　　　　　—Phillip Slater

T he days were getting shorter and colder. It was dark when
I left home for the office, and it was dark when I returned.
Zeroes still glared near my name on the sales report as November slipped into December.

Like the weather, things between Steve and me had cooled off. Our summer brush with intimacy had been real and touching, but neither of us had worked to sustain it. When opportunities presented themselves, I dated other men I found interesting, preferring the early phases of romance, before the rose-colored glasses come off, when the other person sits before you full of promise and compliments. Even so, Steve was a steady presence in my life. We had a strong affinity for one another and I knew I could count on him if I was ever in trouble.

Christmas was new territory, arriving at a time when I didn't want or need a fresh challenge. This would be my first year celebrating. I'd always looked at Christmas as an indulgent pagan celebration that made a mockery of Christ and "pure Christian" worship. Over the years, as part of my Bible study, I'd done extensive reading about the history of the holiday and the role church and politics had played in its creation. I knew Christ was born in the autumn, not the dead of winter. And I'd always been taught to steer clear of birthday celebrations, also fraught

with pagan rituals true Christians avoided. The whole prem-
ise of Christmas was flawed from the Witness point of view.
Up until that year, Christmas had been just another day to me,
sometimes spent in repose, other times skiing with a group of
Witness friends on Mount Hood. Occasionally the entire family came together for dinner, taking advantage of a time when
few of us were working. There was no tree or gift exchange. If
Christmas happened to fall on a regularly scheduled meeting
night, like Tuesday or Thursday, it was often business as usual.

I loved a good party, and that was the tack I chose to create
distance from my years of piety. Like all my other ideas about
faith and religion, I decided to let go of my grip on the old story
and give Christmas a chance. It could be fun, and Lord knows
I needed some light and joy in my life.

I made a point to stroll along Michigan Avenue and see the
sparkling lights of Watertower Place, then throw money into the
Salvation Army tin guarded by a suspiciously thin Santa chim-
ing a bell outside Marshall Fields. Steve and my work friends
Cindy and Catherine were on my shopping list, and I needed
stocking stuffers for my colleagues. For the very first time, I purchased Christmas cards and sent notes to my friends and former
coworkers in Portland. I missed them all and was delighted to
receive many cards in return, some with long, handwritten notes
updating me on their lives. This was how I first came to understand the holiday's power to bring people together, providing an
occasion for them to reflect on the meaning of friendship and
reach out to each other to affirm it. Eventually I got caught up in
the joy of the season, singing along to "Silent Night" on the car
radio, counting the days until Christmas.

One of the high points that month was a girls' night out
to watch a performance of *A Christmas Carol* at the Goodman
Theatre. Cindy organized the logistics with a few other women
from the office. We dressed in various forms of black velvet, red
silk, and pearls and met at my apartment for a toast. Cheeks
rosy and hearts dancing with champagne bubbles, we bundled
up and ventured into the cold night.

I'd never seen the play before, having believed that to do so would be an act of religious treason. As a child, I was never allowed to watch TV movies like *A Charlie Brown Christmas* or *How the Grinch Stole Christmas*; however, I'd loved reading Dickens and was familiar with the story of Ebenezer Scrooge.

Taking our seats, waiting for the show to begin, I scanned the crowd and saw all the families who'd come together. Just in front of me sat a little girl wearing black patent leather shoes, her blond hair falling in ringlets down the back of her lace collar. A sorrowful heat swirled around my heart and throat as I pictured my niece, Sheena, who would have looked much the same if she'd been there with me. I missed my family and knew this was a tradition we would never share. I wasn't even comfortable telling them I had come.

The theater lights dimmed, and the lush velvet curtain opened to reveal another world, beautifully staged. Moment by moment, wonder replaced my sadness as the actors cast their spell over the hushed crowd, carried to another place and time. I was inspired by Scrooge's redemption, how he claimed a future for himself that was filled with happiness and generosity. I carried that feeling of hope and possibility into my dreams that night. It was as inspiring as any church service I'd ever been to.

The office Christmas party was another first. Richard brought all areas of the division together, which totaled a few hundred people. We gathered in the ballroom of a suburban hotel not far from the office and had a buffet dinner, followed by a much-anticipated annual talent show, at which various groups of employees traditionally put on small skits or dressed in costume and lip-synched a pop song. People from all areas of the hierarchy participated, from Richard on down, and I marveled at the spectacle, unable to decide if these people were courageous or fools or both. I can't say I had the time of my life, but I enjoyed being a part of the mix. I didn't have to spend the next workday explaining away my absence or telling people why I didn't celebrate Christmas, because I guess I sort of did now. It was nice to blend in and understand the inside jokes and stories that later became part of the group's shared history—my history.

Steve invited me to spend Christmas Day with his family, and I gladly accepted; I'd met his clan at a summer barbecue and liked them. We decided to exchange gifts in private, before making the one-hour drive to his parents' home in the western suburbs. I'd heard Steve make a passing comment about wanting something to decorate his fireplace mantel. My gift was a rustic pair of bronze candlestick holders, and he seemed pleased with my choice. When he handed me a gift wrapped in tissue, I could tell right away that it held some sort of fabric. Tearing it open, I found a wool muffler, then gray long underwear. I didn't know what to say. "Just doing my part to keep you warm through the winter," Steve said. The underwear was made of fine silk, but still. The long pause between us said it all: our romance was waning. *Welcome to the minefield of the Christmas gift exchange. Another first.* We left our gifts and wrapping paper on the floor and went to the car.

We walked through his parents' front door and were engulfed in the succulent scent of prime rib. Steve's mother, Bernie, was a great cook, and we knew we would dine like royalty. Steve brought flowers, and I came with a worthy Bordeaux.

Steve's father, PFQ, noticed us standing in the foyer removing our coats, and came to greet us. "Merry Christmas, kids." He shook Steve's hand and gave me a hug. We waved to his brothers, who were sitting on the couch, and they smiled and waved back. When PFQ receded to the couch himself, Steve and I went to the kitchen to say hello to Bernie and deposit our offerings. Then Steve joined the men in the other room. I stayed behind, happy to help Bernie.

Throughout the afternoon and evening, I found myself detaching as if hovering, watching myself from a distance. It was like I'd stepped into a Martha Stewart photo shoot, sitting around a beautifully decorated table, eating a gourmet meal, using the silver and crystal, occasionally laughing, sometimes joining the conversation. And there I was, helping to clear the table, stack plates, scoop dollops of whipped cream onto slices of apple pie. Next we were gathering in the room with the Christmas tree, where PFQ and Bernie scanned the gift labels, then set boxes in front of each of their children. I felt like I was in the middle of something that wasn't my business—another family's routines and no place for me. My hosts were kind and hospitable, but just how had I ended up in this living room, especially when I knew Steve and I, though fond of each other, were not meant to last as a couple?

Things went on like this for some time. The next thing I knew, completely out of the blue, Bernie was handing me a medium-size wrapped box. I thought she meant for me to pass it over to PFQ. "Here you are, dear," she said to me, her eyes sparkling. "Merry Christmas." All eyes were on me, and inside my head I heard glass shattering as my brain tried to compute what was happening. I hadn't seen this coming. The full force of their unexpected generosity hit me in a wave of astonishment. I held the box on my lap for a long moment, becoming painfully aware that I hadn't brought them anything, except the wine for dinner. *I should have given them the candlesticks.* I lacked the life experience to understand the nuances and etiquette of this holiday. Collecting myself, I peeled away the smiling Santa paper and found the perfect present, under the circumstances: a pound of dark-roast coffee and a handheld coffee grinder.

"Thank you," I said, bewildered and near tears. One glance at Steve and I knew he was in on this.

"Steve told us you love your morning coffee," Bernie said, beaming at the obvious success of her choice.

"Last week, when you were getting dressed I snuck around your kitchen and realized you didn't have a grinder," Steve said, smiling a little. In that moment, I forgave him for the underwear, though I could still anticipate the groans of my girl-friends. I was deeply moved by the thought and collaborative effort that had gone into this gift. The gesture both warmed my heart and made me feel very alone in the strangest way. It was the kind of thing my own family would have done for me, and I couldn't help but wonder what each of them was doing that day, back home. It was Sunday, so I guessed they had gone to the Kingdom Hall for services, a sermon followed by a discussion of a *Watchtower* article, like any other Sunday. They would have made no special acknowledgment of the "worldly" holiday. I had avoided calling them over the last few days, and they hadn't reached out to me, either. They may have suspected my heathen activities and didn't want to be faced with the truth or a lie. Better to let the whole thing blow over. Every bit the guilty pagan, I felt my heart murmuring with faint echoes of shame.

"It must be hard to be away from your family," Bernie said. "Especially at Christmas."

"It is," I said, my eyes filling with tears. I knew Steve had not shared my situation with her, and that she might misread the meaning behind my emotions. I took a deep breath to recover my bearings. "Being here has helped me along. You are very generous, and this present is perfect for me. Thank you. I'll use it often; I'm sure of it."

Steve placed a Kleenex on my knee, and I dabbed my cheeks, grateful the attention had shifted to the next round of gifts. Without my asking, PFQ brought me another whiskey, which I gladly accepted and sipped through an evening that asked nothing more from me.

Later, after we helped clear the discarded gift wrap and stacked the dishes, we said goodbye. Steve drove us back to the city, where the streets had an eerie stillness and repose, dark and cold as a butcher's locker. Steve and I walked through the deserted lobby of my building and rode the elevator uninterrupted to the fourteenth floor. When we walked through my front door, Steve set down my gift in the kitchen and followed me to the bedroom. The blinds were open, and the city lights cast a blue aura, adding to the spectral mood. In those shadows, we slowly undressed and, without saying a word, curled up in bed and drifted into the sleep of relieved refugees.

Despite the warmth Steve and I shared at Christmas, during the long, soul-searching week leading up to New Year's, I realized our romance was over. On a night when the temperature was seven degrees below with the wind chill, I went out with him for what I knew would be our final dinner. When he walked me to my car, I said, "I think we should stop seeing each other." I felt like I'd stepped into a *Seinfeld* episode. I used all the clichés: "It's not you, it's me," and "I hope we can be friends."

"This just isn't working," I continued.

He didn't resist. "Can't say I didn't see this coming," he said. We kissed once on the lips; then I got in my car and drove away. In the rearview mirror, I saw him step into the black pavement outline where my car had been, under the streetlight. He'd have no trouble finding a cab to take him home.

My relief was much bigger than my sadness. I couldn't muster enough remorse to cry and decided to stop dating for a few months. It took too much energy, and I needed to build my strength, focus on my work, and try to confront the existential dilemmas facing me.

I caught myself staring into space a lot over the coming days, curled up with a kitten I'd adopted from the local shelter, wondering if unsatisfying romantic relationships were punishment from God for leaving my marriage. Scratching his chin while talking to Leo, I got a scary glimpse of my future self, years hence, holed up in my apartment, gray and frail and alone, wearing a quilted bathrobe, surrounded by cats. The neighborhood children would call me the Cat Lady behind my back, and I'd pass out stale hard candy at Halloween.

The next day stretched before me with no plans. I pushed through the void and headed out to an early-afternoon matinee at Watertower Place, then wandered through the shopping mall, finding post holiday crowds surging past the corners of each escalator bank. What weeks earlier had seemed blessed and shiny now felt tired and brassy. The music was irritating, and every face appeared devoid of joy. *This really is an awful holiday.* I decided to leave, but with a free evening looming ahead of me, I was reluctant to return home.

The first thing I did when I got to my apartment was to check the phone for messages. The stutter of the dial tone gave my heart a hopeful lift. Someone had called me. My whole body relaxed as I listened to a call from Deborah, an elder's wife from the local Kingdom Hall whom I'd met a couple months earlier when Lory had come for a three-day visit. She'd convinced me to take her to the local Kingdom Hall for services, and that is when we met Deborah, a compact woman with a jolly, rambunctious nature. At that point in time, I had not preached or attended meetings in over six months. I was irritated by the predictability of the message, but Lory was my guest, so I endured the boredom for her sake. My official status was 'inactive.' Deborah took on the role of hostess and introduced us to other people there. Deborah asked for my phone number and I saw no harm in giving it to her. She and her husband, Ray, were having a few friends (from the Hall, no doubt) over for dinner and charades that evening and wondered if I'd like to come. Feeling like a castaway just discovered on a deserted island, I was thrilled to accept and called her back right away.

Deborah and her husband lived on the third level of a modest brownstone that was less than a mile from my place. Ray greeted me at the door and pointed the way to the living room. "Follow the laughter," he said.

The narrow hall opened to a warm, modestly appointed room where a group of six others were seated comfortably on the overstuffed chair and couch. I recognized most of the faces from that one trip to the Hall. Deborah was seated cross-legged on the floor. She stood to welcome me, then introduced me to the group as a "recent transplant from Portland." Ray brought me a glass of wine, and for a short time I responded to polite questions about where I worked and how I was adjusting to Chicago's weather. I was just as happy when the attention turned to the tall man with graying temples who'd just returned from Indonesia. Except for the prayer of thanks before dinner, there was no overt mention of religion.

Nor was there mention of Christmas, which I found refreshing. I was able to relax and quietly settle in with everyone around the cramped kitchen table. We ate a delectable home-cooked stew and crispy, warm bread. For long stretches during the lively conversation, it felt very natural to be there. As I helped her clear the table, I learned that Deborah was a part-time bookkeeper and a full-time pioneer. Ray drove a bus for the Chicago Transit Authority and had been appointed as a congregation elder five years earlier. I knew they wished me well, seeing me as an "inactive" Witness who might need only a warm welcome to be coaxed back in.

As the evening wore on, I began to find it trying to be around their innocence and certainty. If only they knew how far I'd wandered into worldly ways and thinking: sex, pagan celebrations, grappling with long-held beliefs of evolution, Christian neutrality, and individual expression. Would they still welcome me if they knew my present lifestyle? I felt the room closing in on me, followed by the intense need to bolt. I escaped to the restroom and splashed my face with cool water. I could hear the others' laughter from a distance, as though it were coming from a far horizon, not the room next door. Collecting myself and taking a few deep breaths, I reentered the living room to find Ray organizing the group for charades. I forced a smile and excused myself, saying I needed to work the next day, denying myself the fun so as to escape the discomfort I felt in their company. Part of me envied their certainty, the black-and-white clarity of a long-established set of beliefs. My thinking had pushed beyond that, and their company reminded me of how many questions I was living with. I wasn't even praying anymore, shying away from the face of Jehovah, not even sure what to pray for, yearning for a sense of innocence I thought I'd lost, innocence I imagined this group still possessed.

Deborah saw me to the door, her long, wavy hair still pulled into a ponytail, showing the full bevel curve of her cheeks. "Perhaps we'll see you at the Hall soon," she said in a breezy, off-handed manner. "And we have weekly book study here on Tuesday. You're always welcome. Most of the regulars are people who were here tonight."

"Thank you," I said. "We'll see." I was numb to any feelings about going to the Kingdom Hall. I didn't want to go, per se, but felt compelled to keep the option open. At the very least, it felt good to be known by such a warm soul. I could have a good friend in her if I wanted, I thought.

Traffic along Lake Shore Drive was at a standstill in both directions. I'd slipped out of the office early that afternoon, my first week back after the holiday break, feeling frail and small, possibly coming down with a virus, vacant any ambition, in no condition to conduct business. The lake was at my right, the wind stirring it into a mean, choppy stew that spread out empty, as far as the eye could see. It started to rain.

Traffic reports and news blurbs gave way to music and the beat of my windshield wipers. I had no appointment to keep. No one was waiting for me. My only plan for the evening was to hibernate. There was little else to do but creep forward, following the taillights ahead of me, getting lost in my thoughts.

Earlier that week, I'd received a phone call from my former boss Brian Martin in Portland. He was involved in a new business venture that was recruiting sales talent. He'd thought of me. "Just in case things aren't working out as you'd hoped," he'd said. I was flattered, but of course I declined, explaining how I was just hitting my stride, feeling phony as I talked about how much I loved everything in my new world and yes, thank you, was thriving on all fronts. "I thought it was a long shot," Brian said. "But what could it hurt to make you aware of it?" I was too proud to be honest with Brian, but our conversation triggered several days of ambivalent thinking. In private, I needed to face facts. Did it make sense to at least consider returning to Portland? I'd fallen into a vapid existence, working, sleeping, eating, struggling to retain some warmth, some aliveness, through a dark and frigid season. What was the point of such an existence? If I didn't say yes to these offers, or at least entertain them, they might stop coming, and then where would I be? Stuck. Stuck in traffic, stuck in life, a pitiful divorced woman with uncertain professional prospects and no community. Maybe Mom was right: the world *was* a cold, hard place, and I'd set myself up to get knocked around. "You reap what you sow." "Pride comes before a crash." "Satan is a cruel master—he'll cheat you out of life."

Just then, emanating from the car speakers came the gentle sound of a single acoustic guitar, playing a tune I'd not heard for a while but recognized immediately. It was delicate in tone, each note standing on its own, with a pacing that slowed me down, capturing my attention. I turned up the volume as Bonnie Raitt sang the plaintive tale of "Nobody's Girl," her voice nuanced with a wistful melancholy, *She's fragile like a string of pearls, she's nobody's girl.* I burst into tears. *Yes, that is what I am. Fragile. Alone. Nobody's girl.* I didn't belong anywhere—not in the Chicago banking world, where I couldn't seem to make a sale, but not in Portland, either; not at the Kingdom Hall; not with my family; not with Steve; not with Ross. The lyrics seared my chest like a branding iron. All this internal waffling, this confusion, this feeling deeply and utterly lost. *What have I done with my life? Where do I belong?*

The lament in the lyrics weaved around the raw, simple sounds of the guitar. I was getting very heated and had to unbutton my jacket and crack the windows for air. Was I a fool to think I could have freedom and spiritual fulfillment at the same time? Was that possible for anyone? I cried so hard I got the hiccups. I was perilously close to being completely unstrung, barely holding it together. The final, lilting refrain repeated over and over until it faded out.

Later that week, Lory called to say hello and found me at home, cooking dinner, surrounded by boiling pots of water, colander at the ready, fish wrapped in foil, fresh vegetables waiting to be cleaned and chopped. I'd been so down in the dumps, I'd eaten nothing but takeout food for several days. I'd finally had enough and had sought refuge in my own kitchen. It was a warm way to fill an evening, doing something I enjoyed. Just pulling it all together lifted my spirits, a tangible accomplishment. I chopped and stirred while sipping a pleasant merlot. It was such a contrast to feel some pleasure, and the relief allowed me to let my guard down. I told my sister of my struggles to get through the season, how extreme the weather was, how I didn't want to do anything but hole up in my apartment, hibernate like the bears, wake when it was over. I confided in her about my growing professional insecurities—all those zeros, doubting my abilities, and wondering how long I could keep it all up. I said nothing about breaking up with Steve, but my agony was unmistakable.

I also said nothing about the therapist I'd consulted who'd told me I was in the "emotional boomerang" of processing a divorce, a cross-country move, a new job, and a change of religion. No kidding! It was her professional *opinion* that I was strong enough to get through this; it was also her professional *obligation* to write me a prescription for Prozac to ease the intensity. I had been carrying her scribbled note in my folio, beside my loose change and grocery list, reluctant to cash it in at the pharmacy.

"I've never heard you this distraught," Lory said.

"Distraught?" I continued. "You want to know just how distraught I am? I've even started to miss being married to Ross." And as I spoke, the awful truth of it caught in my throat. I hadn't allowed myself to be this honest before, let alone to say this out loud. "It's not that I miss Ross as much as I miss the comfort born of familiarity. You know, when another person knows you, your little habits, how you like your morning juice at room temperature, water without ice, silly things like that." My voice trailed off.

"You need to go to the Kingdom Hall," Lory said, jarring me out of my reverie. "Really. It would be good for you to go somewhere people are happy to see you."

"Ah, yes, the answer to all my problems," I said, our pocket of intimacy dissolving around me.

"Think about it. You've already made a few friends from there. True friends. It would help you get through the winter."

"I'll take it under advisement," I said, effectively ending the conversation. It didn't occur to her that I was making or could make true friends outside the congregation. I resented the idea that I needed to be fixed, that the problems in my life could be addressed by a trip to the Kingdom Hall. Wasn't it okay just to be in my muck? Life gets confusing at times. That doesn't necessarily mean anything is wrong. I'd made my choices and needed to ride out the consequences. I hung up the phone and finished preparing my meal, but with less vim. I set the table and sat down.

Okay, I said to myself, *look around you. In this moment, you have everything you need. Millions of people are hungry, and you have this delicious meal and new pots and pans to cook it all in. And you have wine.* I toasted the air and took a sip. Leo was sitting in the corner, watching me. *You have the endearing affection of a kitten.* I scanned the rest of the room. *A piano. A TV and VCR. A couch and chair. A warm coat. A roof over your head. A good job. A company car. Good prospects. You're physically strong and healthy. You're just beginning to make new friends.*

This was how I would talk myself down, out of the highest, most delicate branches of the panic tree: by getting my bearings in a single moment and noticing all that was working, large and small. The options seemed to be Prozac, the Kingdom Hall, or continue riding the wave, putting one foot in front of the other, not getting too far ahead of myself with upset and worry. We all need a place to call home, a native habitat that our soul recognizes, and where it exhales with relief upon entry, knowing this is where we belong, where we know and are known. The Hall offered me a place for community and connection. There, I would never have to worry about being alone or forgotten. I often toyed with the idea of returning to my former religion, if only for that security stemming from the familiar, but more than that, I daydreamed about how it would feel to be okay with my family, to walk into Mom and Dad's house, open the refrigerator, help myself to some morsel, and have a mundane conversation about the garden tomatoes. Because what is more native than a daughter being welcomed and accepted by her family?

Chapter 13

Let yourself be drawn by the strange pull of what you really love. It will not lead you astray.

—Rumi

The next weekend, I was sitting with my best work friend, Cindy, in my living room after dinner. The conversation had moved from parents and past boyfriends to a long-standing frustration Cindy had with one of our coworkers.

"I have no room to quibble," I said. "Until I sell something, I don't think I can point fingers at any one else's shortcomings."

Cindy looked down, not saying a word.

"What are people saying about me, Cindy?"

"That's a tough one," she said. "Everyone likes you. Everyone thinks you're capable and smart. No one doubts you've been working hard. The way you revamped our sales proposals is helping everyone."

She paused to sip her wine. I lobbed a round ball across the carpet and watched Leo trace it with his eyes.

"Has anyone ever gone this long without making a sale?" I asked. "It's been six months."

"I'm not sure," she said. "No one can figure out why it's taking you so long."

This question consumed my private thoughts. It had never been this hard or taken me this long to make my mark at work. Was Jehovah punishing me?

"Join the party," I said. "As far as I can tell, I'm doing everything I can, following all the classic sales techniques. I've got several banks *so* close. But they keep dragging their feet."

"We're all rooting for you, and we know Catherine's behind you. That's the biggest thing you have going for you right now."

God, I don't want to let Catherine down.

"Richard can't be happy," Cindy added. "Has he said anything to you?"

"I plan to beat him to the punch," I said. "I've spent too many sleepless nights worrying about what Richard thinks of me or relying on Catherine to be my mouthpiece. I gave Catherine a heads-up and approached Richard about having a meeting to review everything I have in the pipeline."

"That took guts." She stared at me in disbelief.

"He seemed pleasantly surprised by my request. I'm going to walk him through all the deals I'm working on and what I think it will take to close each one. I want him to come out on a few appointments with me, get him involved, show executive support, and see if we can't close a sale or two."

"When is this happening?" Cindy asked, an intrigued smile on her face.

"Next week."

One dreary afternoon, I scrambled some eggs and sat at the dining table to eat and thumb through an audio catalog. I wanted to find a new program to listen to during my two-hour workday commute.

In the "Spiritual Growth" section, the approachable smile of one of the speakers, Marianne Williamson, caught my eye. She had done a series of lectures based on something called a Course in Miracles and was described as a dynamic and uplifting spiritual teacher who'd helped transform the lives of millions. The description of the Course was intriguing: a thought system based on love, instead of fear, in which forgiveness of self and others could free you from judgment, guilt, and anger. The teachings combined spiritual psychology, Christianity, and Eastern philosophy, which I'd always found fascinating but had always been discouraged from exploring.

My long-ingrained suspicions of Christendom lingered, so it was inconceivable for me to attend another church. I was leery about replacing one set of religious dogma for another. But listening to a self-study guide on tape was doable. If I heard anything that seemed too weird or found myself overcome with a feeling of betrayal, the eject button was right there.

The more I thought about it, the stronger my desire became to delve into something, anything that might address a gnawing spiritual void. Listeners were promised insights into maintaining a feeling of connectedness and developing a new awareness of self and God. I'd spent my whole life going to services at the Kingdom Hall, constantly reading Bible-based literature that fostered a feeling of connection to God and spirit. The past year, I'd ripped myself away from those rituals and had not replaced them with anything consistent or satisfying.

A delicate thread of hope and possibility slipped into my heart as I picked up the phone and, grateful for twenty-four-seven customer service, placed my order, happily paying extra for a rush delivery.

Two days later, I got in my car and put the first tape into the console. From the first moment, the message captivated me. Christian terminology created an easy bridge into the concepts, which were ecumenical and inclusive. Marianne started with a prayer, but it wasn't like any prayer I'd ever heard. I'd been taught to pray in a very exact way: always *to* Jehovah, *through* Jesus, invoking his name. Here, the prayer was more of a guided meditation that expanded further and further, to everyone and everything. Unsure how to approach God in my present circumstances, I hadn't prayed in months. Even with open eyes, steering the car along familiar roads toward the expressway, I sensed with my whole body the "golden light" she described.

Marianne was saying that fear comes out of the misguided

perception that we are separate: from others, from love, from wholeness. A cool shiver of recognition pulsed down my spine, as though I were in the presence of a simple truth. It was startling to hear her say there is no such thing as an objective experience—everything is perception. Everything? Everything. Yes, that felt true, too.

As I lapped up every irreverent word, she went on to explain that failure is a perception and the only true failure is a failure to learn, to get back up, and to love. She talked about the patience of the universe, how nobody gets to rush anybody—we each get to determine our own process and timing. When she said, "Nobody gets to look at you and declare, 'You are finished,'" I cheered out loud and slapped the steering wheel with my hands. Hallelujah! I'd been searching for just such phrasing to say to my family but had been too muddled with guilt and confusion to find the right words.

An accident on the expressway had slowed traffic to a crawl, and I didn't even care. I was enthralled by Marianne's voice, her optimism, and her matter-of-factness. She said a life that works, that is happy and clear, comes out of giving up the thought forms of fear—that we aren't good enough—and seeing through the eyes of love. This is simple to say but not easy to do. Amen.

That day at the office, I was buoyed by a new sense of lightness and freedom and found myself looking forward to the commute home, when I could listen to more "church services" in my car. That day I heard a totally new description of "sin" as an archery term, and of "missing the mark" as a mistake in perception, losing sight of our essential goodness, or that of others. The god Marianne described doesn't get angry when we take detours; he doesn't see sins as mistakes he wants to punish. Our only mistake is thinking God ever condemned us in the first place. It was the most radical description of God I'd ever heard. Deep parts of me that had been tense and apologetic for months began to loosen and warm.

Everything she was saying was exactly what I wanted to hear—which made me suspicious. I'd been trained to see the duality, the struggle between good and evil, Jehovah and Satan, the congregation and the World, true religion and false. And here was someone telling me these were perceptions based on fear, creating an illusion of separation—a very harmful dream that was responsible for a great deal of suffering. I wasn't able to embrace—or even understand—everything she was saying, but I was drawn to it. My innate wisdom—the same small voice that had told me to leave my religion one year earlier—encouraged me to keep listening, to mull it over. If God was indeed patient, and I was entitled to the dignity of my own process, then time was on my side.

And yet, for reasons unexplainable in the moment, that very Sunday, I returned to the Kingdom Hall. It had been a brutally cold February, and I'd spent most of that weekend indoors and alone, curled up with the cat, doing laundry, eating, and reading. I longed to get out of the house and be in familiar surroundings, where a few friendly people might say hello to me by name. My homing device for "community" was still wired for the Kingdom Hall. I was experiencing guilty pleasure from listening to the lectures on the Course in Miracles and suspect I wanted to attend a meeting to see if I could capture anything redeeming from the sermon, anything at all to draw me the way the Course was drawing me.

Ten minutes before the service was to begin, I walked into the foyer of the Kingdom Hall. I was relieved to see Deborah and Ray standing by the coat rack, peeling off layers of coats, hats, and scarves. Their greeting was warm and openhearted.

"You're welcome to sit with us," said Ray. "I'm giving the talk today, so Deb would probably appreciate the company."

"Thank you," I said, removing my heavy coat and hanging it next to theirs. The main Hall was filled with people milling around, finding their seats, talking. I recognized several of the faces from the dinner at Deborah and Ray's house. It was oddly comforting when a few of them came up to me and said hello as I followed Ray and Deborah up the aisle to choose our seats. The gray-haired man with all those tales of his travels to Indonesia was off to the side of the stage, buttoning his suit jacket. He approached the microphone, cleared his throat, and called the meeting to order. I was thrilled when he announced that we would be singing one of my favorite songs—"We Thank You Jehovah." I pulled my old *Kingdom Songbook* from my purse, knowing what page to open to before being told, allowing myself to be seduced by the familiar. It felt right to sing along. The mood of the melody is one of awe and gratitude, thanking God for light, guidance, and spirit. Despite my spiritual waffling and confusion, I was unwavering in my appreciation for all that I had.

However, the feeling was short-lived. The third stanza talked of giving praise for Christ's sacrifice, and the honor of preaching and teaching. I felt myself pulling back, unwilling or unable to give voice to that lyric. Sacrifice of any kind seemed brutal, unnecessary. Hadn't we all sacrificed enough?

The opening prayer came next. The brother followed the precise format, asking for forgiveness, and I recoiled inside as he begged for the Holy Spirit to help us conquer the "desires of the flesh." I recognized it as a thought form based on fear, not love. Going on, he asked Jehovah to protect everyone there from the influences of Satan and his worldly, doomed system. Again I saw the fear, and how this religion fostered a feeling of separation as a positive state. And yet my recent experience was of how painful that separation can be. How ironic that I'd come here to feel connected, to experience belonging somewhere.

I was silent as those around me echoed "amen" to that prayer. Deborah and I took our seats. I regretted coming and couldn't wait to leave, but years of training to "be good" kept me in my seat. I pulled my Bible from my purse, set it on my lap, and buckled down to ride out Ray's talk. For most of that hour, I mentally checked out, allowing my mind to wander wherever it wished, without concern or desire to pull it back to the topic at hand. I don't remember what he talked about, except that it was all "old news" to me, nothing new or uplifting. Instead, the messaged weighed on me and I found myself feeling spacey, then sleepy.

At the midpoint of the meeting, after Ray's talk and before the Watchtower discussion, I said goodbye to Deborah under my breath and excused myself. Pulling my coat collar up around my neck and ears, I walked out into the steely air, so sharp it pierced my nostrils. Later that day, I spoke to Mom, who was overjoyed to learn about my trip to the Hall. I told only of going and did not elaborate on my discomfort, my relief in leaving early, or how I'd listened to Marianne Williamson again on the drive home.

The meeting with Richard was the best thing I could have done. He was a banker's banker, a numbers man, and needed to shift his attention away from the big fat zero next to my name and onto all the millions of dollars sitting on the runway. We sat in his corner office and methodically reviewed each opportunity I was pursuing. I was well prepared and had thoughtful answers for every one of his questions. I took the risk of admitting that, after months of deliberate effort, I was baffled that this was taking so long. My honesty took him aback, but he said he shared my disappointment.

"Richard, is there anything you suggest I approach differently, anything I've overlooked?"

He leaned back in his leather chair, his fingers tapping the armrest, and looked at me for what seemed like a very long time. Finally, he shook his head and said something that was music to my ears.

"No. No, there isn't. You've done everything I can think of."

"Would you be willing to come out on a few calls with me?" I asked.

His face lit up. Most of my colleagues tried to keep him at

a distance from the selling process. "It could showcase the commitment of executive management and help our cause."

Over the coming weeks, his secretary arranged for him and me to host several lunches at the executive dining room in downtown Chicago. Richard seemed invigorated by being included, and I got to see a new side—a human side—of him. I came to appreciate his years of experience in the industry and how many people he knew throughout the Chicago banking community. Richard was a gold mine of information; he knew who had worked where and when and for whom. Through these meetings, he got to see me in action, how I handled myself and our prospective clients. He emerged as a supportive ally, and that allowed me to relax some. Feeling less on the defensive, I once again started enjoying the process of selling. The enthusiasm that had eluded me started to percolate.

～∽

One day in March, I returned from a work lunch and discovered I had a voice message from David, a Chicago banker. I'd given him a proposal months earlier, and we'd kept in touch ever since. He consistently encouraged me not to give up on him, and said one day—when the time was right—he'd become a client and tackle the conversion process.

"Linda," the message began, "I hope you're sitting down while you listen to this." David's sanguine tone had me hanging on his every word. "Last week I presented your proposal to our executive committee, and they approved it." A shot of adrenaline whipped through my body as I stood up and continued listening. I could tell David was smiling when he spoke. "That's right. We're ready to go. Give me a call so we can get this ball rolling."

I listened to the message a second time, and a third, allowing the stunned feeling to melt into joy. My first instinct was to hang up the phone and twirl about the room in triumph. Instead, I took a breath and returned David's call. After the mutually congratulatory banter, I promised to send a contract via overnight mail. He was anxious to move forward and thought the legal review could be done that week. This was my second bit of good news, as corporate attorneys can waylay these deals for weeks. David assured me he had an inside track and was confident of the timing, impressing upon me the need to get my team lined up.

Catherine was in closed-door meetings until late that afternoon. I'd been impatient to share this news with her and had refrained from telling anyone else. Poking my head through her office doorway, I caught her eye and she motioned for me to come in. I closed the door behind me and sat down to wait as she finished a phone call. My sense of jubilation and validation were palpable.

"You look like the Cheshire cat," Catherine said, putting her phone down.

"Are you available this Friday to join me in the city for an early-afternoon meeting with Mid-Town Bank?" I asked. Catherine glanced down to check her calendar. "Today I received a verbal commitment from them to move forward."

Catherine froze in place and looked up, a luminous smile across her face. "Well, well," she said. "The moment we've all been waiting for and knew would come. Congratulations."

"The legal review starts tomorrow, and my contact there is committed to pushing it through this week," I said. "I'd love it if you came with me to pick up the contract and welcome them aboard."

"Absolutely," Catherine said. "And after that, there's a small bar just around the corner where we can celebrate."

"One more thing," I said. "Unless you disagree, I'd prefer that this not be announced to Richard or anyone else until the ink is dry on the contract."

"Good call," Catherine said. "Remind me of the numbers again."

"Fifty million dollars in annual volume." It would move me from last to third in sales for the team.

That week unfolded with excitement and ease. David made good on his promise, returning the contract to me within days, and our in-house risk managers supported my request for a rush review. The final contract would be ready to sign by the end of the week.

Mid-Town Bank was a short walk from my apartment. I parked my car at home and floated down Clark Street toward the Friday afternoon meeting, poised and confident, breath visible with each step.

The encounter went off without a hitch. Catherine and I emerged with the signed contract and a clear plan to move forward.

"Cheers," she said, raising her glass of chardonnay in the neighborhood bar where we went afterward. "I never lost faith this day would come." We clinked glasses. I thanked her for her support and sipped my wine. I was practically levitating off the barstool with relief. The stalemate had ended.

Catherine used her cell phone to share the good news with Richard, paid the tab, and departed for her long drive to the suburbs. I walked toward home along Lincoln Park West, turning back toward Clark Street in time to visit my favorite shoe boutique. I told the owner I was celebrating, and he got right into the swing of things, helping me select a new pair of pumps as my reward. It was five o'clock when I walked into my apartment, no one but my cat to party with. Richard had left a message congratulating me.

The first person I called to share my good news with was Cindy. She would be assigned to manage the relationship, and we were thrilled about the chance to roll up our sleeves and work on a specific project together. She was still at the office, where a large whiteboard was kept with an ever-growing list of new sales for each month. She promised to post my win "with your name next to it, so everyone knows." My ego loved that idea.

Next, I phoned Steve. The month before, I'd sent him a birthday card as a small peace offering. I couldn't bear the thought of losing him as a friend. He'd done so much to help me get acclimated in Chicago, and I really did care about him. Out of that gesture had come a casual dinner the week before, where we'd both admitted that friendship suited us way better than romance.

He had always listened patiently to my work anxieties, and I knew he would be happy about my news. He promised to buy me dinner sometime in the next month to celebrate. "Or maybe you should pay," he said. "You're the one getting the big fat commission check." And I laughed. Without the burden of romantic expectations, we were much freer with each other.

So there I was, alone in my apartment. I took a long, hot shower then opened a bottle of wine. As I sipped a glass and scanned takeout menus, I noticed a complete absence of loneliness. In fact, I was grateful for the solitude. Managing details all week was intense, and the victory sustained me. Many questions had been answered that week. The fulcrum I'd organized my life around had come through. I could do this job and fashion a life in this town. What now seemed like trite and tedious doubts about the future vanished with David's signature and commitment. I was staying in Chicago.

Chapter 14

◦◦◦

I was born into the Hebrew persuasion, but then I converted to narcissism.

—Woody Allen

The next week, temperatures plunged back to single dig-
its and a blizzard canceled out all views from my balcony.
There was possibility in the fresh and consuming whiteness.
Brio and bounce had returned to my countenance. More than
ever, work took center stage, as I immersed myself in the conversion phase that comes with each sale. I kept appointments
with David's staff and held internal meetings with Cindy and
others following through on the promises I'd made. I learned
as much about the practical side of the industry in those four or
five weeks as I'd learned in the previous eight months. It was
unusual for the salesperson to be so involved in a conversion, but
I wanted to understand the practical aspects of our "back room"
operation. It was very satisfying to see it all come together and
provide David with regular updates of our progress. We were
both happy with the end result.

My focus was split between the conversion and ongoing sales
efforts in Chicago and beyond. I started flying to Houston every
other week, where I had to establish relationships from scratch
through cold calling. This was much different from being in the
close-knit Chicago banking community, where I could rely on
Harris Bank's regional dominance and reputation to open doors.

One early spring day I was enjoying lunch at an outdoor

café in Houston's Galleria area, basking in sunshine and seventy-degree temperatures as bleak weather persisted at home. It was a nice break; I was often overwhelmed with the scope of intention and diligence needed to get things off the ground: learning my way around yet another new city, identifying the people of influence there, crafting a compelling enough story to get a foot in the door. As the waitress set down my sandwich plate, I thought about how much I dined solo. When I wasn't at work, I spent a lot of time in my own company, traipsing through airports, using the treadmill in some vacuous hotel fitness center, reading a novel, or gazing out the window of an airplane. Munching on my potato salad, I felt oddly assured about my new capacity for self-sufficiency. I was standing on my own two feet in every way; emotionally, financially, spiritually, physically. It was lonely at times, but even that opened the way for richly textured thoughts and ideas about life to bubble up and nourish me. My days had become so full of people and problem-solving that I welcomed quiet moments like these, free to reflect, uninterested or unable to muster energy for socializing.

About that time, another Chicago bank I'd pursued for months decided to go with us, requiring me to negotiate a second contract. I greeted the news with glee and gratitude on the inside but a lack of fanfare on the outside, attempting to project the persona of an old-hand salesperson. I'd inched up to second place in sales for the year. There was an avalanche of work to do, and I allowed myself to be carried away by the mass of details and meetings, which made it easier to dismiss fears about my future and unexpected explosions of homesickness.

But then one balmy evening in May, as I arrived home, I heard the muffled sound of my phone ringing.

"Hello," I said, irritation slipping into my cadence.

"Hey, Linda." The lethargic, Eeyore-like voice belonged to Ross. I immediately regretted having answered the phone.

"Hey," I said, forcing some enthusiasm into my reply.

"How are you?" It was a perfunctory question.

"Fine," I said, instinctively aware that he was pressing on

to some end, some bit of news or something important to say. "And you?" I said. "To what do I owe this pleasure?"

"I'll come straight to the point," he said. I started pacing back and forth in the kitchen: two steps, turn; two steps, turn.

"Linda, I've met someone." I stopped pacing. He told me her name and what a great sense of humor she had. She and her family had recently moved into the congregation. I got the impression she was in her early twenties. "She's fantastic, and for some crazy reason she likes me, too. But I can't date her, now can I?" His voice was taut, anger rippling just under each syllable. My stomach twisted.

"Can I?" Ross repeated the question.

I wanted to tell him the truth right then and there. I felt the words collecting in my throat, the incantation that would release him, release me, from this retched spell.

"Linda, am I free?" he asked, mewling now.

I knew what I had to do. If I told him what he so desperately wanted to hear, he'd jump off the phone and broadcast the news to all his friends. But I couldn't do that to my family. This was the sort of confession I wanted to make in person. There could be no more hemming and hawing. My next steps were clear and poignant and absolute.

"No, Ross," I paused. "No, you're not free."

I could hear a deep sigh from him that turned into a groan.

"Woman," he said, "you're killing me."

"Guilty as charged," I said. It was seven o'clock in Portland, and this was a Tuesday night, when he would usually have been at the Kingdom Hall.

"No meeting tonight?" I asked.

"Couldn't do it tonight," Ross said. "Just feeling too down to be around people. I've been trying to reach you since six."

"Should I be worried about you?" I asked pacing again.

"No. Don't do me any favors. I've got plenty of people here covering that territory."

"Well, then," I said, "if there is nothing else you wish to harass me about, I'll be going."

"Good night." And I heard the click of the phone line trail off into oblivion.

I opened a can of soup to warm on the stove and drew a hot bath. I didn't feel guilty anymore for lying, if indeed withholding private information can be called lying. I had a plan, and Ross would be thanking me soon enough. It was a relief to know he'd found someone else to love. A solitary lifestyle had never suited him. I was ready to take the stand for my freedom to a whole new level. I'd been bucking the current—pushing against reality—and it was exhausting. It was bigger than I was, and it was time to surrender to the call of my heart, without reservation. This would require me to tell my family and the elders the truth, My Truth, to bear witness to my own story, the only one I could fully vouch for.

The next evening, I started working a plan that was fine-tuned over several therapy sessions. I phoned Deborah's husband, Ray and requested a visit—known as a shepherding call—to discuss a "pressing personal matter." We found a mutually agreeable time, contingent on his finding another elder to come along. It was unthinkable for him to visit the home of a single woman alone or meet with me in a public place.

Next, I called my parents. Some weeks earlier, they'd raised the possibility of my flying home in the summer and joining them for a vacation in Central Oregon. For about five years running, we had rented the same large house in a resort town there. We'd always found it a fun and restorative place to go together. I'd stalled my mom when she'd first suggested it, but that night I told her I'd been able to schedule some vacation time, and we agreed to secure the house after all.

I set down the phone receiver. I could almost smell the sweet perfume of the pine trees that lined the meadows there. It would be the best place to tell them the truth about my life. It held enough happy memories to feel safe, but it was a place we could all leave behind. I'd enjoy our time together. I'd absorb as much of their love and affection as possible—the emotional equivalent of storing nuts for the winter. And then I'd sit them down for a talk the morning before our drive back to Portland and tell them the truth. I couldn't be sure how they'd react in the moment. But I was absolutely sure of one thing: they would shun me.

They'd believe they had no choice, that it was what Jehovah wanted and a rightful rebuke for someone this haughty. I knew this was the last vacation I'd have with my family for some time to come, if ever. They, of course, would be oblivious to this plan, anticipating my visit as always, glad to see me, hoping for some glimmer of humility in my spiritual state. It would be a shock—but then again, maybe not. I knew only that I had to move forward, to free Ross, to free myself—and telling them in person was the only dignified thing to do.

Chapter 15

The truth is rarely pure and never simple.
—Oscar Wilde

I'd alerted Demitri to the elders' impending arrival and requested that he let them in. He called just after they passed through the lobby, heading toward the elevator and my apartment. It was a Sunday afternoon. I'd spent a relaxed morning reading the paper, then biked along the lakefront to the Shedd Aquarium and back. The ride allowed me to clear my head and think through what I might say later. I'd come home and cleaned up, then stalled a bit in front of my opened closet. *What are the kids wearing these days to confess their sins?* I settled on jeans and a plain white blouse.

There was a knock on my door. I stroked the cat, who had been watching me from the edge of the dresser.

"Wish me luck, Leo."

I opened the door to greet Ray and the elder who'd traveled to Indonesia.

"Hi, Linda," Ray said turning to the side. "This is Jeremy Schwartz. He tells me you two have already met at my house, which I have no recollection of, but I'll take his word for it."

"Hello," he said, and smiled as he reached out to shake my hand.

"Yes," I said. "Nice to see you again. Please come in."

They were both wearing suits, no doubt the same ones they'd worn to the Kingdom Hall that morning. But neither wore a tie, and only Ray carried a briefcase. I supposed one Bible was enough to pound me over the head with, just as Vince Lloyd had done before I left Portland. I'd planned on "confessing my sins" to them, knowing they would take it from there. Earlier that week, I'd pulled out from an unpacked box the Witness book *Organized to Accomplish our Ministry*—a sort of policies-and-procedures book for congregational order. I'd looked up the section for expelling unrepentant sinners and came across this Scripture from First Corinthians:

"But now I am writing you to quit mixing in company with anyone called a brother that is a fornicator or a greedy person or an idolater or a reviler or a drunkard or an extortioner, not even eating with such a man. For what do I have to do with judging those outside? Do you not judge those inside, while God judges those outside. Remove the wicked man from among yourselves."

That was me. A fornicator. And greedy, too. The book of James was quoted:

"My brothers, if anyone among you is misled from the truth and another turns him back, know that he who turns a sinner back from the error of his way will save his soul from death and will cover a multitude of sins."

In other words, you get spiritual bonus points if you bring someone back into the fold. That's what these elders would try to do now.

"Look at that view," Jeremy said, pushing past Ray and walking straight through the living room. In the distance was the true-blue lake, dotted with sailboats. Jeremy had stopped short at the closed screen.

"Feel free to go onto the balcony," I said. Jeremy pushed open the screen and stepped outside. Ray set down his briefcase and stood in the living room, hands at his waist, smiling.

"What a great place," he said, scanning the living room, the kitchen.

"Thanks. The apartment isn't anything special, but the view is priceless. I can sit on the balcony for hours and not get bored."

Jeremy had removed his jacket and folded it over his arm

without looking away from the view. But as Ray took a seat at the farthest corner of the couch, Jeremy followed his lead, came in, and sat in the side chair. I took a seat on the opposite end of the couch from Ray, one cushion between us.

After a brief silence, Ray started speaking to Jeremy, detailing what he already knew about me.

"Linda was raised in The Truth and moved here from Portland," he said. Turning to me, he asked, "And you pioneered for several years, didn't you, Linda?"

"Yes," I said. "Five in total." I was already growing impatient with memory lane and thought it odd Ray hadn't told Jeremy any of this before arriving. To my surprise, Jeremy looked thoroughly engaged.

"How can we help you?" Ray asked.

I turned to lean against the arm of the couch so I could face them both. "For a while now, I've had something on my mind that I'd like to share." I spoke directly to Jeremy, to bring him up to speed.

"About a year and a half ago, I started experiencing doubts about this religion. I was raised a Witness, married a Witness, really knew no other way of living or thinking. I found myself curious about the world and, much to my husband and family's chagrin, became inactive. I thought if I got some distance from the religion, I could also get some perspective. I divorced my husband of nine years, on the grounds of irreconcilable differences. We were married young. It wasn't a bad marriage, but it wasn't great, either, and I wanted to free us both to live our separate lives. About that time, Harris Bank recruited me and moved me here to Chicago, and not a moment too soon. I was quite happy to get away."

Both men were looking at me, following along in earnest.

"This past year has been tough—so much transition. But I can't say I have any regrets. I'm no longer afraid of the world, like it's something to be avoided. I feel like I have a new lease on life—there's so much to learn and discover."

"How do you feel about The Truth?" asked Jeremy.

I remembered his prayer, and all that talk about Satan and the "desires of the flesh."

"Being at the Kingdom Hall is very uncomfortable," I said.

"That's not uncommon for someone in your situation," said Ray. Jeremy nodded his head in agreement. I knew I needed to get more direct in my language. This was turning out to be easier than I thought, perhaps because I lacked history with these men and was not seeking their approval.

"Teachings that once comforted me now seem archaic. There are rules for everything, and I don't care to live that way. I've become curious about other religions, other ideas. I haven't pursued anything yet, but I'm open to it. One thing I'm clear about is that I don't plan to attend meetings at all anymore."

Ray sat expressionless. "What does your family say to this?"

"I'm traveling to Portland in two weeks. I'll tell them then."

"I'm sure they'll be very disappointed."

"No doubt." I said. "Even more so when I tell them one more thing, which is why I really asked you here today."

I could hear a police siren in the distance and getting closer, probably from Lake Shore Drive.

"I've gotten involved with someone, a lovely man." I'd decided in advance I wasn't going to reveal that my dalliances had started over a year ago, or that there had been more than one. I felt foolish enough talking about something so personal with near strangers. But this was official business, part of the process, so I pressed on. "When I go home, I'll also be telling my ex-husband that he is free." They correctly understood I meant Ross was now free to remarry.

I'd expected to feel lighter, freer, but I didn't. Part of me felt sorry these decent people had to spend a beautiful Sunday afternoon talking about this soap opera that was my life.

"When were you dedicated and baptized?" Ray asked, wanting to clarify my official standing with the organization.

"Ages ago," I said. "I was sixteen." I felt like I was remembering something from another person's life.

"This is very serious for you," Ray said.

"Yes," I said. "Life-changing."

I expected him to pull out his Bible and beseech me with Scripture, but both men sat still for a moment, observing my determined expression.

"Is there anything we can say to help you change your mind?" Jeremy asked.

"No," I said. "I know you consider this a gross sin."

"It is on the Bible's authority that we call it a sin," Jeremy said, correcting me.

"I no longer share that view, nor do I feel any remorse."

"That is clear," said Ray. He was resting his hands on his thighs. Leo had curled up in a ball next to him to sleep.

"I wanted to meet with you before I go to Portland, to see what this means for me."

Ray looked solemn as he spoke. "I don't think there's any need for action at this moment," he said. "I'd like to wait until you see your family. I know you have elders and people there who know you better than us. Perhaps after you see them all, you'll feel differently."

"My family has a poor record of talking me out of anything," I said.

"All the same," Ray said, "at least you can indulge us in hope. Being disfellowshipped is a serious matter. What's the rush?"

This was not what I'd expected. I'd wanted action, to be condemned for my rebellious attitude, to be put on notice, anything but more waiting, more time. I'd confessed to a grave sin and showed no remorse, and this elder was buying time, lingering on the possibility that I'd come around. If I showed any signs of sorrow or shame, they'd try to work with me. I maintained a calm exterior, but inside I was stewing. Until he stalled, I hadn't realized how much I really wanted out.

"You have my number, then," Ray said, standing up, tugging up on his pants by the belt loops. "Please call me when you return. We'll take it from there."

Jeremy and I stood up in unison. Without saying a word, he put his jacket back on.

"Fair enough," I said. They had been there thirty minutes and had never once broken out a Bible or preached to me in any way. I walked them to the door and said goodbye. The apartment was still again. The first step in my plan was done.

⤜⤏

The next day it rained, beginning a long string of morose, gray days. I came down with a cold and had to force myself out the door to work each morning. The end of my nose was red and tender from all the Kleenex I rubbed against it, and the smell of menthol cough drops was my constant companion. I'd be traveling to Portland in a week's time, and I needed to build strength for the journey.

My parents had been successful in reserving the Black Butte house for a long weekend in June. The plan was for me to fly to Portland on Thursday and spend the night at my parents' house. The next afternoon, the entire family would make the drive together to Central Oregon, arriving in time for dinner. That left me time in the morning to meet Ross for breakfast.

When the day arrived to pack my bags and catch a cab to O'Hare, a heavy melancholy came over me. My family was unaware, but I was coming as the hapless bearer of bad news. Grave news. Life-altering news. I sank into my window seat and tried to lose myself in the newspaper and in-flight movie.

On the ground in Portland, I'd expected my sister to pick me up at curbside, as we'd discussed. As I disembarked from the plane, I was surprised to see Dad and Lory waiting for me at the gate. The moment I saw them, my heart skipped a beat and I was practically overcome by the love and affection I felt for them. It brought tears to my eyes. I'd missed them more than I'd allowed myself to admit. It was Thursday night, so they were both missing meetings at the Kingdom Hall. Their presence elevated my dreary mood, and we all talked excitedly on the car ride to my parents' house. When we arrived, I walked through the front door and called out to Mom, who was already there, preparing a light dinner of soup and salad. I heard her exclaim from the kitchen to no one, "Lindy's here." She dropped what she was doing and came out to give me a hug. As much as she had irritated me over the months with her nagging, it was all forgotten in that moment. I was so happy to see her, standing there, smiling, in her quilted bathrobe and slippers.

When I carried my suitcase into my old bedroom, I found a WELCOME HOME sign tacked up at each corner of the closet. It felt magical, a rainbow of bright metallic colors strung together, as if the letters were dancing arm in arm, saluting me. No one had ever done something like that for me, and I understood what it must feel like to celebrate one's birthday or discover an unexpected surprise in one's honor.

"That was Lory's idea," Dad said, popping his head in to call me to dinner.

Mom, Dad, Lory, and I sat around the kitchen table, slurping soup, chatting idly about this and that. Ove had gone to conduct the meeting at the Kingdom Hall and was expected to drop by later to say hello and take Lory home.

"Where's Randy?" I asked, realizing no one had uttered a word about my brother since my arrival.

Lory stopped chewing.

"We're not going to see him, I'm afraid." Mom's voice was weary. Dad shook his head as she spoke, staring into his soup bowl.

"They've decided to skip this trip," he said, still looking down.

My chest tightened, and I swallowed hard.

"Because of me?" I asked, looking from person to person, seeing confirmation in each downcast expression. Just then, bread popped out of the toaster. No one moved. "They're boycotting Black Butte because of me?"

The annoyed looks on their faces told me Randy's decision was controversial. I surmised it had generated a fair amount of consternation among them in the days leading up to my arrival. The entire family had always gone to Black Butte together. It would be a completely different experience without the presence of my niece and nephew, giggling at the pool, having tickle fights before bedtime, letting me give them piggyback rides to the clubhouse, Sheena sitting in front of me at the fire, asking for a "rub back." I could feel my cheeks warming.

"Maybe I should stop in to see them before we leave tomorrow," I said, grasping at the high road. Randy lived just a few blocks from my parents. The corners of Mom's mouth sank at the suggestion.

"I don't think that's such a good idea," she said. "Randy made a point that he would avoid our home during your visit, and that you were not welcome to go there."

My throat stung. "Wow," I said. I felt like a large hammer had just pounded me into place. It was a curt reminder of what I was going to face from each of them. They would all be on the same side soon enough. I also realized with sadness that I would not get to see Sheena and Tyler, probably for a long while. The WELCOME HOME sign and surprise greeting at the airport suddenly made more sense. My family was compensating for my brother's absence, attempting to ease the sting of his condemnation.

"Their loss," I said, shaking off the bad news, at least at the surface. "What's the shower schedule for the morning?" And we went back to our banter, talking through the logistics of the next day. We couldn't recapture our riant mood, but I could feel everyone's relief in having delivered this bitter news.

After clearing the table and helping with the dishes, I retreated to my room to unpack and absorb this setback. I unzipped my suitcase and slid the closet door open. *I can't have it both ways*, I thought, shaking the wrinkles out of a pair of pants. *My choices are freedom or family. What a lousy set of options. Why couldn't I have been satisfied with my life the way it was? Was it really so bad? Why couldn't I have come from a religion or a family where differing lifestyles were met with tolerance?* I sank into bed, drifting to sleep on a sea of sepia-toned memories.

The next morning, I rose early, showered, dressed, and repacked my bags. Mom had offered to lend me her car for my drive into the city, where I was to meet Ross for breakfast. I sought her out to borrow her keys and found her in the kitchen, counting out vitamin pills and dropping them into a container with separate compartments for each day of the week. She was wearing the same bathrobe and slippers she'd had on the night before.

"The keys are on the piano," she said, and stopped what she was doing, turning to look at me.

"And, Lindy, dear," she said. "When you meet with Ross, don't be too haughty. You've put him through a lot, and the only chance you have at forgiveness will be to eat some crow."

I stopped in my tracks, speechless. These comments came out of the blue. Did she think I'd come home to seek forgiveness from Ross, to reconcile with him? I searched my memory for some conversation—any conversation—that would have caused her to expect this and came up short. I'd never told my parents, or even Ross, the full nature of my intent in seeing him. He had a car title and other papers he wanted me to sign off on, and as far as he or anyone else knew, that was the main purpose of our meeting. After my initial shock wore off, I felt anger jump through me, a freight train of emotions that I caught in my throat—just in time.

"Thanks, Mother," I said, hearing, as I'm sure she did, the thinly veiled agitation in my voice. *Forgiveness for what? For following my heart? For moving away from fearing the world to see instead a world of vibrant possibility? For this I must ask for forgiveness?* It was too big to take on then and there. The weekend was just beginning, and I had an appointment to keep. This didn't lessen my resolve, but it did make me dread my moment of truth, as I realized anew the full force of disappointment awaiting my mother.

Ross was already seated at the table of my favorite breakfast spot in the city. I'd suggested this diner, an enclave for local writers and actors, because it was unlikely that we'd run into anyone we knew. I caught his eye and walked over to greet him. He smiled and stood, kissing me formally on the cheek. He looked as though he'd dropped a few pounds.

"You look like you've lost weight," he said.

"I was just thinking the same thing about you," I said, settling into the seat opposite his.

"I owe it all to stress," he said.

"Me too."

"I already ordered you a latte," he said, still familiar with some of my habits.

The conversation was very ordinary, like one between two old friends who hadn't seen each other in a while. I asked about his job, his boss, his mom, and certain friends of ours. Things were easy between us. We ordered our usual meals, and then I pulled out a manila envelope stuffed with old photographs.

"I thought you should have these," I said. In the stress and confusion of our separation, I'd ended up with nine years' worth of photos from our time together. In preparation for seeing him this last time, I'd gone through them all and pulled out things I knew Ross would like to have, pictures that were more his memories than mine. There were pictures of him at work, another of him with Ellen Kyte on the day of his baptism, another of he and his mom at the Portland Rose Garden.

"I'd forgotten all about these," he said, sifting through the pictures. "Thanks. I'll take a closer look at them later." He stuffed the photos back in the envelope, pushed it aside, and sipped his coffee. "Enough about me. How are you doing?"

It was my opening, but I couldn't bear to ruffle his feathers before our food had even arrived. I started by telling him more about Chicago—where I lived, how city living compared to the suburbs, and how worried I was to make my first sale. Our food was served, and I became aware of how hungry I was, slathering my biscuits with butter as I rattled on about the weather, midwestern sensibilities, and the Cubs cult of the North Side. He laughed in all the right places.

"Can I bring you more coffee?" asked our waiter, a local theater actor who'd worked at the café for years. The question brought me back to Portland and the moment.

"Yes, thank you," I said, then turned to look out the window.

A meter maid was ticketing a car just in front of the restaurant. "We leave this afternoon for Black Butte."

"So I heard. I ran into Ove, and he told me," Ross said. The grapevine was alive and well. "No Randy this year?"

"No Randy, no Ross," I said, the words catching in my throat. Ross looked older then, his freckles faded, his hair more burnished than red. His blue eyes looked right through me.

"Do you have anything else you want to tell me?" he asked. He knew why I'd come. I just needed to say the words.

"Yes," I said, just as the waiter refilled our coffee cups. Ross didn't take his eyes away from mine. I took a deep breath. "I've moved on, Ross. I've gotten involved with someone."

As I held his gaze, his eyes filled with tears.

"So here are the words you've been wanting to hear: you're free."

He kept looking at me, expressionless except for the watery eyes.

"Free, free, free," I said in a gentle, steady tone.

Ross leaned his head back to keep the tears from streaming down his face. He worked to regain his composure.

"I've expected this for a long while," he said, "but hearing it feels terrible." He wiped his nose with the napkin. "I thought I'd be happy to hear this, but I'm not."

Relief and a bone-tired peace came over me, sitting there, being honest, telling him the truth. Never underestimate the power of an honest answer, even if it means disappointing someone you love. We can all recover from disappointment, but lying about who we really are and how we really feel keeps everyone in chains. Just saying these words made me stronger, more resolved. I sat back in my chair and let out a sigh.

"What's his name?"

"No names," I said, adamant.

"I'm afraid to ask how long this has been going on," he said.

"Then don't ask," I said, my voice clipped. I felt the absurdity of the situation, confessing to something that happened a year ago, as if it were occurring in the present. "I wanted to tell you sooner, but it's not exactly the kind of thing you say to a person over the phone."

"I suppose not," Ross nodded, resigned.

"And I was afraid you'd blab to everyone, and I couldn't do that to my family. I want them to hear this from me, not through the grapevine."

"Probably a good call," he said. The check was delivered to our table, and Ross picked it up. "Let me get this—a small price to pay for news of my freedom."

He had become distant and lethargic. "Your family will be devastated not to be able to see you."

"As if they have no choice as to how they'll react or treat me." I could feel anger rising in my throat.

"They won't see it that way, and you know it."

"No kidding." I knew he was right. He understood, as I did, that my family would turn away from me if I were to be disfellowshipped. "Mom thinks I'm having breakfast with you to discuss getting back together."

"Hope springs eternal," Ross said. "She's in for a grim reckoning."

We sat for a moment, contemplating this, nodding our heads.

"My plan is to enjoy their company over the weekend, then sit them down and tell them before we leave on Sunday. I know how selfish that sounds, but I want to have some time just being with them."

"Before you drop the bomb?"

"Before the hammer comes down," I said. "But this is none of your concern. It's my challenge to face, not yours. It's time for you to get on with your life. You deserve that."

"Thanks for finally being straight with me," he said.

We both sat quiet for a long moment.

"Linda, forget about me, us, everything—you're walking away from Jehovah." He shook his head, his voice pleading. "It's a dangerous game you're in—like playing Russian roulette with your life. I just hate to think about it."

I didn't reply, having developed a Teflon coating against that line of thinking.

We stood without saying a word and walked to the street corner together.

"Goodbye, Ross," I said.

"Goodbye, Linda."

We gave each other a hug and walked in opposite directions.

⁓

I'd expected to feel sad. Instead, as I drove my mother's car through Portland's city streets, I was relieved and a little gleeful. The conversation had freed me from the yearlong weight of a secret life. Over the year, I'd started to locate—to remember—a wise, ancient, knowing part of myself, a more authentic self, and had risked showing it. She wasn't fully fleshed out, this new self, but I was proud of her and I liked hanging out with her. I'd come this far in overhauling my life and decided to put it all on the line. I had just seen with my own eyes and heart that Ross would be fine, and so would I.

We'd come together at an important time in each other's lives, and together we'd learned a lot about how to do life. We'd taken it as far as we could as a team. I could tell by Ross's response that he loved me in a way that was genuine. Given his convictions, he feared for the path I'd chosen, but he wasn't going to argue or stand in my way. I felt as if we had come full circle and I'd just participated in an honorable completion.

As I turned the car into my parents' driveway, I saw that my father had backed his Trooper up to the garage and was loading our luggage into the back. The unexpected advantage of Randy's not traveling with us was that all five of us could ride together in one vehicle, rather than creating a caravan of many cars. Dad gestured for me to park to the side. As I did, Lory and Ove pulled up in their Volvo and parked next to me. My excitement was building. Relieved by how well the morning had gone, and clear of my plan not to talk to my family until the end of the weekend, I was able to give myself to the moment. Everyone seemed in a jovial, expectant mood. It was early enough on Friday to assume we'd beat the weekend traffic. We got into the Trooper. I sat in the backseat, between Lory and Ove. Mom sat in the front passenger seat, fastened her seat belt, and turned to me.

"How was your breakfast with Ross?" she asked, reading too much, I feared, into the radiant smile on my face. Everyone in the car stopped what they were doing and fell silent.

I needed to set a realistic expectation for the sake of everyone's sanity.

"Nice," I said, nodding at my mom. "It was great to see Ross. We had a very good talk, and I want to tell you all about it, but not now. It's time to have fun. I'll let you know when I'm ready to share, and we can all gather around the table."

This seemed to satisfy everyone.

"Good idea," my dad said, looking at me through the rear-view mirror. "Let's get this show on the road." I imagined he was worn out by the situation and happy to postpone any serious talk for later. He turned the key and put the car in gear, and we were off.

Chapter 16

❦

We must be willing to get rid of the life we've planned, so as to have the life that is waiting for us.
—Joseph Campbell

We arrived at the house by midafternoon, the sun high in the sky, the pine trees' succulent aroma seducing me to relax. For all my talk of loving big-city life and embracing the concrete jungle, I noticed how much I missed the intense green of Oregon, white-capped Cascades touching heaven, the tree line of noble evergreens pointing upward. There was a sameness and stability here; any changes were slow, imperceptible, lacking human contrivance.

We found the house as always, in quiet repose, the blinds pulled down like resting eyelids. We broke through the silence with one turn of a key and began our habitation routines. Everything was as I'd remembered it, barstools lined up in an even row under the tiled kitchen counter, macramé wall hanging over the river-rock fireplace. I set a few decks of cards and poker chips on the long wood dining table and then followed my dad through the sliding glass doors leading to the back deck. He stopped still and took a deep, satisfying breath, then walked over to open an outdoor cupboard to the rear of the garage. I joined him there, and, without a word, he handed me several cushions. Together we laid them on the empty patio chairs like pieces of a puzzle.

We went inside and joined the others to finish settling in. I avoided the upstairs bedroom Ross and I used to share, choosing instead to sleep in one of the smallest rooms, tucked downstairs behind the kitchen. Because it had twin beds, it was usually reserved for Sheena and Tyler. Without the children, the house felt empty, and without Randy and Marlene there were whole rooms left unattended, which made everything feel off kilter.

Returning to the kitchen, I found Mom putting away the last of the groceries. Ove was already in the garage, pulling out the bikes. We all went for a short ride through the area, past familiar homes and vistas. It felt good to move, to get my heart pumping, shaking loose the odd awareness of being there, knowing what faced me, what faced us all that weekend.

I wanted to capture each moment like an emotional photograph: the lighthearted mood, the genuine goodwill, the ease born of familiarity, the love. Part of me was relaxing, but another was vigilant and intent to soak it in, to remember every nuance.

Ordinary things, like chopping vegetables with my sister or doing dishes with Mom, were potent with a bittersweet melancholy. I wondered if they felt it, too, the small stone in the pit of my belly. Friday turned to Saturday, and the time unfurled like ribbons in a gentle breeze. Breakfast slipped into pool time, which naturally led to another, longer bike ride, which naturally led to lunch together on the shady deck—cold fried chicken and potato salad. With full bellies, we settled in for a lazy afternoon. Dad disappeared into his room for a nap, and Ove went out to play golf. The women hung out on the deck, reading whatever books and magazines we'd brought, whiling away the hours until dinner. Mom talked about her work in the insurance agency, and Lory described a recent trip to Denmark to visit Ove's relatives. Eventually we fell quiet and gazed up to the sky. Lory dozed off. Mom and I went back to reading.

As night approached, everyone naturally gathered inside, near the kitchen, drinking wine or beer, laughing, joking as the meal came together.

Dad sat at the head of the table; Mom and I were side by

side, across from Lory and Ove. Dad asked Ove to say the prayer, and then we reveled in a simple feast of grilled salmon and vegetables. The wine and sun and exercise had finally gotten to me. I was happy, content, noticing everything that was right with that moment. I began to see that Randy's absence was for the best. Having him, Marlene, and the kids there would have complicated everything. Mom and Dad were less distracted. I was able to have more of their attention. Yes, this was the right group and the right time.

We cleared the dishes, then got out the decks of playing cards.

"What should we play?" Dad asked, shuffling the first deck.

"Hearts," Lory and I said in unison. Dad had taught us how to play the game when we were little kids, on a family camping trip. Satisfied with the shuffling, he dealt the first hand and then led with a two of clubs.

"Smoking out the queen, are we?" I asked.

"Maybe, maybe not." He grinned and shrugged his shoulders.

The rest of us were organizing the cards we'd been dealt, reviewing our hands. How auspicious, I thought, that I'd been dealt nothing but hearts and thus had no choice but to lead with one, known in the game as "breaking hearts." Once you paint a trick like that, you might as well go for it, and after many tense moments, I was able to pull off a slam.

"That was too easy," I said, gathering all the cards to shuffle before the next hand. "What's wrong with you people?"

"Hey, hey," Dad said, "we're just getting warmed up. Subtract your points and deal."

By the end of the night, Dad came out the clear winner, with the lowest score. All our boisterous laughter during the game had shaken my tension away. That night I fell asleep the moment my head hit the pillow.

I was the first to rise Sunday morning. *Don't chicken out*, I thought. I got up and slipped into the quiet kitchen to brew the coffee. Sipping from my mug, I watched two deer milling about in the meadow. I wished Dad was there to see them. *How many times in my future will I wish the same thing?*

I busied myself in the kitchen, cracking the eggs and setting up everything for Dad to make omelets, his specialty. Still alone, I poured a second cup of coffee, grabbed a blanket, and went outside to sit on the deck. *I hope this comes out all right. How will I begin? When? Before breakfast? After? Will they stop talking to me right away?*

None of these were new thoughts. I'd rehearsed different phrases over and over, but it was always a mental exercise. Surrounded by such bucolic conditions, did I really want to spoil everything?

A sound came from the kitchen. The doe and her speckled fawn froze in place for a moment, then resumed chewing. Dad poured himself a cup of coffee and then came outside. He'd dressed in jeans and a T-shirt, but his hair was uncombed.

"We have company," I said softly.

"I see," he said, sitting down on the lounge chair next to mine. Just then, another sound came from the kitchen. It was Lory, pouring herself some orange juice. Mom was up next, and soon we four were all sitting on the deck, lined up in a row, looking out at the deer. It meant so much to be there, together, in peace. Every cell in my body was alive, knowing I stood on the edge of a moment that would change everything. We engaged in idle chatter and read the Sunday paper.

"You got up early," Mom said to me. Behind the comment, I felt her anticipation. She would not have forgotten my promise from two days earlier, to tell them all about my conversation with Ross. There wasn't much time left at the house; it was our tradition to begin washing linens during breakfast, then throw them in the dryer while we took a final bike ride together. This morning was all I had left.

"I guess I'm still on Chicago time," I said.

The screen door slid open, and Ove emerged barefoot in his bathrobe, coffee mug in hand. "My head hurts," he said. "I'm not used to drinking that much wine."

"I'll be sure to make your omelet extra greasy," Dad said, then stood up and went in to the kitchen. Soon the scent of bacon and hash browns was floating around and drew us inside. Lory set the table, and I made more coffee. We sat down, and Dad served us up one by one.

I noticed that no one had remembered to start the first load of laundry. I considered getting up, and the thought preoccupied me for the longest while, as I chewed my eggs and watched Lory spread jam on her toast. But I didn't get up. I sat where I'd sat the night before, next to Mom, across from Lory and Ove, Dad at the head of the long table.

Soon the dining table was cluttered with empty plates and rumpled paper napkins. The pace of the conversation was winding down. I sensed anxiety and expectation hanging over the group, like a tiger waiting to pounce. I knew this was the moment. We were all together. *It's now or never.*

A knot formed in my stomach, like tennis shoes tossed in a clothes dryer, each thud pulsing in my ears. I was feeling small, wanting to curl up in a ball and forget my name.

"I suppose we should start washing the first load of towels," Mom said, listless.

"No, wait," I said with a start, resting my hand on her arm. She looked at me, expectant. "I want to give you all that update I promised."

Mom's shoulders dropped, and everyone settled in. I rested both hands on my lap, gazed down at them as I gained my composure. When I glanced up, all eyes were on me. They'd been waiting for this moment, too. A breeze came through the open screen door, curling pages of the newspaper stacked at the far end of the table. I started by looking directly at Mom. Her eyes still had some of the hopeful bounce of the night before, when she had shot the moon and won. But this was no game. I knew my words would be difficult to absorb or accept, so I spoke slowly.

"First, I want you to understand—really hear—that Ross and I will never, ever, ever, ever get back together." The light in her eye flickered out to a hard darkness. "That relationship is over. Really over." There was a long pause, a cloak of gloom slipping in where the lightheartedness had been. "When Ross and I had breakfast, I told him he was free. I told him that I'd met someone else, been with someone else."

Mom, Lory, and Ove looked at me in stunned silence. Dad stared out the window, arms crossed at his chest. My heart was tightening, and I could feel little compartments of each chamber shrinking to close. "In anticipation of my visit here, I met with two elders in Chicago. They came by my apartment to discuss this."

"What did they say?" Ove perked up at the mention of elder business.

"Of course, they were looking for some expression of remorse," I said, my voice flat, matter-of-fact now, detached from my body. "But I've searched my heart and can find no regrets. If I told them I was sorry, it would be a lie. A lie of convenience."

"Convenience?' Mom said, and her eyes opened wide. "There's nothing convenient about this." She was angry now, or afraid, or both.

"Least of all for me," I said.

"This isn't just about you," Lory said, her voice and eyes laden with disgust. "This affects all of us."

"I'm well aware of that," I said, bracing myself up against the roiling of emotion that was brewing around that table.

"What else did the elders say?" Dad asked, and I was surprised to see that he, too, was engaging, trying to understand.

"They didn't want to do anything until I'd been here to see you all. They're hoping I'll have a change of heart while I'm here in your company. They asked me to call them with an update when I return."

"So you went to the elders for what reason?" asked Ove. "If not to repent, then why?"

It was a fair question.

"It seemed like the right thing to do." I said. "I realize I could have written a few letters and been done with this, but I wanted to be honorable about it."

The mention of the word "honorable" seemed to provoke them.

"You may not have regrets now, but you will," Lory said. "Trust me. One day, your foolishness will hit you like a ton of bricks, and you will feel terrible."

"Perhaps." I didn't think that was likely, but I knew I could always return to the congregation if she was right. Everyone was quiet for a moment. I felt like a recalcitrant child, standing for the required scolding, waiting to be sent to my room. But I was a grown woman making rightful decisions about my life.

"Why would you do this?" Mom asked. "Was your life really so bad here? Is your life really so much better now?"

"Yes and yes," I said. "This last year has been a roller coaster. But something inside me that wasn't there before has come to life. I'm so glad I moved. I was suffocating here in an unhappy marriage, boring routines, an unfulfilling spiritual life."

"And how does an adulterous relationship support your unfolding spiritual fulfillment?" Ove asked.

Rage fomented inside me; I was so angry to have my journey belittled, reduced to nothing more than a sexual excursion. They could not fathom how any thinking person could find spiritual truths outside the Witness organization. I had always been so zealous, such a good girl. It was easier for them to conclude that hormones, rather than the deeper stirrings of the soul, were at play. But I tamped down my anger, just wanting to get through this conversation. *Let them take their shots as me. This will soon be over, and I can go home.* I felt myself becoming emotionally cool and rigid.

"In the world I inhabit, no adultery has been committed," I said, not caring how belligerent this sounded. "I'm free to do as I please."

"All things are lawful," Ove said, quoting Scripture. "But not all things are advantageous."

"With an attitude like that," Mom said, "you're just asking to be disfellowshipped."

I said nothing.

"If that happens, we won't be able to help you," Mom said, urgent now. "We won't be able to talk to you."

"Not *if*—when." Lory looked at her. "*When* she gets disfellowshipped, we won't be able to help her."

"It will kill us," Mom said, looking down. There was a jagged desperation in her voice. She tucked her hands under her knees and started to rock forward and back. "It will absolutely kill us, but we'll do it. It's for your own good." Dad nodded in agreement as she spoke, looking aggrieved, his eyes dark and beady.

"I know," I said. Hearing these words, spoken out loud by my shattered mother, pierced right through my heart. Mental rehearsals had not prepared me for the visceral pain that hit me as I watched their faces, pinched with alarm and trepidation for my soul. Their expressions would haunt my dreams for years.

"Lindy"—Mom was pleading now—"you surprise me at every turn. When I think of all those people you've helped over the years, whom you've studied the Bible with and encouraged in a thousand different ways—none of that means anything if you leave The Truth."

"Now, Mother," I said, slapping my hand on the table. I wouldn't have my life minimized like that. "Don't insult me. I refuse to believe exercising free choice negates my entire life. Anyone I've helped is still the better for it, no matter what happens to me."

She looked at me long and hard, possibly searching for the agreeable woman she'd raised, not this unwavering, contentious person before her. I was as taken aback as she was by my long-stifled passion and vehemence, but I was proud of this new self and felt protective of her daring emergence. I wanted to stretch my arms around her, keeping everyone at bay as she got her bearings and stood steady. I was asking myself the same question they were: *Who is this person?* Whoever she was, I liked and admired her, needed her to get through this fierce onslaught of once trusted voices, to heed now only the wise voice from inside.

Mom turned to my dad.

"What do you say to all of this, Frank?"

"I don't know, Mom," he said, shrugging his shoulders. "It's terrible news, of course. But when Lindy makes up her mind about something, you just gotta get out of her way." He looked at me, and I saw something in his eyes I'd never seen before. Was it resentment or disappointment? The father who raised me—the pragmatic, independent thinker who bristled at rules and resented fearmongering—he was gone. We'd switched places in the family dynamic. I rued the day he was baptized, and harbored a wish that he would be sensible and support me in secret. That he did not speak to me directly shattered that fantasy.

Lory looked at me hard.

"When you have children someday, I want you to promise you'll tell them the truth about why we don't talk to you."

She had done as I had done and mapped this out into the future, in which months or years would slip by without contact.

"Do you plan to have children?" Mom asked. "Is the man someone you plan to marry?" As with the elders and Ross, I had chosen not to go into detail about "the man."

"No plans like that, no."

"What *are* your plans, then?" Lory challenged me. "What are your goals?"

Ah, my goals. Any reply would sound feeble to their way of thinking.

"I don't know," I said, feeling pressure to sound more "together." The truth was, I didn't have any clear, defined goals, spiritual or otherwise. I knew only that I was enjoying the freedom of not having all the answers, reveling in a state of curiosity and discovery about the world. I wasn't certain that I even wanted to have children of my own. I knew I'd eventually wish to settle down with someone special but suspected that was years away. I'd been lucky enough to meet plenty of good men. I enjoyed dating for fun, unburdened from the Witness presumption of marriage. For the time being, I'd be happy to achieve some post-religious, post-marriage emotional stasis, to continue moving forward in my career, to become financially strong, and to travel. "I'd like to get in good physical shape and ride my bike around France." It sounded trite, but it was an answer I could live with.

"And what is your hope for the future, and for conditions to improve on the earth, if you don't have The Truth?" Lory pressed. "If you don't put faith in Jehovah or The Kingdom, then *what*? Your job? Your bank account? Your health?"

Though I maintained a facade of confidence, inside I squirmed at these questions. I had no answers here, trite or otherwise. I was floating in a spiritual void, where existential questions about God and spirit swirled about me, unsolved, a far cry from the certainty of my whole life up to that point, the same certainty Lory still had. Exposure to ideas like the Course in Miracles had created a new context for thoughts on love, heaven, and God. These were the types of questions that I could resolve only with time, inquiry, solitude, and a quality of faith that felt new and important to develop. I was uneasy about my lack of spiritual clarity, but I was willing to put in the time, trusting the answers would come. For now, I was happy enough suspending ossified beliefs about a jealous old Jehovah, an imminent Armageddon, and fixed ideas about what made a person good or bad.

"I haven't had a chance to sort out a whole new belief system."

Everyone at the table sat still, staring at me.

"Listen," I said. "I spent thirty-some years in one religion. You can't expect me—at least I don't expect myself—to have a whole new spiritual structure all figured out in one year. That's crazy."

There was more silence.

"All I know is that I used to be very unhappy. Besides my frustrations with Ross, there was an undeniable pull to feel a part of the world—to expose myself to all of it: career, people, politics, ideas, and religions. I understand the idea of that repels you, but it excites me. I feel like part of me is coming to life. And along the way I met someone and had a relationship. Big deal. I'm happy. Happier, anyway, than I was. To me, that counts for something."

The silence from the group held.

"The downside of all this," I said, "is obvious." There was a crack in my brittle mask. I could feel my face twitch. I looked down and caught my breath. "The downside is the cost—the cost of my relationships with you." A fly buzzed around and landed on a dirty plate. "I do hate that part, but I'll accept it if I must."

"Well, as long as you've thought it *all* the way through," Lory said, her voice riddled with sarcasm.

"No regrets, huh?" Ove asked, watching me closely with his elder's eye.

"Only one," I said, which caused everyone to perk up. "So many blessings came out of being raised a Witness. I really mean that. But I regret that I grew up in a religion that requires members in good standing to shun people who leave. Damn, why couldn't we all have been Catholics or Methodists?"

My attempt at levity fell flat. No one was amused.

"I think we're done here," Dad said, and began to stack the dirty dishes. "Time to get organized."

The next little while was very awkward. Everyone went about the business of getting the house back in order, doing the dishes, collecting used linens, or clearing the living room of books and magazines. A heavy pall fell over these ordinary chores. No one spoke much, and anger was present in the subtle aversion of Mom's eyes. I could feel Lory's impatience and intolerance as I handed her the storage unit key and she snatched it from my hand with brisk efficiency.

Before we sat down to breakfast, the plan had been to set out for a final bike ride while we waited for the washing machine to finish its cycle. The others started dressing for this, but I chose to stay behind. I was welcome to go along, but it didn't feel right. I was numb from holding it all together and preferred to be alone, to collect my energy before the drive home. I announced that I would run the vacuum while they were out and even caught myself having the childish notion that if I did more of the chores, they might not be as angry with me.

As they prepared to leave on their bikes, I retreated to my room to pull the sheets off the bed. I was moving like a robot. I didn't know what else to do, so I cleaned—anything to keep moving. Until everyone was out of the house, I didn't dare sit still, not sure whether I would explode into tears or cave in upon myself and go to sleep.

While the others waited for him in the driveway, holding their bikes, Ove passed my open door and stuck his head in to see me.

"Hey," he said.

"Hey," I replied.

"I just don't understand," he said, standing in the doorway, putting on biking gloves. "How can you be so calm, cool, and collected?"

The words were like a fist to my stomach. I gasped for air. I could feel ripples of tension releasing in my middle, making it difficult to stand up. After several moments, I managed to get my breath.

"What are you talking about?" I said, through tears and hiccups.

"You've been so cool, so matter-of-fact." His manner was firm, despite my emotional outburst. I had wanted to hold it together until I was alone. And if I did lose my composure, the last person I wanted to see me was Ove. Somehow I managed to get enough oxygen to speak.

"You think this is *easy* for me?" I said, my voice trembling with anger. "This is one of the hardest things I've ever done." The low rumble in my tone surprised me. I pulled myself up to look directly at him. "Don't you people know me well enough to know that?"

"We can't know anything about you for sure anymore," he said, genuinely puzzled. "You've done so much to shock us. Your family needs to *see* that this is hard for you. That might make it easier for them to accept."

"Go," I demanded, sitting down on the bed, sobbing. "Please go."

And he left. I collapsed in tears. As my mind replayed snippets of the whole showdown, I was infuriated that I was also being judged on how I comported myself while confessing. I'd fooled myself into thinking my calm honesty would be seen as noble. Instead, I was accused of being cold, unemotional, detached.

Soon I was all cried out, exhausted and relieved from the outburst. I called Cindy back in Chicago. She was perfect. She listened but didn't condemn my family—that would have been too much to handle along with my own anger. She reminded me I had a right to happiness, to choose my own path, that life wasn't black and white. She told me she admired my courage. She told me everything would work out for me, even if the "how" wasn't clear at the moment.

My calm resolve gradually returned. My eyes were red and puffy, but the storm had passed. Where was my family? I got dressed, finished packing, and sat down to read a novel. Were they trying to punish me? It felt like they'd been gone a long time. I couldn't concentrate on the book. I took out a deck of cards, sat at the table, and played solitaire. *How fitting. A game for one.* A free-floating paranoia came over me, sitting in the stillness, at the same table where I'd laughed so hard the night before.

Finally, Dad walked in the front door, his face flushed, his T-shirt damp with perspiration. Mom and Lory followed him, then Ove. I was a little disappointed that they should find me in this outwardly placid state.

"Thank God you're back," I said. "I was starting to worry."

"No need for you to worry about us," Dad said as he stood at the kitchen sink, filling a glass of water.

"What's that supposed to mean?" I said, anxiety stirring in me. Everyone stood around the kitchen, breathless, crowding the faucet with empty glasses in hand.

"It means you don't need to concern yourself with our well-being," Mom said. "We're fine. Your worry would be wasted on us."

I was no longer one of them. I was on the outside now.

Within the hour, we were on the road to Portland. Conversation was sparse, the mood one of quiet resignation—everyone lost in private thoughts. From time to time, Mom or Lory would ask a question, trying to get their minds around the root cause of this situation. "Did Ross push you to work so you could afford to buy a house?" "No, Mother. That was my idea." "We knew there was tension between you—was it over The Truth?" "Sometimes yes, sometimes no." The questions painted a picture of their suspicions about all the elements leading to my spiritual demise: that I was first led astray by the glamour of my job, which demanded an inordinate amount of my time and wore down my Christian defenses through close proximity to worldly people; my professional success then preyed upon my ego, which remained unsatisfied, and stimulated a desire for material goods; and once I made enough money to live on my own, I blithely discarded my marriage. They implied that if Ross had been a stronger spiritual head—his God-given role in the Christian family—I might not have drifted so far so fast. Everyone had the hundred-mile-stare of emotional exhaustion. There was tut-tutting and hand wringing, but it wasn't aggressive or done with the intent to persuade me. That would come later.

We were all aware of the next steps for me: a judicial hearing with the elders in Chicago. As with the process for approving candidates for baptism, a coterie of three elders would convene, to assure a balance of opinion and break any tied decisions, and would make a very deliberate effort to find any sign of shame or remorse on my part, not taking pleasure in rebuking anyone.

That night, I slept in my old bedroom. Warm memories of childhood pressed in on me. This was once a place of rest and refuge, the room where I played with Barbie dolls, sang Earth, Wind & Fire songs into my hairbrush, and first applied frosted blue eye shadow. It was where I started keeping a journal, finding my voice through writing, dreaming of the day I'd grow up to be an adult, a grown woman. It was where Mom told us bedtime Bible stories, and where I said my nighttime prayers. Lory's WELCOME HOME sign was still hanging over the closet. I took it down and folded the letters like an accordion on top of one another, placing it in my suitcase for safekeeping.

"It's not too late, Lindy," Mom implored the next morning.

We sat next to each other in the backseat of the car on the way to the airport. Dad drove and Lory sat in the passenger seat in front of me. "You can turn this whole thing around. Just look at your sister. She had her troubles and went outside her first marriage, causing all sorts of problems for herself. But she took her licks and got back on the straight and narrow. Look at her now, happy, living in a beautiful home, married to a good man."

The idea of living my sister's life made me shudder—it was the life I'd spent the last year escaping.

"It was a long, tough road back to 'good standing,'" Lory said, twisting herself around from the front seat to face me. "But you're a lot stronger than I am. If I can do it, you can, too."

"You can come back home," Mom said. "You can live with us; we'll support you on the condition that you start attending meetings again."

Dad was watching my face in the rearview mirror. I tried to keep my face blank. I didn't want to seem ungrateful for the offer, but it was the furthest thing from my mind. I was a few weeks shy of my thirty-third birthday. I had a good job and good prospects. But more than anything, I had my freedom. Under these circumstances, why would I move home? Once again, I felt entirely misunderstood. All support from them was conditional: a shared religion. They refused to see any other path for me. I wanted to laugh out loud, giddy from the absurdity of it all, but I knew that would mock their desperation.

"Listen, everyone," I said, glancing out the window, grateful to see we had just turned onto the airport exit. "I appreciate your offer, really I do, but that's not going to happen. My life is in Chicago now. Coming back to Portland is inconceivable. It just feels like I'd be going backward."

Mom looked away, out the window, collecting herself. "Just keep it in mind." She paused and turned back to face me. "And don't be too haughty when you meet with the elders."

We all knew I was doomed. I'd meet with the elders, and I'd get disfellowshipped. We were resting in the final moments of togetherness, and I felt compelled to talk about that future.

"I wish you could understand my point of view, but I see that isn't possible. I hope we can keep in touch somehow." The words were coming out strong and clear. I marveled at my equanimity. "And if you ever need anything, you can always ask me."

Mom looked blankly at me. Dad kept his eyes on the road. It was Lory who spoke, still twisted around, her hand holding the back of the seat to keep herself in place.

"I assure you, if we ever need anything, you're not someone we would come to for help." She let go with her hand and turned to face the road. We drove the last few miles in silence, until Dad slowed and stopped at the curb. This time, they would not see me to the gate. Everyone got out of the car and stood to watch Dad get my suitcase from the back. Despite the mix of anguish and disgust on each of their faces, they each gave me a firm hug.

"Goodbye," I said. They stood side by side in front of the car and watched me walk away. I had to detach from what was happening in order to move forward. I felt like I was playing a part in a play and this was where the script said, "EXIT STAGE LEFT." I drifted through the airport entrance in a trance, arriving at my gate with surprise, unable to recall checking in or going through security. I wandered aimlessly through the shops, suspended between worlds, floating between the old and new, grief and joy, certainty and ambiguity. My old life was over. There was no turning back. If the black hooded riders showed up tomorrow, I'd be in trouble—my list of sins was growing longer. Satan and his demons might be off somewhere, celebrating the victory over my soul.

Over the next several hours, though, as the plane soared east, these worries lost their luster. *What's done is done*, I thought. Whatever happened next, I knew I could manage. When the airplane approached Chicago, flying above the shoreline of Lake Michigan, I caught sight of the city lights outlining the many harbors and high-rises, and my heart heard the bell tone and fluttered with recognition. With some concentration, I could just make out my apartment building. *There's my place. My place. My Place.*

"Ladies and gentlemen," came the flight attendant's voice across the audio system. "If Chicago is not your final destination, please consult the gate agent for connecting information." The plane veered right, away from Lake Michigan, following the continuous string of car headlights on the Kennedy to O'Hare.

Was Chicago my final destination? Who could predict? But something seemed different. For the first time, landing there felt like home.

Chapter 17

‿๑

You must learn one thing. The world was made to be free in. Give up all the other worlds except the one to which you belong.

—David Whyte

The door to the Kingdom Hall creaked as I pulled it open and entered the quiet, empty foyer. Ray Thomas came through the open door of a small back room to greet me. He reached out to shake my hand. "We're going to meet in the library." I followed him there.

Jeremy Schwartz and another man stood as I entered the small room.

"Nice to see you again, Linda," Jeremy said, his eyes kind as he took my extended hand and held it briefly between his palms. "But I wish it were under different circumstances. This is Brother Potter."

I'd seen Brother Potter at the Hall but had never been introduced. I was going to ask for his first name but thought better of it. He was the required Third Man, stout and potbellied, with a bushy mustache that disguised any expression. He seemed uncomfortable in his suit, which pulled at the buttoned waist.

The room was lined with folding chairs set in a circle, which the elders had broken into a subcircle for the four of us. We all sat, our knees just inches from our neighbor on either side. It was Saturday afternoon, about a month after my return from

Portland. I'd phoned Ray within days of my return, to keep the momentum going, and this was the earliest time he could coordinate having three elders in one place with me. It was summertime, and there were family vacations to organize around. My case wasn't urgent, since I was not actively associating with any Witnesses in the area.

"How was your visit with your family?" Ray asked, straight-faced.

"Bittersweet," I said. "We had a lovely time together in Central Oregon. But things went downhill the day we left there, once I told them the truth of my 'spiritual condition.'"

"How so?" asked Jeremy.

"They believe I'm foolish and quite selfish," I said. I felt very calm and sure of what I was doing, clear and articulate, like a TV news reporter discussing something that was vivid and real but didn't affect me personally. This conversation was just a formality, and I was going through the motions. "But I expected that. They're very angry and disappointed in me."

"Can you blame them?" said Potter.

"Of course not," I replied, annoyed by the suggestion of blame, as if I'd set out to do something malicious. I was just trying to live my life on my own terms.

"Your brothers are both elders, aren't they?" Ray asked.

"Yes, my older brother is an elder, but I didn't see him on this trip. He's ahead of the rest of the family—he started avoiding me the moment I filed for divorce from my husband and moved to my own apartment. My brother-in-law is also an elder, and he was with us." I wondered what this had to do with anything.

"Did he spend any time talking to you, ministering to you?" Ray asked.

I laughed. "If making me wrong is ministering, then yes, he did." I remembered Mom's caution about sounding haughty, but I found the question amusing. "He didn't pull out the Bible and read any Scriptures to me, if that's what you mean. We were sitting around the breakfast table when I told them I'd had a sexual relationship with someone who was not my husband."

I felt absurd saying the word "sexual" in the company of these men. "And I told them I was not sorry about it. I told them, and my husband, that he was free. And telling them this made *me* feel free."

All three men watched my expressions closely as they listened. Potter was leaning back, stroking the edges of his mustache. Ray and Jeremy sat still in their seats.

"I tried to explain to them that this isn't about sex, but I don't think they heard that part."

"What *is* it about, then?" asked Ray.

"It's about feeling like I belong in the world, instead of separating myself from it—embracing it, versus condemning it. And, it's about taking the time to explore other spiritual ideas, about God, love, what it means to have faith." I knew this last part was worse than admitting to any "sexual misconduct," which was why my family had refused to hear it. Openness to other beliefs was a step toward apostasy, an unforgivable sin. Adultery was one thing. Even if I had no regrets then, they hoped for some future dark night of the soul when I'd see the error of my ways and return, riddled with guilt. Of course they'd welcome me. But apostasy was the worst kind of sin, a denial of Christ and his sacrifice; the bridges back from there were not so easily mended.

"Have you joined another church?" Ray asked, possibly trying to clarify if I'd already become an apostate.

"No," I said. *I've had such a hard time getting out of this religion, why would I join another?*

Everyone sat in the gaping quiet.

Ray looked at the other elders. "Does either of you have any more questions for Linda?"

Jeremy and the Third Man shook their heads.

"Then, Linda," Ray said, "will you please excuse us while we confer?"

I got up and walked through the foyer, out to the front steps of the Hall. Inside they were discussing my situation, making an official decision about my standing in the congregation.

I thought of resting on the steps but felt too energized to sit still and walked down the sidewalk to the parking lot. I paced around the lot, my car the only one there.

Years later, I would look back and realize I could have simply written a letter and been done with the whole matter, without putting myself through this formal process. But I was still in the clutches of a certain way of thinking, responding to the experience of being evaluated. I adapted my exit to the religion's terms, believing that was the only way to be decent and noble. While I'd made huge strides in expanding my point of view about life and the world, I hadn't fully developed my capacity for independent thinking and still slipped into my pattern of "being good."

I had waited about twenty minutes when Ray came out to get me. I followed him back into the library, where Jeremy was now standing, leaning against one of the bookshelves with his arms folded at his chest. There was a solemn mood about the room. I sensed there was a protocol, so I sat and waited. Ray spoke first.

"As a judicial elder body, we've made the decision to expel you from the true Christian congregation. The charge is adultery. The biblical grounds for this ruling can be found in many places in the Scriptures. I'll read just one of them." His Bible was already opened to the passage he now read from. "First Corinthians 5:11–13: 'But now I am writing you to quit mixing in company with anyone called a brother that is a fornicator or a greedy person or an idolater or a reviler or a drunkard or an extortioner, not even eating with such a man. Remove the wicked man from among yourselves.'

"You have openly confessed your sins and we, regrettably, see no sign of remorse or repentance. Therefore, it is our responsibility to keep the rest of the congregation spiritually clean." He turned to another Scripture. "Second Thessalonians 3:14. 'But if anyone is not obedient to our word through this letter keep this one marked, stop associating with him, that he may become ashamed.'"

Potter broke in now, raising his opened Bible. "And 1 Timothy 1:20 says to 'reprove before all onlookers persons who practice sin, that the rest also may have fear.' For this reason, Linda, to cultivate a healthy fear of sin within the congregation, we will publicly announce your disfellowshipping in one week, from the stage, at the beginning of the service meeting."

I remembered times gone by when I'd sat in those meetings and heard similar announcements. They were brief and stated with a lot of gravity and always made me sad for the person who had so clearly lost their way. It was tantamount to hearing a death sentence, since the person was no longer guaranteed life. It was not outside the bounds of kindness to offer sympathy to the family members still in The Truth. Now, my family members were the ones in line to receive such condolences. One of the elders, probably Ray, would be invited to the stage. He'd pull out a piece of paper from his suit pocket, clear his throat, and say, "It is with regret that we inform the North Side congregation that Linda Ann has been disfellowshipped from the Christian congregation for conduct unbecoming a Christian." He'd fold the paper back into his pocket and leave the stage, and the meeting would resume.

Jeremy spoke up from the corner of the room. "If you have any dispute about this ruling and wish to appeal the decision, you have one week, exactly seven days from today, to do so."

I did the mental math and realized this would be just a few days after my birthday. Though I'd spent my life abiding by this religion and was now being expelled, I didn't feel any shame, just a detached marvel that I, the ever-vigilant, law-abiding citizen, was being rebuked.

"Trust me, Linda," Jeremy said, "we don't take any pleasure from this. And neither does Jehovah." It was his turn to read a Scripture. "Matthew 18:12–14 says, 'If a certain man comes to have a hundred sheep and one of them strays, will he not leave the ninety-nine upon the mountains and set out on a search for the one that is straying? And if he happens to find it, I certainly tell you, he rejoices more over it than over the ninety-nine that have not strayed. Likewise it is not a desirable thing with my Father, who is in heaven for one of these little ones to perish.'" He paused for a moment, looking at the page, perhaps for emphasis. "If you ever, ever wish to return to the congregation, any one of us would welcome a phone call from you. There is always room for forgiveness on Jehovah's part.

"And though the official reason for this is adultery, we also heard something very disturbing from you—your interest in exploring other religions." I couldn't believe Ray was still finding more to say, turning to yet another Scripture as he spoke. Boring! "We urge you not to deny the power of Christ by denouncing your faith or pursuing other pagan, non-Christian beliefs. Hebrews 10:26–27 says, 'For if we practice sin willfully after having received the accurate knowledge of the truth, there is no longer any sacrifice for sins left, but there is a certain fearful expectation of judgment and there is a fiery jealousy that is going to consume those in opposition.'"

They never took time to delve into the meaning of these Scriptures, the way we would in Bible study, which added to the official tone, each reading a pronouncement. They were legally and religiously obligated to delineate and justify what they were doing. Over the years, many people have sued over judicial decisions handed down by the elders, charging slander or defamation of character. But I had come to them voluntarily, and they knew I was aware of the literal interpretation of each verse. I waited a moment to see if anyone had anything else to say.

"Do you have any questions?" Ray asked.

"No." Asking questions would only prolong the meeting. I had no questions and really could not have cared less about their opinion of me. Everyone stood up. I shook each of their hands and thanked them ever so politely, because I thought that was the "proper" thing to do, but felt nothing. No pain, no relief, just another thing to check off my list.

I walked out the door, never to return.

The next day, I went through the mental and emotional gymnastics of preparing to call my parents. They were not aware of the exact timing of my appointment with the elders, and I was sure they were anxious for any news, gearing themselves up for a dreaded outcome. We all needed closure.

I paced in front of the phone, wearing my bathrobe. It was ten o'clock—eight o'clock in Portland. I'd been awake for hours. My parents were early risers, but I talked myself out of calling. *Give them time to wake up.* I paced some more. *Let Dad enjoy his first cup of coffee.* I'd been unable to concentrate on the morning paper and clicked on some mind-numbing TV. Eleven o'clock Chicago time. *They'll need to focus on getting ready for the meeting. That will help them feel stronger. I'll call this afternoon.*

Having bought myself several hours, I got dressed and took a long walk to my favorite coffeehouse in Wrigleyville. It was a warm, sunny weekend. As I walked, I noticed cyclists heading to the lake and a pair of women wearing flip-flops and sundresses, chatting happily. The streets seemed filled with people who didn't have a care in the world. I envied their lightheartedness. I'd not had much occasion in life to deliver bad news, but it seemed arduous, as if I was announcing something just as final as a terminal diagnosis. Except that an illness would garner sympathy, understanding, promises of unconditional support. My news would not be met so kindly.

I arrived at the coffee shop and got in line to order. A quote of the day posted on a blackboard near the menu read DON'T CUT WHAT CAN BE UNTIED. —ANONYMOUS.

Perhaps my guardian angel had posted this to encourage me. Hadn't I tried hard to "untie" myself from a religion that no longer worked for me? I'd searched for ways to be myself and still "fit in" with my family. I'd wanted to live openly—not doing so felt dishonest and had cost me some happiness. It was unsustainable. Drastic measures were inevitable. I'd always known it. I wasn't convinced God was as conditional as this man-made system, but there would be time to sort that out later.

I walked home, determined and clear again.

At one o'clock in the afternoon, Portland time, Mom answered the phone.

"Are you sitting down?" I asked. I was pacing back and forth in my kitchen.

"I'm ready for whatever you have to say," Mom said, her voice wobbly and thin. I told her the verdict. She just sighed.

"Well, Lindy," she said, "you're getting what you deserve."

It was a painful thing to hear, despite my clarity.

"Just remember," she said, "there is always, *always* room for you to return to Jehovah. If you ever decide to make your peace with Him, you'll have our full support."

Comments like that are what make this easy for me. I'll miss my family, but I won't miss being pounded with these warped ultimatums. Can this be love?

She said goodbye and gave the phone to my dad. He must have been sitting nearby, because she didn't need to call out for him.

"I gather the news is not good," Dad said.

"I'll write you both every once in a while, Dad, so you know what I'm up to and don't have to worry about me."

"Don't forget our phone number," he said, resigned and forlorn.

"Nor you mine."

"Mom wants the phone back. Goodbye, Lindy." *Goodbye. Goodbye.*

In the background, I heard him scold her for rushing him.

"Lindy," Mom said, "be sure to call your sister."

"Yes, Mother. I plan to."

"You owe her that after all the support she's given you."

"I'll do it, Mother, because I *want* to, not because I *owe* her."

I was tempted to quote her the Scripture 'do not you people be owing anyone a single thing except to love one another' but thought better of it. It was no time to quibble.

After she hung up the phone, I sat mesmerized by the dial tone in my ear. It became hollow and distant as it followed her and Dad on their way, like those white lines left in the sky behind airplanes, blurring in the blueness, eventually fading.

⌒∽

My sister was out of town, and we were not able to speak for several days. I was at the office when we finally connected. I slipped into an empty conference room to use the phone. By the time I reached her, I knew Mom would have delivered the news. I was disappointed when Ove answered the phone. I'd hoped to avoid speaking with him.

"You're denying Jehovah and choosing Satan as your god," he said.

Enough already!

"And one more thing," he said, and his voice was softer, as if he'd caught himself. "Your mother is devastated. We all are. You must never doubt how much we care for you."

"I've never doubted that." I was not able to meet his moment of vulnerability. I didn't want his assurances. I knew my family's experience of love was exactly what drove their actions and made this so awful. I was repressing my anger so I could get through this phase, and also because I'd been taught the folly of anger and the lofty virtue of forgiveness. I had not yet learned that anger has its own wisdom.

"I'll go get your sister," Ove said. "She's been a wreck, unable to leave the house. I've never seen her like this."

Indeed, when my sister greeted me, her voice sounded hoarse and husky.

"I have just two questions for you," she said.

"What are they?"

"First, did my example or anything I said make it easier for you or encourage you to get divorced?"

"Not in the least," I said, surprised. "Please don't worry about that. I see our situations as completely different. My divorce was inevitable."

She didn't say anything.

"Lory, are you still there?"

"Second, do you think if our family were closer, you might not have gotten so weird?"

Her bluntness was stunning.

"You think I'm *weird*?"

"Well, yeah," she said. "You've become a self-centered, worldly person, and that's weird."

"There's no need to insult me." I knew this was to be our last conversation for a very long time. I was pushing back the tears.

"I just don't get it," she said.

"I've got news for you, Lory." My breathing had deepened. "It's not necessary for you to 'get it.' I'm tired of wishing and waiting for you, or anyone else in this family, to 'get it.' So good-bye." And I startled myself by slamming the phone in its cradle.

How's that for weird?

I sat there, panting, still trying hard to keep my tears at bay, for several minutes. Lory's brusque choice of words had allowed me to avoid answering her: Was our family dynamic at the root of my rebellion? It was a question that would surface many times in the months to come. Certainly, self-denial and perfectionism had been cultivated throughout my upbringing and made me bristle now. My mother (and her parents before her) had always been unquestioning and hyper-vigilant in applying the Society's teachings. And despite the acrimony it caused in my parents' marriage, I was grateful that Dad was not a Witness when I was very young, because it exposed me to independent thinking and the humanness of "worldly" people. Even when they argued about evolution or Christmas or after-school sports, I never doubted my father's love for my mother, which would now show up in his loyalty to her and the religion.

I was calm again. I rose from the chair, grabbed the work files I had brought in as a decoy, and returned to my desk. There was only one thing left to do: carry on.

Chapter 18

$\mathcal{C}\!\!-\!\!\circlearrowleft$

Too much of a good thing can be wonderful.
—Mae West

Massive waves of energy were freed up now that I was no longer hiding my life from my family. Like a spring held tightly in the hand, then released, I bounced through life loose and free. It was the middle of summer—time to party. I crammed the months with activity. I missed my family, of course, and in quiet moments I felt forlorn, but more than anything I was giddy in the absence of their pestering.

I believed the worst of the experience was behind me; the full scale of my loss hadn't hit yet. Little did I know how many heart-wrenching moments lay ahead. But early on I made excuses for my family's behavior, as I had been taught to do. Hadn't I, through the years, shunned people who'd been disfellowshipped, turning my head, avoiding the gaze of someone I passed on the street or in a store? I repeatedly told myself that my family had no choice but to do the same if they wanted to stay true to God and their religion. No matter, I thought, as I practically levitated from the freedom from having to please them, the elders, and angry old Jehovah. Those days had an urgency, as though I needed to swallow life whole and satisfy the pent-up and greedy hungers of my soul. So I decided to try everything that called to me, explore all ideas, and keep my dance card full. Armageddon may or may not have been coming—I hadn't sorted that out—but I'd come this far, and I might as well have a good time.

My career continued to blossom, and my sales numbers skyrocketed. I was comfortable navigating around greater Chicagoland and was regularly flying to Houston, where I was starting to get traction in that banking community. When talking about the industry, I spoke with authority. I had a steady paycheck, a commission check in the queue, and the respect of my peers.

That summer, I also set a goal of participating in three century rides—organized cycling events where participants bike one hundred miles over one or two days. Training for these rides, playing beach volleyball with a team I'd joined in the spring, and personal-training sessions at my gym helped fill my evenings and burn off stress.

In addition, eligible, attractive men were everywhere, and I had no trouble meeting them. I enjoyed playing the field, no longer anchored by the obligation to think of each suitor as a potential marriage mate. I was living the life my new friends had lived in their college years and early twenties, back when I was newly married and knocking on doors full-time.

David and I met when I responded to his personal ad in the *Reader*. He was fair-haired and sturdy, wore cool wire-frame glasses that accentuated his genuine intelligence, and had a wicked, self-deprecating Jewish sense of humor. After one date, it was clear we would be no more than friends, but friends indeed. He became like a brother to me, and we sought each other out to sort through the nuances of our respective encounters with the opposite sex. At one point, which David affectionately referred to as my "slut period," I was dating five men and "knowing" them all in the biblical sense. The men included a pediatrician who lived in my building and hinted at giving me a mink coat for Christmas; a mortgage broker I rendezvoused with whenever I traveled to Houston; a ponytailed graphic artist who tended bar at night; Harper, who'd become a cherished friend and steady cycling partner; and Andrew, a seductive man, eight years my junior, from my beach volleyball team. (Because of our age difference, David referred to him as my "boy toy.")

"Do you even *have* a type?" David asked one day, as we steered our bikes out of his garage and toward the lakefront. I laughed at the question as I put my helmet on.

Ever attentive to doing things the "right way," I'd been honest with each beau about my level of commitment, declaring I was newly divorced and not interested in getting tied down. Everyone proclaimed acceptance of my terms, a few finding my detachment liberating, others seeing it as an irresistible challenge to win me over. I told myself as long as I was practicing safe sex, no harm would come to me.

David was right. These men couldn't have been more different, in their ages, their accomplishments, their politics, their boundaries, and the way they made love. It was fascinating to observe the different sensations, techniques, and positions each one favored. Every encounter provided a place to experiment, seeking some hint of who I was in the reflection of each lover's eyes.

Around this time, my work friend Debbie invited me to rent the top-level apartment of her three-story brownstone. The apartment was huge, with two bedrooms, a separate dining room, and a sitting area off the living room that led through French doors to a spacious balcony. It oozed with architectural charm, hardwood floors, high ceilings, and a claw-foot tub. Accepting her offer allowed me to triple my living space and reduce my rent expense by hundreds of dollars each month.

The more I settled into my work and home, the more I noticed the lack of spirituality in my life and an ever-present yearning to find meaning in my situation. I continued listening to the taped lectures on a Course in Miracles but wanted to branch out in my quest for understanding. Seeking a replacement for my lifelong habit of reading the Society's literature, I picked up the book *The Seven Spiritual Laws of Success*, by Deepak Chopra, to read at bedtime. Chopra spoke of energy and spirit in a fresh, approachable way and introduced me to the novel idea that we can be in the presence of divinity without a godhead. In the past, this would have struck me as blasphemy, but now I was intrigued. It was also the first time I heard an explanation of karma directly from a Hindu practitioner. Up until that point, my sole exposure to that principle had come from *Watchtower* discussions, which dismissed karma as unnecessary if you exercised faith in the redeeming value of Christ's ransom. This new perspective made me feel light and quietly determined. It was a message of self-responsibility: I as The Creator. Chopra's writings about the power of our intentions put words to the truth of my own experience. Hadn't I shaped and molded a new, compelling life for myself? It was the perfect thing to read at night, closing each day with fresh, affirming ideas about the never-ending nature of all things.

On top of everything else I was doing, I started pursuing my undergraduate degree through night classes at DePaul University and volunteering one Saturday a month for various community projects. I felt a strong desire to give something back to the city that had taken me in. From an early age, I'd been taught the importance of making a contribution to one's community by preaching and teaching, and now I felt the vacuum of an abandoned habit. Also, I wanted to deliberately place myself in environments that were different from my WASPy, white-bread world. My motives were as much self-preserving as they were charitable.

This desire led me to a nonprofit group called Chicago Cares, which organizes all sorts of community projects in such a way that "busy professionals" can participate. Everything was hands-on. I selected a different project each month, taking my pick from environmental programs like maintaining a city park, sorting donations at a food depository, or working with seniors. I succeeded in filling my Saturdays and exposing myself to the underbelly of Chicago, compared to which my own situation seemed quite charmed.

After several months of this full and intense lifestyle, I realized that, while I wouldn't give up my volunteering, friendships, work, night classes, or soul searching, I could not handle the emotional demands of juggling so many men. My ego loved the adoration and variety, but the pace was exhausting. I missed the comfort and simplicity of monogamy. The pediatrician did me a favor and broke up with me soon after I moved. David, who'd confirmed his reputation as a real mensch, was consulted about how to further narrow the field. Steve also weighed in like the true friend and brother he'd become. They both agreed that the long-distance Houston romance could be shut down quickly and without a lot of fuss. Done. That alleviated some of the pressure right away. For several weeks, I continued carrying on with three men. I vacillated between needing to take care of my emotional well-being and wanting to spare feelings. I was haunted by fears of being alone, which weighed down the process with a much bigger significance than it warranted.

"What do you *want*?" Cindy asked me over the phone, exasperated by my indecisiveness. It was a simple question, the one question I'd forgotten to ask myself. Nothing in my upbringing had encouraged me to think that way. I was still caught in the delusion that to ask that question was selfish. And out of Cindy's clear reminder came clarity.

I knew I wanted to be with Harper—not for a lifetime, but for now. We'd been training together over the summer, and he'd kept me and my girlfriends looked after and entertained when he joined us on the first Wisconsin ride. The Michigan ride was also behind me now, and I was filled with a growing sense of accomplishment. My last hurrah would be the Hilly Hundred Century in late October. As summer turned to fall, Harper was the last person still committed to doing the ride, and I was glad for his company on the drive to southern Indiana. He was handsome and easy company, and I'd grown quite fond of him. My decision set, I brought the other entanglements to an end and was happy with my choice.

When it was time for us to make the drive to Indiana for our century ride there, we stuffed Harper's Subaru with riding and camping gear. After months of training and preparation, we were off. The next day, we joined thousands of riders from all over the country, covering the first fifty miles, pedaling past acres of freshly tilled earth where cornfields had stood.

The weather cooperated beautifully both days, with dewy October mornings followed by sunny afternoons, red leaves flashing against a bright blue sky. I was in the best physical shape of my life. Volunteers waved flags and cheered us on as we approached the ninety-mile mark. Inside my head, I could hear my gym trainer's mantra as he pushed me through a difficult series of weights. *This is you, Linda, commanding your body to perform. This is you, exceeding your own limitations. Come on, now—send oxygen to those muscles.*

I knew I would finish as long as I kept breathing and refused to listen to the barking pain in my legs and rear. We crossed over a series of railroad tracks, and the houses started getting closer together. After a sweeping downward turn, we passed more volunteers, cheering us home. We'd reentered Bloomington, and the route flattened out.

"We're almost there!" Harper shouted. "I can almost taste the cold beer." We crossed the line and raised our arms overhead, as if we'd just won the yellow jersey at the Tour de France.

I was completely worn out and elated, both proud to have followed through on my goal and relieved this century season was over. I thought about calling my parents and sharing the moment with them but pushed the idea aside. That wasn't what we did with each other anymore, and they would not have welcomed a call from me. Instead, I accepted a hug and a cold beer from Harper and partied with my fellow bikers.

Chapter 19

❧

I want to stand as close to the edge as I can. Out on the edge you see all kinds of things you can't see from the center.
—Kurt Vonnegut

It was a muggy summer night, and I stood alone at the edge of Lake Michigan, near the north end of Oak Street Beach, gazing at the bright lights of my sparkling city. I saw the gallant lines of the Hancock Building, its two spires saluting the heavens, top lights blinking green, and, beyond it, the twin Sears Tower. All the buildings, large and small, seemed to dance in the sudorific night. Several months earlier, I had begun to immerse myself in the study of spirit and inspiration and was seeing the world with fresh eyes. It occurred to me all of this was a gigantic creative expression, a living testament to the collective dream of hundreds of people, architects, designers, government officials, laborers, and craftsmen.

The reflection of these buildings sparkled across the still waters of the lake, right up to my toes. I felt a familiar yearning to be a contributor to this scene, to belong. What was my creative expression to be? What could I offer this world, a place I had been taught to keep at arm's length? I was told as a young girl that the ancient Greek word "inspired" translates to "God breathed." He breathed the essence of his message through the beings of each Bible writer and onto those ancient scrolls. I'd just begun to accept the idea that he'd done the same with Buddha and Muhammad. It was not hard to imagine his hot whisper in the muggy breeze of this night.

How would God breathe through me? I had been greedily turning the pages of many books on spirituality and personal growth and had found myself riveted by a new world of ideas. Without reservation, I swung open the mental doors to my private sacristy and kept them open. I allowed the dusty old relics of monotheism to sit next to shiny new metaphysical concepts that required no god at all. The juxtaposition was awkward at times, with old and new thoughts eyeing one another suspiciously. The more I studied, the less I feared I was jousting with death. Concerns about the black hooded riders diminished. As I turned away and began to stroll home, I knew that just below my pristine exhilaration was a longing to find my place in the grand scheme of things.

The night after these beach ponderings, I walked through the side entrance of Old St. Patrick's Catholic Church and rode the elevator to the second floor. It was the third gathering of my Artist's Way group, which I'd joined after reading the book by Julia Cameron. I rounded a corner to the airy meeting room. One side was lined with windows level to the streetlights. Twenty chairs were set in a circle, and several women had already arrived and taken their seats. Paulette, our facilitator, was sitting at the far end of the circle and waved me in with a smile. Her delicate frame could barely contain her fierce and fiery energy. She'd taken to calling me Linda, dear, with a gentle affection that charmed me. My friend Carol had already arrived and had saved me the seat to her right.

Carol and I had met some months earlier at a meditation workshop that ran over three consecutive Saturdays. New to meditation, we were eager to share our experiences. We were each at a crossroads in our lives. We were all single and busy, with successful corporate careers. We had stories of love gone wrong but remained hopeful that true love would find us. We thought of ourselves as spiritual seekers. Carol and our other good friend in the group, Kathy, were both lapsed Catholics trying to make peace with a religion that had not kept pace with their values. When Carol and I heard about Paulette's twelve-week workshop, using principles from *The Artist's Way: A Spiritual Path to Higher Creativity*, we signed up right away. Kathy's work schedule did not allow her to join us, but she enjoyed listening to our updates over scrambled eggs on Sunday.

"My mom will be thrilled to hear I'm attending weekly services at the church," Carol said, her eyes gleaming with mischief. "She doesn't need to know the priests aren't involved."

I saw it as my chance to have spiritual communion in a group without participating in organized religion.

We used written and experiential exercises inside and outside class and were asked to journal every morning. As the weeks passed, I experienced a deepening sense of safety and saw new possibilities for expressing my creativity. We identified many of our outdated, negative beliefs and made a list of our "crazy-makers" and creative "monsters." I began to see how all humans express creative flair in the smallest acts, including how we dress or arrange a bouquet of flowers, even through the innovation I brought to problems at work. That led to my thinking about my job as not just a secular endeavor but also a conduit for making a spiritual contribution, not through preaching or imposing my beliefs on others, but through the quality of my interactions and the choices I made in business. Every part of my life could be an expression of my creativity, and I started living in the question of "what do I want to create here, right now, in this moment?"

That night in the church meeting room, to lay the groundwork for a class exercise, Paulette asked me to read out loud a paragraph from *The Artist's Way*. I cleared my throat and started reading. Points were made about synchronicity, and how much seen and unseen support is available for artistic expression, once we accept the idea that it is natural to create. "Learn to accept the possibility that the universe is helping you with what you are doing. Become willing to see the hand of God and accept it as a friend's offer to help with what you are doing. Try to remember that God is the Great Artist. Artists like other artists."

Paulette thanked me and carried on with the class, but her voice receded into the background. At my core was the welcome bell tone of truth, and my mind was turning over a simple yet profound connection. *God is the Great Artist.* What an appealing, approachable image. I still spoke of God as a He, more out of habit than out of belief, and whether he was a he, a she, or a benevolent force was not something I was ready or able to define. But I could agree that everything I observed in the natural world showed evidence not necessarily of a creator, but of dynamism and artistry. This was a God, a Source, I could relate to. And if God is a Great Artist, and artists like other artists, maybe, just maybe, God liked and cared about me. It was my own private Sally Field moment. *God likes me. He likes me! He really, really likes me!*

How different this was from the jealous old Jehovah of my former faith. This God could meet me in the field of creative expression, absent "shoulds" and rules and preconceived form. The very idea pierced a hole through my guilt and spiritual neurosis, a fresh breeze swirling through the sacristy. Could it be that simple? Was God truly a benevolent artist, up in heaven, donning a beret and painter's smock, cheering me on? Years later I would see this as a morphing of the concept of God as a male personage, but at least this version didn't give a damn about my sins—he just wanted me to take a shot with this fresh canvas.

If so, and please *let it be so*, I thought, *it changes everything.*

After that, every escapade into the world held potential to touch the divine. I sat ten feet from Amhad Jamal as he pounded the ivories in a passionate tribute to Miles Davis and wondered how many angels were dancing on his shoulder. I shimmered and swayed with the crowd as B. B. King stroked Lucille and made her wail, lowering my head from time to time to sip a cold beer beneath the layer of smoke filling the bar. Walking through a Degas exhibit at the Art Institute, I was struck by his midlife transition from paint to bronze sculpture, drawn as he was by a strong internal directive, the call of spirit, to shift to a new medium. Watching Aretha Franklin belt out "Respect" in the summer breezes of Petrillo Music Shell, I decided that if there was such a thing as reincarnation, I wanted to return as one of her backup singers. There were lesser-known and esoteric attractions to enjoy, like Howard Levy's funky harmonica, Béla Fleck's jazz banjo, and the handmade jewelry and textiles on display in the street booths of the summer art fairs. Regardless of the venue, the degree of polish or fame, I felt I was in the presence of something sacred, enjoying everyday life as a place of worship, a way to experience truth and beauty for its own sake. Had the world been like this all along—rich, full, and fascinating—and I had failed to notice? My heart mourned the thirty-five years I had spent waiting for God to bring paradise, when here it had been all along, right under my nose.

Carrying a program and a single yellow rose, given to all first-time visitors by the smiling greeter at the entry, I took one of the few open seats toward the back of the church just as the program was about to begin. To the left of the raised platform and pulpit were an electronic keyboard, a bass guitar, and a standing microphone. Along with a feeling of gaiety and relaxed anticipation, the large hall was filled with light. This was Unity of Chicago.

As I waited for the service to begin, I scanned the program. The front cover read: "A Church of Light, Love, and Laughter. We honor people from all races, colors, creeds, and lifestyles, seeing God's expression in the faces of everyone."

As the opportunity presented itself, I had started attending a variety of church services throughout Chicago: Catholic, Christian Science, and Episcopalian. In each case, I was glad for the experience but felt like a bored observer on a school field trip, an outsider looking in, untouched by the message.

I could tell right away that Unity would be different. At

the top of the hour, a woman and two men entered the hall and walked over to the waiting instruments. The woman had an ethereal quality, her long hair flowing unencumbered to her waist. She smiled and greeted the audience as she adjusted the height of the microphone. The man at the keyboard removed his slip-on shoes, applied a bare foot to the pedal, and ran a few scales, making minor adjustments at the controls. The bearded base player was ready to go and waited patiently for the others. They made eye contact, nodded their heads three times in unison, and started to play the happiest melody. It wasn't cloying or overly sincere—it was rock and roll! In church! Speakers in front and in back started thumping with a joyful sound, electronic percussion pulsing from the keyboard; then the bass kicked in and the woman started singing, "Walking beyond the border, beyond right and wrong, is where I'll be." The audience was swaying to the music, some sang along, and the energy picked up until everyone was clapping their hands or nodding to the beat. To my far right was an especially boisterous group, and two women at the center stood up and danced through one verse, right there in the middle of the row. No one seemed to mind.

I'd been drawn to come that particular day after calling a prerecorded number for service times and learning the sermon was about the Lord's Prayer. I hadn't prayed since I'd left Portland, and wondered what this group might have to say about it. The senior pastor turned out to be female, something you would never see at the Kingdom Hall, where women were not allowed to speak "before the congregation." I'd come to see that prohibition as wasteful of rich talents and neglecting an essential feminine perspective.

The pastor asked the first-time visitors to raise their hands, and the audience was peppered with a few other hands beside my own. "Welcome," she said, and I believed her.

What stood out most was the absence of any dire predictions for the future or judgmental comments about nonbelievers. The pastor's language was uplifting, hopeful, and inclusive. She described prayer as a compact formula for attuning the attitude and dwelled for a long time on the expression "*Our* Father," showing that we are not alone even when we pray alone. "Our" can always remind us of the whole. "We're all in this together," she said. "It is a fact of metaphysics that we are interconnected. Every thought, every action, affects the whole." She went on to discuss the role of self-responsibility. "There is really only one of us here." I found solace in that idea, which was revolutionary to my way of thinking. She went on to describe the church as a family and a hotbed of humanity, how through living it is only natural that we will bump up against each other with our patterns and problems, how we are always presented with the choice to grow in our capacity to be in relationship. She didn't spend a lot of time quoting Scripture and verse, but everything she said felt sane and Christlike. More than that, it felt grounded in love and acceptance. As she spoke of the challenges people encounter in relationships, she said something completely foreign to me: "There is no such thing as bad people, only unskillful behavior." It didn't make anyone wrong or assign blame or shame.

I thought about all the ways I'd been pissy and unskillful with my family, and they with me, as I'd struggled to find my way, and I knew we had all done the best we could with one another. Tears filled my eyes as I realized anew the widening philosophical gap between my family and I, wishing with my whole being that they could open to this new way of thinking, too, not needing us to be part of the same religion to be together. Even if they insisted on rejecting my beliefs and lifestyle, did they have to reject *me*? What did it matter, if we were all one anyway? It's a grievous and harmful thing, I thought, to shun another person. It's a sort of emotional terrorism, the worst sort of coercion, at least the worst form I'd ever experienced. The sermon was a sharp, bitter contrast with how I was treated. I felt the aspiration of this community to practice a living compassion and remembered Jesus's barometer of wise teaching—recognizable by its fruits.

As the pastor concluded her sermon, every molecule of my

heart felt tender and malleable. Old hurts had been stirred and mended, and I was being reconfigured somehow—stirred up, electrified, and relieved to discover a church like this existed.

"Finally, my friends," the pastor said, "I'd like to ask Jean and her group to stand up for an acknowledgment." About twenty people stood up, many arm in arm, including the two women who had danced during the first song. "This group will be representing our congregation next week in the gay pride parade, marching through the streets, right behind Mayor Daly's car, spreading peace and tolerance and love. If you get a chance, please go down and show your support. Remember, we're all family and we're all in this together."

The applause grew riotous. This level of acceptance was too much to absorb, and my tears came quickly. I was stunned to find a house of worship that didn't concern itself with what people did in their bedrooms.

There was a call to prayer. I grabbed a tissue from my purse and bowed my head, relieved for some privacy. I was too full to hear more, so I anchored my feet and breathed into the place in my heart that was swirling with emotion. When the program was over, I was reluctant to leave and sat alone in my seat for a while, enjoying the parade of people around me.

Lying in bed that night, I prayed for the first time in a long while. It was more like releasing a balloon into the ether, launching wishes and gratitude, whispering my request for wisdom, trusting it would be heard somehow. Even if my higher self and I were the only ones listening, that was enough. I drifted off to sleep in the middle of it but didn't feel guilty for leaving God hanging, as I might have done in days gone by. And I took heart in knowing that the separation gripping my family was only an illusion—on some bigger playing field, we were still connected.

Chapter 20

Out beyond ideas of wrongdoing and rightdoing, there is a field. I'll meet you there.

—Rumi

Just home from a day's work, I stood on the porch of my brownstone building, flipped open the rusty mailbox, and reached in for the solitary letter. The writing, with its tidy, just-so slant to the right, was familiar: my mother's hand. My breathing stopped short and my legs wobbled as I dropped down to sit on the cool concrete stairs, resting my purse and briefcase, staring at the envelope. The return address was the house where I was raised on Mapleleaf Street, where my parents had lived for over thirty years. She still wrote her ones the same way, in a crazy-eight style, with the last loop arching down, the same way she wrote her twos. Whatever grief and upset my exit had caused her three years earlier, it didn't show here.

I could hear the telephone ring in my apartment one story up but couldn't move. My body felt like lead. My mind swirled with curiosity and worry. Why would my mother be writing me? If someone in the family had been in trouble or seriously ill, she would have called. Or would she? Lory's parting salvo had made it clear I wouldn't be someone they would reach out to for help. What would have caused Mom to break The Rules and reach out to me now? Taking a deep breath, I stood up, dropped the letter into my briefcase, and rummaged for my keys. Unlocking the door, I walked up the stairs to my apartment.

Once inside, I removed the letter from the briefcase and set it in the center of my coffee table. My two cats, Leo and Tucker, had come to greet me, twisting their bodies around my ankles begging for dinner. One by one I picked them up, as was my custom. The envelope looked back at me. I turned away and walked down the long hall toward the kitchen, beginning the evening routine. I washed my hands and fed the cats. I walked back into the living room to open the French doors and air out the house. The envelope glared at me. The phone rang again, and again I let it go. It was only the envelope and me. I left the room, took a quick shower, and went to the kitchen, tossing leftovers in the oven to warm. Pouring myself a glass of wine, I walked to the living room and settled on the couch.

I sensed something unwelcome was about to be thrust upon me. My life was going well. I'd become stronger emotionally and spiritually. The outline of a blessed life was taking shape. Regular visits to a therapist were helping me work through the guilt and heartbreak of my losses, but this was always done on my own terms and in my own time. Whenever the sadness was too much, I could pace myself or wriggle out of the discomfort, seizing upon some distraction from the long list available to me. But this letter could not be avoided.

I opened the envelope to find a card with a photograph of the tulip fields of Oregon's Willamette Valley, the ones we always passed when driving to the Assembly Hall in Woodburn twice a year. Inside was written:

Dear Linda,
This is to let you know that I will be making a business trip to Indiana next month and will be passing through Chicago. I want to see you on my way back, which will be Saturday, October 11. I will call you that morning at your house. I wanted you to know this so you don't go into shock when I call.
Looking forward to seeing you!
Love, Mom

I felt like all the blood was draining out of my body, leaving me deflated and lifeless, like a leaky inner tube. I leaned back on the couch and stared across the room. Leo walked in, his tail up high, the end curled around in a question mark. Was she *really* looking forward to seeing me? Or was I being summoned for a grilling? She had given me one week's notice. How should I prepare?

Looking around my living room, I saw the furnishings through my mother's eyes. She would be impressed by the arched doorways, my choice of colors, and the layout. I would take her out the French doors to the balcony and show her the flower garden I had nurtured through a Chicago summer. She'd be surprised to find such a peaceful place in the middle of the city. If things went well between us and I was feeling vulnerable and brave, I might tell her how I'd felt connected to her when I planted those flowers, despite our estrangement. I imagined her commenting on the impressionist painting hung above the television or the Venetian mask on a side wall, giving me an opening to tell her about my trips to France and Italy, where I'd purchased them. She would scan the framed photographs on top of the piano and see me with my new friends caught in various moments of fun and celebration. Through the photos, I could introduce her to everyone who now mattered in my life.

There was the photograph of David and me in my kitchen after Thanksgiving dinner, surrounded by dirty dishes, toasting each other. We had hosted a meal for all our single friends, people like us with no family in town. Steve was there, and Geoff even flew in. When the feast was over we all played a contentious game of charades, with everyone yelling and screaming over each other. Later we strolled the neighborhood in a tryptophan haze while David and Geoff smoked cigars. Mom would cringe at that. Nor would she be pleased by the photo of me blowing out the candles of my very first birthday cake—at thirty-five years of age—surrounded by my girlfriends singing "Happy Birthday." There was a photo of me and some friends hamming it up on a sailboat in Monroe Harbor, and a picture of Cindy and me on our bikes, the Tuscan hill towns behind us.

I wondered if she would notice the nondenominational prayer books on my shelves or the esoteric spiritual titles, like *The Feminine Face of God* and *Anatomy of the Spirit*, next to Dickens and Du Maurier. Better to hide the brochure from Unity Church and avoid mentioning my current exploration into shamanism or that I had met my two best friends at a meditation workshop.

The next day, swimming in uncertainty about what Mom intended for our time together or how long she would be in town, I placed an emergency call to my therapist. She encouraged me to get clear about what I wanted. I still needed other people to remind me it was okay to want things, that it wasn't selfish or un-Christian. I wanted to hear news about the family. Details. Stories. Was everyone healthy? Had Mom and Dad grown a big vegetable garden? Where had they gone for vacation? What funny thing had my nephew said lately? I wanted a good old-fashioned catch-up session with my mom. There was also the matter of my pride. I wanted her to see me happy, successful, and prospering in my new life—no worse for wear, so to speak.

As the week progressed and my mother's visit got closer, anticipation and dread increased in equal measure. The eternal optimist in me believed we could have fun together. Each day I cleaned and tidied a certain room of the house, hiding piles of clutter and scanning the bookshelves for potentially offensive items. I finally got around to buying houseplants for the empty spots in each room. I swept and organized the pantry. I polished my shoes and got a haircut. I called all my friends and asked them to say a prayer for me.

I considered introducing Mom to some of my friends. Her communication left me with few details to plan around. After showing her around my apartment, I thought about taking her sightseeing around Chicago. My boyfriend offered to take us sailing. "There isn't a better way to take in the grandeur of the skyline," he said, "than from a boat in Lake Michigan." We'd both agreed that, should this happen, we'd simplify things by telling Mom we were just friends. He agreed to keep his day open, awaiting my call.

The day before her visit, I bought fresh flowers for the house. That evening I stayed home, just in case Mom called. She did not call. Had I not been disfellowshipped, she would be sitting there with me on the couch, sipping chamomile tea and giving my spare bedroom some use. Curious about where she was, I started phoning hotels that cater to the business traveler but gave up after a few tries. Mom did not want to connect until the morning, and that was that.

The phone rang at ten o'clock sharp. I'd been carrying a cordless phone around the house and was on the deck, watering the flowers. I answered the call.

"Hi, Lindy. How are you, my dear?" It was my mother.

"Are you actually here, in *my* city?"

"Sort of. I'm staying at the Hilton near O'Hare."

I cringed at the idea of her staying near the airport, when the heart of the city had so many great hotel options with class and character. If only she'd called me, I could have guided her to them.

"I was beginning to wonder when I would hear from you."

"I wasn't sure if Saturdays were a day you liked to sleep in, but I decided to take time off this morning. I've been racing around all week. I'm not used to business travel, and it's worn me out."

"I was so excited to see you that I woke up hours ago," I said. "I'm ready to go whenever you are."

"How far is my hotel from the city?" she asked.

"It's about a thirty-minute cab ride. All you need to do is give my address to the driver and then sit back and relax. The driver will see that you get here safe and sound."

This is going well. I was about to tell her some of the fun activities I had in mind for the day so she could contemplate the options on her ride over. If we ended up on a sailboat, I thought she might want to bring a change of clothes or something warm to wrap around her shoulders.

"Oh, Lindy, I'm sorry, dear, but I'm just not comfortable coming over to your house." She sounded determined and prepared for this part of the conversation. I put down the watering can and stiffened in place. "One day, after you return to Jehovah, I look forward to having a big party to celebrate, but until then it just wouldn't be right."

Wouldn't be right? Right, you say? What is *right about this whole ridiculous situation?*

"Is there a nearby restaurant where I can meet you for lunch?"

Well, of course—there are a bazillion restaurants in Chicago. The idea of meeting in a restaurant was appalling, though, because I wasn't sure how I would react upon seeing her. I might break down into hot tears or loud, baleful sobs. The possibility of her declining to come to my home had not even entered my mind. I felt foolish for indulging in fantasies of a weekend armistice. I sat down slowly in the lawn chair.

"Yeah. I guess so. There are lots of restaurant options." My mind was pounding through the shock. "You won't even pop in for a few minutes and see where I live?" My voice was feeble and thin. "I don't have to 'entertain' you or anything."

"No, Lindy. I'm sorry, but I just wouldn't feel right about that."

Now up from the lawn chair, I began pacing, hoping the movement would stimulate some rational thought, understanding that I needed to choose a venue where I would be comfortable.

"Fine, Mother," I said in a flinty voice. "Tell the cab driver to bring you to Bistro Zinc on Southport, just North of Roscoe. Does eleven thirty work for you?"

"Yes, but don't I need the address?"

"No, Mother. Just tell him Bistro Zinc, on Southport at Roscoe. That's all you need to say." I could hear the edge in my voice and feel my throat gripping. "This is Chicago. The big city.

The cab drivers know what they're doing." *Do you?* I wanted to add, but refrained.

When I hung up, my breath was labored, tears came to my eyes, and I started to perspire. Pacing the floors, I looked desperately for something to throw. Leo crouched in the corner as I stormed past him to my room. Landing in a belly flop on my bed, I buried my head in the pillows and screamed. And screamed again. Grabbing a pillow, I pounded it against the bed, over and over, like a petulant child. Dread overcame me, and I lay on the bed, breathing deeply. This lunch was now something to be endured. How long did it take for red, puffy eyes to recede? Not more than an hour, I hoped, because that was all the time I had.

Fortunately, it was a bright, sunny day in Chicago, the kind that invites hope and desire. As I walked through the streets from my apartment to the restaurant, a fresh conviction emerged. This was a rare chance to spend time with my mother. I'd need to keep my guard up—who knew what other surprises were in store?—but I decided I didn't want to waste this precious time mired in offense. All I could do was show up and eke out whatever I could from the encounter.

I'd chosen Bistro Zinc for its ambience and familiarity. It was a regular weekend lunch spot for Carol, Kathy, and me. We'd hang out there and get caught up on each other's weeks, sharing war stories from the office, laughing or crying over the men in our lives. As I turned the corner to Southport, I saw they had opened the French doors, unfurled the awning, and set tables on the sidewalk. Each table had a delicate vase of fresh pink and yellow freesia. The waiters were always friendly and never looked down their nose if you mispronounced *l'agneau grillé*, *niçoise*, or *confit*.

The yeasty aroma of fresh croissants greeted me as I walked through the entrance. The black-and-white tile floors and mahogany bar warmed the room. It was tidy and charming. Mom would like that. I arrived early and claimed a corner table just inside the open door so I could see the cab delivering my mother.

The moment the car stopped in front, I could make out my mom's silhouette through the car window, wavy hair barely gracing her narrow shoulders. A bittersweet pain clutched at my heart. She got out of the cab and stepped on to the curb. Dusting herself off, she turned to size up the entrance, securing her purse tight under her arm, like a shield. As she came through the revolving mahogany door, I saw that she was dressed impeccably, in white pants, a black-and-white-striped sweater, pearls at her neck, and white sandals. She squinted as her eyes adjusted to the light until she saw me standing, waving her to our table. She smiled stiffly, revealing only her bottom teeth. Her walk was unnatural and labored. Emily Post doesn't cover the rules of engagement for greeting estranged relatives, and I was unclear on how to receive my mother. A handshake seemed absurd and distant. Would a hug feel contrived? If she didn't want to visit me in my home, what other boundaries did she have? But I wanted to hug her and was glad when she reached our table, set down her purse, and extended her arms. At five foot eight, I towered over my mom's petite frame. Our embrace was swift and awkward. She moved like a cat that allows itself to be picked up, then quickly wriggles to get free.

"You look beautiful, Mother." It seemed like the right place to start. She had more gray hair than I remembered, and her eyes turned down at the corners in an unfamiliar way. Was she weary from the journey, or was this grief? I pulled out her chair and gestured for the waitress to bring coffee.

"You look good, too, my dear," she said. "I see you've managed to stay slim." She took her first sip of coffee. "This looks like a fun street. Is this far from where you live?"

"This is my neighborhood. My brownstone is only six blocks away. I just love it here. There is a nice mix of families and single people my age. It's about equal parts people who've lived here their whole life and transplants like me. We're only eight blocks from Wrigley Field, so this place gets crazy on game days." I was babbling and couldn't seem to stop myself. "I love the hustle-bustle of this street, and yet, just one block over in either direction, are tree-lined, quiet residential streets. All of these restaurants are regular haunts of mine. The Music Box Theatre shows great, artsy movies. I can walk to the grocery store, and we're a five-minute bike ride to the lakefront."

"You sound like a tour guide," Mom said, "but you've always been a city girl at heart." As she lifted the menu, I noticed her hands had not changed. Her nails were short, unpolished, and clean, yet they had the dry toughness of long summer hours tending to her roses.

The waitress brought fresh bread and took our order. I served myself, and as the butter melted in my mouth, I realized how hungry and hollow I felt. I'd been up for hours and had been too stirred up to eat.

"I feel very at home here," I continued. "The great thing about Chicago is the range. One day you can go casual to the baseball game and then out for beer and blues, and the very next night dress in black tie for the opera."

"And I suppose you've done both?"

"Sure. And Midwesterners are so friendly. There's something very easy and unassuming about them. Once, I struck up a conversation with a couple sitting next to me at a Cubs game and ended up joining them at their house later for a barbecue. They live just around the corner from here, and I still see them from time to time."

"You weren't concerned about going to the home of complete strangers?"

"Once you've been through extra innings with someone and your team still loses, you're no longer strangers—you're old friends. The Cubs have an odd way of bringing people together."

She nodded her head, and the corners of her mouth turned up, but she didn't smile. She'd set one elbow on the table and was resting her chin on her hand as she listened. We were keeping the conversation alive, but I wasn't feeling connected to her.

"How has your trip been?" I asked. As far as I knew, Mom still worked as an underwriter for a well-respected insurance agency. "I've never known you to travel on business. Did you change jobs?"

"I'm working exclusively on commercial lines now, and my agency has this enormous new client with buildings in Indiana. Because the potential liability is in the hundreds of millions of dollars, we require someone to come and personally see it and meet with the developers." The waitress set down our plates of salad, quiche, and beef burgundy. "I've spent more time on this than anyone else on the team, so the owner of the agency asked me to go. He thought it would be nice for me to meet the client, and he knew I had a daughter in Chicago. Of course, he has no idea of our situation and I'm sure the work will be piled high on my desk Monday morning."

Our situation. Yes, we definitely have a situation. We started eating.

"You'd better be careful of too much business travel," I teased, hoping she'd get the joke. "It puts you in contact with all sorts of worldly people, and before you know it you're letting your guard down. Then any number of untoward things can happen."

"Yes, I've observed this phenomenon." She rolled her eyes, mildly disgusted. Then she set down her fork, signaling the end of small talk. "Listen, sweetheart," she said, "I'm really happy to see you. Everyone in the family misses you *so much.* Our dinners just aren't the same without you. And things will not be the same until you come back. I know you probably want to hear news about everyone, but I'm going to tell you only that everyone is healthy and doing well. If you want to know more, you're going to have to make things right with Jehovah first."

I slowly chewed my last bite of food, then swallowed hard as I absorbed this last stipulation. The one thing I'd wanted was being withheld.

"Then why did you come here, Mother? If you won't come to my home or share any family news, why are you here?" My voice was shaky, hysteria bubbling just below the surface. "Why?"

"Oh, Lindy, I told your dad I couldn't come this close to Chicago and not see you. And since I don't plan on making a *practice* of seeing you, I told myself it was understandable, even forgivable. I wanted to see you with my own eyes and perhaps talk some sense into you." Her hands were resting on her lap, and her jaw was clenched.

"I see. So, are you counting your time? Will this show up on this month's field ministry report for Ruth Tucker?"

"No, Lindy, of course not. You know this is hard for Dad and me, but especially for me. You are my daughter, and I thought we would have all this time together. Whenever we go to the assemblies, people still ask about you. 'How's Lindy?' 'Have you heard from Lindy?' And we never have good news to share with them." She looked down at the hands in her lap.

"Have you ever thought, Mom, about how hard this has been for *me*? I left everything and *everyone* behind—my entire community of support. People don't make changes like that unless they sincerely believe it is the right choice. I know this has been hard for you, but at least you get to struggle through it with the support of everyone you've ever known your whole life. I've had to start over completely."

With each blink, the brown in her eyes seemed to deepen.

"Yes, Lindy. It's amazing what you've done. We never doubted that you would make new friends or that you would be successful at whatever you put your mind to. But this is *your life* we're talking about. Tell me, with these new friends of yours, do you celebrate Christmas?"

I nodded, thinking about my merry band of slightly sauced friends who'd donned Santa hats and sung Christmas carols at the Music Box Theatre, just before the annual showing of *It's a Wonderful Life*.

"And birthdays?"

I nodded again. She looked up to the ceiling and shook her head. Neither of us was eating much, and the food was getting cold.

"Here's the thing, Mom. You might as well know that I've gone completely to hell in a hand basket. It's just that simple. If you keep asking me questions like this, I guarantee you are not going to like the answers." My voice was getting stronger and clearer. "I'm not going to have this conversation with you. I'm very aware of your beliefs, but you don't have a clue what mine are. Suffice it to say, you and I believe differently. Maybe someday I'll get into the details with you, but that day is not today. I haven't seen my mother in over three years. *Three years.* So enough of the interrogation. I just want to sit here and enjoy your company. Is there anything wrong with that?"

Her shoulders dropped, and she let out a sigh. "No, honey." She leaned toward me. "But don't forget, time is running out. You know what the Scriptures say, and all the nightly news reports confirm we are only getting closer to Armageddon with each passing day. Just don't stay out in the world too long."

Excusing myself, I went to the restroom to regroup. Splashing cold water on my face, I looked intently at myself in the mirror. *What happens now?* Given the gist of the conversation, we were running out of things to talk about. On some level, I suspected Mom found my company disturbing, and I was very disappointed that she could not set aside her objections for one rare afternoon and simply be with me.

I returned to the table just as the waitress was serving two glasses of white wine.

"Given the conversation, I thought this was in order," she said. "What the heck? It's Saturday, and I'm on vacation."

Just in time, I remembered that Witnesses don't clink glasses, seeing it as a pagan superstition. Of course, I'd discarded that as a needless concern long before. We raised our glasses and took the first sip. Mom smiled with resignation and seemed to relax a bit.

"I need to ask," Mom said. "Are you taking good care of yourself, eating well, and seeing the doctor for regular checkups?" For a number of reasons, including the fact that Mom had been diagnosed, my sister and I have a statistically high risk for ovarian cancer. I'd always been mindful about preventing it and testing for it. But her question angered me, even though it was a logical, caring question for a mother to ask. But I wanted my whole mother—one who would laugh and cry with me unconditionally—not this one-sided aspect prodding me about medical testing and my self-care routine. *You can't have it both ways. Be my mom either all the way or no way.* The anger that emerged from this question caught me off guard. I struggled for a long moment to gain my composure.

"Of course," I said, dismissing the topic outwardly with a flick of my wrist, signaling my lack of willingness to pursue the subject.

"How is your work going?" she asked.

There was so much I could have told her. I'd been promoted to vice president and become a national sales manager and was struggling to assume the role of leader among people who had previously been my peers. I could have told her about my first ride in a corporate jet sent to take our team of executives to New York, all part of our due diligence with a new vendor. After a few years in sales, I found it fun to be on the receiving side of a business courtship. But I was brief in my answer. Other parents might take pride in these accomplishments. She wanted to hear only that I was doing well, and might find these developments more disturbing than impressive.

"What are your plans for the rest of the afternoon? Would you like to go for a walk along the lake or do some shopping?" I was hopeful that we could salvage some good times from the day. "I have a friend standing by who has offered to take us sailing."

"That is very generous, but my hotel has an outdoor pool I want to take advantage of," she said, swirling her wine by the stem of her glass. "I never get a chance at home to while away the afternoon with a good book. It's been a full week, and I'd like to rest."

I couldn't believe what I was hearing. I fought an urge to plead with her, the way I used to beg for more ice cream as a child. It was a perfect day to play tourist. Within a month, snow could be falling to the ground. Was she seriously going to sit around an airport pool, 747s flying overhead, when she could be basking in the skyline of a grand city, a city other people clamor to visit? Yes, she was.

We paid and left, and as I walked out to the street with her, I felt the sidewalk underfoot giving like a cushion, either from the growing heat or from my state of mind. All passersby faded into the distance. I hailed a cab and turned to her as it pulled alongside the curb.

"Stay healthy, and be sure to allow yourself enough time to rest," she said.

"Yes, Mom." We hugged goodbye. "Have a safe flight home, and give Dad a hug for me."

It was all very civilized, but I was crumbling inside. As her cab disappeared into northbound traffic, I pulled out my cell phone and made a quick call.

"There will be no sailing today," I said. Then I walked home and collapsed on the couch to stew in anger and sorrow.

PART THREE

The Death Exemption,
2006

Chapter 21

There is no need for temples, no need for complicated philosophy. . . . Our own heart is our temple; the philosophy is kindness.

—His Holiness the Dalai Lama

Ten years passed, during which I had little contact from my family. In the early years of my newfound freedom, they were never far from my thoughts. Mundane moments like stumbling upon Mom's famous apple pie recipe or listening to a friend describe a fun night out with his dad could evoke sorrow or envy. Hearing Kenny Loggins sing "Celebrate Me Home" on the radio could leave me unsettled for hours, betwixt and between the world I now reveled in and the fold I left behind.

When we leave one world for another, poignant moments like that are inescapable. The emotional pain fuels our initiation into the life that is ours to claim if we dare. Initiations usually involve purification, letting go, burning through the agony. With time I was able to reconcile the paradox of feeling sadness and relief, loss and liberation, all at once. I could not imagine returning to my old life or religion. What choice did I have but to put one foot in front of the other and cultivate compassion and acceptance for the predicament? Minus that resolution, I would never be free in the fullest sense.

I was committed to freedom. It made no sense to go through the turmoil of being shunned only to be trapped by self-pity or resentment, which are just different forms of dogma.

Over time, my family seldom came to mind, and then with only a twinge of melancholy and matter-of-factness. Agony faded to discomfort, which then morphed into a faint emotional bruise that caused an occasional cringe when a random song or memory pressed against it. The black hooded riders rode into the same world occupied by Mother Goose. I did not feel possessed of blame, anger, or fear. The world felt safe as I found my place in it, as I discovered my own unique "worldliness."

Over that transformational decade, I kept my word and sent my parents a card whenever I changed addresses or phone numbers. Clear lines had been drawn, but I wanted my family always to know where I lived and how to reach me.

The world prepared for Y2K, which I quietly mocked as another man-made Armageddon. By my thirty-eighth birthday, I was living in California. Visa recruited me to oversee one of its emerging-market segments and offered to move me to San Francisco, near its headquarters. After shivering through five Chicago winters, I was happy for a new scene and professional challenge. Daffodils bloomed in February, and the mild Mediterranean climate allowed for hiking and biking year-round. I was in a state of continuous rapture over the beauty of the area.

Working for a leading global brand was an eye-opener, and I had to step up my professional game to keep up and flourish. Over the years, I held a variety of leadership positions, interacting with executives at all levels of our banking system. During that time, I grew dismayed by the suffering caused by unskillful leadership and the foolish decisions smart people make when they lose connection with their heart and soul. I wanted to contribute to a shift in how leaders show up and sensed this would require leaving corporate life. I decided to pursue a career as an executive coach and devised an exit strategy that including being trained in that field.

After five years at Visa, I resigned and hung my shingle as an independent consultant. No more corporate plastic, first-class flights, or quarterly bonus checks. In the early months of self-employment, I had several panic attacks, jolted awake in the middle of the night, soaked with perspiration, fearing

244

abject poverty and the disgrace of failure. Thankfully, within six months I was busy with client work and have never looked back.

One year after moving to San Francisco, I met Bob Curtis while attending a fundraiser for my friend Lynne's nonprofit. Bob had known Lynne for more than thirty years; they had been colleagues in the human-potential movement, for the eradication of world hunger, and now worked on environmental sustainability. That day, I had several pressing work matters that made it challenging for me to break away midmorning, and I came close to canceling attendance, but something about Lynne's dynamism and enthusiasm compelled me to say yes, and that yes changed my life.

It was a glorious spring day, and the program was held in the largest room of the St. Francis Yacht Club. Blue waters lapped against the banks of the bay next to the wall of windows lining one side of the room. The Golden Gate Bridge graced the horizon to the west, and the Bay Bridge strung across to Treasure Island like a pearl necklace. The room was overflowing with more than two hundred people.

I met the other guests at my assigned table and took a seat. I thumbed through the program and noticed a quote printed from a South American indigenous leader on the front:

If you are coming to help me,
you are wasting your time.
But if you are coming
because your liberation is bound up with mine,
then let us work together.

The words gave me pause, and I felt that familiar, harmonious bell tone, my internal tuning fork humming major C, which I'd come to recognize as "major see." It was such an eloquent acknowledgment of our interconnectedness and shared humanity, the opposite of the Witness edict to "go forth and save," the arrogance of which had originally opened me to my doubts.

Let us work together . . . together!

The program was a revelation to me. Here I was, a success-ful executive negotiating multimillion-dollar marketing deals with Fortune 500 companies. I considered myself well traveled and well read. I tell you with sheepish honesty and a red face that I thought recycling my newspaper made me a conserva-tionist. That day, I was humbled by my lack of awareness at just how quickly the Amazon was being pillaged for oil and other resources. By some estimates, over ten million trees are felled every day. That's about a football field a minute. *That can't be right*, I thought. But it was true and I had found a group that was doing important work, in true partnership with the indigenous people who'd made their home in the rainforest for centuries. I wanted to be part of that effort somehow.

When the event was over, I sought out Lynne and thanked her for inviting me. Seeing how moved I was, she invited me to travel with her group to the Amazon to meet their indige-nous partners—and one year later, I did just that. But after we spoke, I was still flying high from all I had seen and heard and was reluctant to break the spell by returning to my office. So I went to the coffee line, and that is where I met Bob. He was a founding board member of the nonprofit and had traveled to the jungle with Lynne and her husband, Bill, several years ear-lier. We found a lot to talk about. The spark between us led to dinner a few weeks later. Months after our first date, he told me he'd made a rare exception to his dating practice; at the time, the fact that I lived a half-hour drive beyond his acceptable dat-ing radius made me "geographically undesirable." Thankfully, he liked me enough to set that rule aside, which is just another example of how saying yes to something slightly inconvenient can be the smart choice. Three years later, we were married and that is hands down one of the best decisions I've ever made.

The first thing I noticed about Bob was his strong, six-foot-two frame and Irish charm, which shone through a ras-cally smile and lighthearted laugh. He was divorced, with two children, an eleven-year-old son, Will, and a fourteen-year-old daughter, Christine, who lived with him half-time. He and his

ex-wife had been apart ten years and had a warm, cooperative relationship.

Possessing both an engineering and law degree, Bob was a sharp man who had run dozens of successful businesses all around the world, though he was never flashy about his accomplishments. He had a reputation for being one of the smartest and most humble of people in whatever group he belonged. I recall standing in our kitchen, getting exasperated as I sorted through our Tupperware cupboard, trying to find a bowl and matching lid. I threw up my hands, turned to Bob, and said, "This is chaos"—to which he replied, "No, my dear, that is entropy." Rascally smile. Lighthearted laugh. Kiss on the cheek. Never have I known anyone better at balancing such a keen intellect with a warm heart. His sense of humor never came at another person's expense. He thought the Catholic religion he was raised in was hypocritical and backward, particularly when it came to women's reproductive rights and gay rights. He embraced the magic and mystery of life and had a very tender and reverential spiritual life that showed up in his love of nature, poetry, philosophy, and art. When you combine that with his mental prowess and generous spirit, you have a very elegant man. Stories of his generosity with time and resources are legion.

Becoming a stepmother was challenging for me. I was over forty and had conceded that I would not have my own children in this lifetime, a decision made easier by Bob, who did not want more kids. It took a while for me to get my bearings. Will and I warmed to each other right away. At first, Christine was not sure she liked having me in the picture, and I found her adolescent moods a bore. My stepkids were raised in privileged circumstances: private schools, tutors, music lessons, a swimming pool in the backyard, Hawaiian vacations. It was a far cry from my own upbringing and sometimes triggered judgments and resentments that I needed to let go of in order to deepen my relationship with them and their father. It was a deliberate choice that I did not assume any parenting responsibilities—

these children already had two engaged parents, so that base was covered. Over the years, I assumed the role of a steady and supportive adult who loved them.

We made our home in Marin County, surrounded by redwoods in a tri-story house tucked into a canyon on Mount Tam. Raven families nest in the boughs of my favorite tree while a pair of turquoise hummingbirds sustain themselves on our lavender and Mexican sage. Life and work unfolded in rich and surprising ways as I entered a period of deep peace, joy, and productivity. Like everyone, I had my share of garden-variety life challenges, but I could always find much to be grateful for.

⁓

One evening I was home alone, reading a fine book. The telephone rang, and it was my dad. I'd been married two years, but we had not spoken in over eight years. His age—now seventy—came through the receiver; his voice, scratchy from the flu, sounded dull as a used pencil. He got right to the details, like someone pressed for time. His mother, my ninety-four-year-old grandmother, had been in decline for many months, he said, and had just been admitted to a hospice home. She was in and out—but mostly out—of consciousness, and no one expected her to live more than a week or two.

"It's been a long haul," said Dad. "Your mom is over there every day, checking in with the hospice staff. It's starting to take its toll on all of us. We're ready for this to be over. Grandma just needs to die." He seemed resigned to the waiting.

Growing up, I never felt a sustained closeness with Grandma T., a nickname she encouraged. Like the rest of my father's family, she was not a Witness, and we had limited contact with the "worldly" side of the family. She was always kind to me, though, and I thought of her with fondness. I recall her dismay with my choice to skip college and go into full-time pioneer work. "You're smart, Lindy," she said. "Think of all the goodness you could bring to the world if you had an education." At the time,

I dismissed her point of view. I was pursuing a noble path and believed what I had been taught: chasing higher education would distract me from my spiritual ideals. Armageddon would soon come, followed by the New System here on Earth. Calling attention to that event was my way of serving humanity. I always assured Grandma that my spiritual education would be more than sufficient to get me through the time remaining in this old, doomed system. She'd roll her eyes and take a sip of tea.

Dad wanted me to know about Grandma's condition, in case I wanted to visit her before she passed away. He had begun planning a service at the local funeral home.

Disconnecting the call, I felt a warmth and inclusion I hadn't experienced for a long while. A gust of winter wind thrust itself against the window beside me, and rain beat down on the overhead skylight. I sent a silent prayer to Grandma T., wishing her well and thanking her for creating this opening. I was being granted some kind of death exemption.

In the years since I'd left the religion, I'd wondered how my family would manage around me during a crisis. Dad's call started to answer that question, a question that weighed on me. With months, then years, passing without substantive communication, during which I had no idea about their health or other circumstances, my imagination gave birth to scenarios where I was excluded. True to their word, Lory and Randy had avoided all contact with me.

As a result, I had been unsure of how—or even if—my family would communicate about illness or death closer to home. Today that worry was assuaged. If they called me now, *before* Grandma passed away, I knew they would grant me the same courtesy in the future. This was a dry run for the inevitable. I saw my chance to "test out" how to be with them before another loss occurred, one that would cause me a much deeper sense of loss. As much as I scoffed at the reasons we needed a death exemption, it was better than the alternative.

That night I talked to Bob, reviewed my calendar, and searched the Internet for flight options. I slept on my decision but knew in my heart it was the right thing to go before Grandma T. passed away. Something unsaid in my father's voice told me it would mean a great deal to him. It was perhaps the only form of support he could accept from me, and thus the only one that mattered.

The next day, I phoned Dad to declare my intentions to visit in two days, hoping Grandma would hold on. I could fly in and out of Portland on the same day, with time to spare. That would be more than enough time to drive from the airport, get my bearings in the old neighborhood, visit Grandma, and have a bite to eat. I'd rent a car, I assured him, and didn't expect anyone to show me around. If someone gave me the address of the hospice home, I'd locate it on my own. Bob would join me later to attend the memorial service, whenever that was, but I would make this first trip alone.

Dad set the phone aside and succinctly recited my plan to Mom. There was a pause while she took it in, then a muffled reply. Back on the phone, Dad said that would be fine, except Mom had to work that day and he remained sick with the flu, quarantined from seeing Grandma. Again, I assured him I could manage alone. I never expected them to spend time with me. Dad had explained in his phone call the day before that Mom was still working part-time at a commercial insurance agency. Between that work, attending meetings at the Kingdom Hall, and keeping in daily communication with the hospice workers, she was at the outer limits of what she could take on. I had accepted the possibility I wouldn't see her at all and predicted the memorial service would be our next encounter.

Dad insisted I come by the house, where, he said, he would give me directions. I was excited to see him and hoped we would have some time alone together. I saw the day unfolding in my mind: after a brief visit with Dad, I'd drive alone to the nearby hospice home and pay my respects to Grandma. I would offer to pick up some warm soup, eat lunch with my father, and then be off to the airport in time for my five o'clock flight home.

The next day, I arose at dawn to catch the early flight to

Portland. As I dressed in brown slacks and a crisp blue blouse, I thought I could just as easily have been headed to a business meeting in the city. I slipped on my coat, grabbed an umbrella, and headed out the door. A faint yet persistent restlessness hung over me, a hollow anticipation that comes whenever I have to speak in front of a group, when there is nothing to do but hang out and wait, every cell of your being ready to begin.

I had last been to my parents' home six years prior, when I had traveled to Portland to attend the wedding of a girlfriend's daughter. Coincidentally, it was within a week of my parents' wedding anniversary. Following the protocol my mother established years earlier, I mailed them a letter informing them of my plans and my desire to stop in and pay my respects. Though I had no assurances they would receive me, when I phoned upon arrival, my mother invited me over the following day. In honor of the occasion, I brought them flowers and wine. I believe they were happy to see me, but they offered only coffee—much less than the easy hospitality I was raised with—which I took as subtle encouragement to keep my visit short. Based on that experience, I did not expect Dad to offer me a meal now, so I ate breakfast on the plane.

The flight was uneventful. As the plane touched down, I felt a stirring of nerves and foreboding. It was the last day of January, and the weather was bleak and soggy. Dad said it had been raining there incessantly for a full month. After securing the rental car, I called Dad from my cell phone to let him know I was on the ground and headed for his house. I was ready to put the car in gear and leave the parking garage. It was then that he informed me Mom had taken the day off work and was going to accompany me to see Grandma. Not only that, but my sister had also rearranged her schedule to be with us. Mom would fix us breakfast while we waited for Lory to arrive.

I felt like a steel elevator dropped from my chest to my stomach. An immediate increase in my blood pressure shattered whatever shards of tranquility I possessed. I almost missed the turnoff from the airport feeder road onto the Banfield freeway, a route I knew by heart. My well-planned day was taking a turn. Was it for better or for worse? What would it be like to see her after all these years? What would she look like?

I did the math. Lory was forty-nine years old. When I had last found myself in Portland, for the wedding and the brief pilgrimage to see my parents, we had sat drinking coffee on their back patio, on the part of my parents' property that abuts Lory's backyard. At that time, Lory had refused to come over, choosing to hole up in her house instead. Mom made excuses, saying she was not up for seeing me—though I wasn't sure whether she meant Lory found it emotionally trying or morally objectionable.

So what had changed now? Back then I'd felt regret that my sister was suffering and wished her some peace. Did her choice to see me today indicate a sign of healing or resignation?

As I drove along the I-5 interchange, the city of Portland came into view. The US Bank Tower dominated the horizon. Under sheets of rain, the Willamette River was the same gray as the retaining walls of the boat docks. The skyscrapers seemed hunched in a protective stance, a hopeless effort to shield themselves from inclement weather. This day held more potential than I'd originally anticipated. In the twelve years since I'd left Portland, I had owned my choices and their consequences. I'd made peace with the past. But it's easy to fool oneself. Those claims were about to be tested. Could I stay openhearted, remaining both kind to my family and true to myself?

As I steered into the old neighborhood, my anxiety increased, clammy hands clutching the steering wheel. It occurred to me there might be an organized plot among my relatives to gang up and try to talk some sense into me. Maybe Lory and Mom would pull me aside and talk about my getting reinstated. Maybe Lory was coming to judge for herself how far I'd slipped from the path. Was it too much to hope she just wanted to spend time with me?

The rain stopped, but a forlorn mood hung over the neighborhood. Most of the old houses still stood on Mapleleaf Street. Some were pristine and well cared for. Others were dark and frowsy. Here and there, larger lots had been divided into twos and threes by developers, who'd built new houses that shared a common driveway. It felt erratic, with no rhyme or reason.

I turned into my parents' driveway. They had one of the pristine houses. Gone were the two maple trees that dominated the yard of my childhood, but the row of rhododendrons still flanked the flower bed closest to the foundation. A retaining wall had been built to the side of the driveway. The place had the barren look of a long winter. I turned off the ignition and adjusted the rearview mirror to take a final look at myself. I took a deep breath. Inside my head, I heard Bette Davis saying, *Fasten your seat belts—it's going to be a bumpy night.*

Chapter 22

I am he as you are he as you are me and we are all together.
—John Lennon and Paul McCartney

Dad greeted me at the door before I had a chance to knock. One hand rested on his belly; the other was extended wide to greet me. He had the scruffy, unshaven look of the convalescing, dressed in jeans, worn leather slippers, long-sleeved T-shirt, and vest.

"Hi, Lindy." He smiled as I stepped inside. We came together naturally in an unabashed full-body hug that was an enormous comfort to me. After pulling away, he looked me up and down.

"You look good," he said with a bashful grin.

Mom walked around the corner from the kitchen to greet me. "Hi, Mom," I said, and we embraced. Right away, I was filled with concern for her. She was so thin, I felt as if I could pick her up and toss her in the air like a small child. Stress had always melted the pounds off my mother. I wished I'd heard about Grandma T.'s condition sooner. Perhaps I could have helped Mom navigate the chores. Would she have accepted my help? If I'd known she was going to rearrange her schedule, I would have consulted her about the best time for my arrival, the way normal families who are talking to each other do. "I didn't expect you to rearrange your whole day for this," I said. "I know you have a lot going on." *Not to mention the shunning*.

"That's okay, Lindy," she said, still hugging me. She pulled away and looked me over. Her chin-length hair had filled with even more soft strands of gray. She looked up at me with tired, red-rimmed eyes. "I don't want you to be alone when you see Grandma. She's very weak and depleted. I hope you've prepared yourself for that."

"I have," I said. "At least I think I have." I realized I'd spent more time thinking about seeing my parents than preparing myself for the impact of Grandma's frailty. I took off my shoes and followed Mom and Dad into the kitchen.

"Would you like some coffee?" Mom asked. "I thought I'd make us some breakfast—fresh fruit and cereal—while we wait for Lory to arrive. She'll be here in about an hour."

There I was, standing in the surreal reality of my parents' kitchen, chatting about life like any ordinary group of relatives. Maybe I'd dropped into some parallel universe. Dad went into more detail about his virus, how he struggled to sleep. While he spoke, I noticed his white head of hair, unfamiliar creases around his eyes, poignant reminders of time slipping by. Mom sliced apples and pineapple for the fruit salad, refusing any assistance from me. Through the kitchen window I could see the patio and expansive backyard, also barren from the long winter, the only color coming from the green lawn. Beyond their garden stood the house Lory and Ove had built five or so years earlier, where they still lived. It was a home I would never be inside, because I would never be invited there. All of the other houses weren't much different than I remembered, but a new log cabin had been erected between two of the established homes.

"What an odd style choice," I said. "A log cabin in the suburbs, twenty feet from the next house, no forest for miles."

"It's just awful," Mom said. "This neighborhood has been sliced and diced so many ways."

There was an unmistakable tension in the room—or maybe it was inside me. I sensed I was being watched, observed, for signs of who I was now, my level of happiness, what I believed, what motivated me, how I lived my life. Cupping my coffee mug, I wandered around the corner to the living room. Mom had completely redecorated, with a new couch, wingback chairs, and billowing window coverings—objects unfamiliar to me. But the paneling remained on one wall, and Dad's leather recliner. The TV cabinet and bookshelf were there, too. In between the books, stereo, and CDs were small frames containing family photos. Dad joined with his coffee cup in hand just as I came across a recent photograph of Bob and me.

"You have our wedding picture here," I said, surprised at first, then relaxing as particles of joy sprang up inside my heart. It felt like a talisman to unexpectedly see my dear husband and me, out of doors in our wedding finery, smiling under the shade of a tree on the banks of Richardson Bay, Mount Tam in the background. There was a solace in being included, a sense of being honored, even, to be displayed in such a prominent place in my parents' home, a room they sat in every day.

Mom and Dad had declined the invitation to attend our wedding. As soon as we'd set a wedding date, I'd dispatched a letter to them, announcing our engagement and plans to marry. They would be receiving a formal invitation, I assured them, but I wanted to share enough details of our plans that if they chose to join us, they'd be prepared. We expected about ninety guests. I made a point to "warn" them the ceremony would be officiated by a woman who had become a spiritual mentor and friend to me. Though the ceremony would be nondenominational, I told them Bob and I would be actively involved in seeing that it reflected our spiritual values. I'd been careful to keep my language warm yet unattached to the outcome.

It would mean a lot to me if you would come share in our happiness. Your attendance would not be interpreted as anything more than a wish to meet my community of friends and remain connected despite our different choices.

Over the many weeks that followed, however, I realized I'd fooled myself as their silence obliterated my so-called unattachment. My yearning for their presence and participation was excruciating. Every day I'd listen for the postal delivery and open the mailbox with the same expectation a child brings to

Christmas morning. Day after day, the mailman failed me. As our wedding plans proceeded, the dangling question of their presence clouded my joy. I was wishing for a wedding exemption, a truce for one day when we could simply rejoice in our shared humanity.

A month before the wedding, I received this letter:

Dear Linda [she used my given name, rather than the more familial Lindy]:

I apologize for being so late in writing this letter. I have agonized over how to tell you that Dad and I will not be attending your wedding. We know you will be very disappointed. In thinking it over, we feel that our being there would be even more painful to you as it would be to us, as we would not be comfortable under the circumstances. It's better that we just not attend.

But this is not to say that we aren't happy about your marriage. We all hope for the time when we get to meet Bob and enjoy both of you. Of course, this all depends on whether you can make room in your heart to set things straight between you and Jehovah. I am sure this is far from your mind right now but will always be something we hope for.

In the meantime, you are in our minds and hearts and especially so on October 4.
Love you always,
Dad and Mom

In the end, this letter was the best thing that could have happened to ensure a happy wedding day. Of course I cried my eyes out upon first reading it. On the second reading, I flamed with anger at her judgments, believing my relationship with God was none of her damn business. By the twentieth or thirtieth reading, I surrendered and found relief. The question of their presence was resolved; I could make peace with their absence and move on. I had always known their attendance was a stretch. And my mother was right about one thing: on your wedding day, you want to be surrounded only by unconditional love and support. Since they were unable to provide that, it was not their place to be there. In the final weeks before our wedding, I found a joy and lightheartedness that comes solely with true acceptance and love.

The day before the ceremony, we received a large box from them, filled with wedding gifts. There was a rustic platter, a bottle of Oregon pinot noir, and a card. Lory enclosed a letter to Bob, welcoming him to the family and complimenting him on his choice in me. *Linda is an equal mix of our parents. Frank is a storyteller, and Ruth is gracious, loved by all. On your wedding day, I wish you all the happiness the world has to offer.*

We had a blast at our wedding. I felt connected to everyone there by a deep bond, sensing the presence of my "soul family," a heart connection that transcends DNA. I missed my parents, but the only tears I shed that day were tears of joy. I was completely swept away by my love for Bob.

A few weeks later, we sent my parents a card thanking them for their gifts, and I included the wedding picture I now held in my hands, elegantly framed in silver.

Mom had set the table with place mats and cloth napkins and invited me to take a seat. Dad poured us more coffee and joined me. Mom placed large bowls of fruit and oatmeal in front of us and then sat down.

"Dad, would you like to say the prayer?" she said, as Dad and I both became sheepishly aware that we had already started eating, chunks of pineapple and grapes in our mouths. Dad wiped his mouth with the cloth napkin and bowed his head. I followed his lead, closing my eyes. His prayer was brief, sticking to the basics.

"Thank you, Jehovah, for this day, and this food, and please be with Grandma and those looking after her. In Jesus' name we pray. Amen." He rushed over the words, but his reverence was genuine, unmistakable. Apparently, my father had deepened his spiritual practice while I had been away. I admired him for it.

After taking a few bites of food, Mom stood up and fished out a glossy brochure from the desk near the dining table and gave it to me. It was for barge cruises in France, and the page was turned to the trip they'd taken the year before, to celebrate their fiftieth wedding anniversary. They spoke of Dad's disdain for Paris, Mom dragging him through the sites, pleading for a photo on the Pont Neuf. Dad preferred the tranquility of the barge cruise through rural communities and told funny stories about the captain and other characters they met along the way.

"Congratulations," I said. "Fifty years. That's amazing."

The very ordinariness of such mundane chatter was a quiet thrill for me. I missed this. It was almost as good as spending time alone with my dad.

"We were so surprised when we got your letter saying you'd left Chicago," Dad said. "You were crazy about that city."

"I still am. I didn't think I would ever leave. But Visa offered me a great job and the chance to relocate me to paradise on their dime. How could I refuse?"

I went on to describe the joys and challenges of working for Visa, and my decision to resign and launch my own business. Over the years, I had established a warm and reliable community of friends and wanted to share what that meant to me, and how meeting Bob had expanded the web of connection I felt to the world. I remembered Mom's warning, proclaimed at this very table: *your only true friends can be found in The Truth— worldly people will always let you down.* Part of me wanted to tell her how wrong she was, to emphasize the good and true companions I had in my life. But I hadn't come for that purpose and was enjoying the connection too much to clutter the experience with comments she would dismiss as quixotic.

Lory's arrival was imminent, and my angst about seeing her was mounting. The two breakfasts I'd consumed—one on the plane, this second one to be polite—were churning in my belly. I could feel the entirety of my body tensing in anticipation.

While Mom cleared the table, Dad offered to show me the rest of the house. Few things had changed. We were downstairs in the pantry when I heard a door open and close upstairs, then two women talking. My sister had arrived. I waited for Lory to join us downstairs, but she did not. Dad was talking, and I was growing impatient.

"Dad," I said, "I hate to interrupt, but I wanna go upstairs and see Lory." He paused midsentence and nodded in surrender.

I clipped up the stairs, two at a time, bracing myself for an awkward moment. I called out, "Is that my sister's voice I hear?"

As I pushed through the door, I saw Mom doing dishes and Lory leaning against the counter. They were in the middle of a conversation. Lory's appearance hadn't changed. She had beautiful brown eyes and the same clear, olive complexion. She was wearing her usual fine wool skirt, blouse, and cardigan. Her long black hair fell in waves around her face. She turned her gaze toward me and uttered a question I could not have predicted.

"Lindy, do you color your hair?"

Of all the questions I'd imagined, this was not one of them. A small pause fell among us, broken by Dad's arrival just behind me, at the top of the stairs.

"What kind of a question is that?" I said. "You don't see me in twelve years, and you ask me about hair color?" I opened my arms and took the few steps toward her. "Come on, give me a hug."

She smiled and we embraced. I could feel the tension in her limbs. She had never been outwardly affectionate toward others, and our hug was brief. It was reassuring to know she was nervous, too. As we pulled away, I really looked at her and saw only a hint of her age, in the faint lines around her mouth.

Once again I found myself enjoying the everyday conversation that occur among families, the four of us leaning against various portions of the L-shaped kitchen counter. Something inside me relaxed as the topics swung from vitamin supplements to gardening. Then Lory brought the conversation back to Grandma. It was time to go see her. Dad took aspirin and lay down. Lory, Mom, and I put on our raincoats and hurried through the drizzle to Lory's car. As we drove, the conversation was easy enough. They asked more questions about my life that day than they had over the previous twelve years combined, taking an interest in my work, my move to San Francisco, my two stepchildren, Bob. I was still feeling skittish, wondering when the preaching might start, but I was happy to answer their questions, not caring if they were judging me as worldly or selfish to think I could get away with living as I pleased. No matter what, I was doomed in their eyes, but perhaps they could acknowledge my happiness as I tumbled toward Judgment Day. I didn't avoid details that would reveal just how far I'd drifted. At one point it felt natural to make a passing comment about the joy of my yoga practice, something my former religion forbade, given its associations with the Hindu religion.

Soon we entered a suburban sprawl that was new to me, large housing developments stretched out over acres where we used to pick strawberries in the summer. Lory turned the car into one of these developments, winding through a series of tract houses, and parked in front of a one-level ranch-style house.

"Here we are," Mom said from the backseat. "When we go in, I'll get an update from the hospice nurse, and then we'll sit with Grandma a bit."

Grandma T.'s small room was gobbled up by the hospital bed that dominated one corner. The bed was perched up, and Grandma was lying there, eyes not quite open and not quite shut, eyelids thin, with barely a trace of lashes. The full reality of her impending death hit me as I observed Mom coaxing this once lively and self-possessed woman to take a few sips of water through a curled plastic straw. "Look who's here to see you, Grandma. It's Lindy."

I pulled a chair up to her bedside, sat down, and slipped both arms through the frigid metal railings, taking hold of her cool, knobby hands. Her blank expression did not change. I believe she was drawing inward, resting between the dimensions, pulling together the energy she needed to pass over into another world. I was raised to believe that death is a state of nonexistence, no consciousness, living only in Jehovah's memory, until some far-off time when he resurrects people back to physical form in the New World. But I didn't believe that anymore. Deeply saddened as I contemplated the months of pain and suffering leading to her death, I was comforted to think the universe would never be without the essence of Grandma T.'s kind soul, and that soon she would be released from the confines of corporeal form, free to grace us all again from benevolent realms.

Soon it was time to leave, so I said my last goodbye and we headed back down the dark corridor, through the foyer, dodging raindrops as we dashed toward the car. All three of us were quiet for a while, in a reflective, respectful way, but I don't think any of us was overcome with grief or emotion. I was grateful to see Grandma one last time, feeling the melancholy and mystery of the situation. I guessed Lory and Mom would feel some relief upon her death; in their view, it would open the way for her to potentially be resurrected into the New System on a perfect physical earth, if that was Jehovah's will for her soul.

The windshield wipers kept the beat as we drove past my old high school and Lory updated me on her life. She and Ove continued to work together on his home construction business while she pursued her real estate license. They did not have children, so she was free to remain very active in preaching work. Ove's position as a congregation elder also kept him busy. As we drove past certain streets and neighborhoods, I asked about people from the congregation who had once lived there. Each time, Lory gave me a thorough update. There was no hesitation in her responses, no stinginess with details.

Mom spoke up from the backseat and turned the conversation toward Randy. *Is this the same woman who visited me in Chicago and refused to share even the smallest tidbit of family news, preferring instead to grill me about my beliefs?*

Mom said my big brother and his wife, Marlene, were living in eastern Oregon, a stone's throw from the Snake River at the

Idaho border. Sheena had married and was expecting her first child within the month. This was big news to me, as I'd always been especially fond of her. *If Grandma weren't dying, how would I ever learn of these exciting and joyous developments?* According to Mom, Dad was gloomy about the prospect that Grandma might not live long enough to see the arrival of this fourth generation, but everyone anticipated the happy event nevertheless. Mom didn't say much about my nephew, Tyler, except that he was experiencing the usual struggles of teenage years.

It was unclear why Mom was suddenly so relaxed and comfortable sharing so many family details, or why my sister was speaking to me at all, but I refused to question it outright. Grandma's imminent death had been the catalyst, and, as with her passing, this level of intimacy was temporary. I preferred to enjoy it for its own sake.

We arrived at my parents' home. Dad sat with us in the dining room as we gave him the update on Grandma's condition. Mom clicked on the heat, and we all sat in a circle around the floor vent to get warm, like we used to do when I was little. It felt foreign and familiar all at once. Falling into such communal routines is what I love about family life, and the tug at my heart reminded me of how much I had missed these simple rituals. Mom consulted Lory and me to weigh in on the printed program for Grandma's memorial, what the picture caption should say, which poem and verse to use. And just then, I realized I had just enough time to comfortably reach the airport for an on-time departure. The day had slipped by like a warm breeze.

"It's time for me to go," I said, standing to gather my things. "Thank you for calling me, and thank you for taking me over to see Grandma. Is there anything Bob and I can do to help right now?"

Dad shook his head. "No," he said. "Just show up when we call you."

Chapter 23

❦

The end of our exploring will be to arrive at where we started, and to know the place for the first time.

—T. S. Eliot

Grandma died two days later.

Dad called to tell me the date and time of the memorial service. Bob and I had one week to make our travel plans, but those arrangements were small potatoes compared with the questions running through my head. My first trip to Portland had been an antidote for years of anxiety; I'd been treated with respect, and no one had preached at me. But a crowded memorial service promised a new set of dynamics. I started a mental list of relatives and Witnesses who might be there. Could I stay openhearted through this second round?

My dominant concern was whether or not Randy would talk to me. It had been twelve years since our parting conversation in the mall parking lot. But if Lory could find a way to speak to me, maybe Randy could, too.

A few days before our departure, my mother telephoned. She wanted to be sure our travel arrangements were in place, but I sensed she had more than logistics on her mind.

"We'd like to invite you and Bob over for dinner after the memorial service," she said. "I hope you haven't made other plans."

Other plans? Was she suggesting we might go out and paint the town after this solemn occasion, or was she just trying to be gracious and give us a social "out"? I'd just spent a thousand dollars on airfare. What else was there to do but show up fully?

"We'd love to come," I said. "It would be nice for Bob to see the house I grew up in."

"Now, Lindy, I want to prepare you," she said, in a careful-on-the-playground tone. "A lot of friends from the congregation will be at the service, and several of them are dropping food by afterward so I don't have to cook."

I was pacing between my kitchen and my dining room. "That's exactly the kind of thing I'd expect from the friends, Mom."

"Several of them have asked about you, and many of them are looking forward to seeing you. But, Lindy"—there was a long pause—"I must warn you, dear, there will be some people who won't talk to you. They want to, of course, but their Christian conscience won't allow it. You need to be prepared for that."

I stopped pacing. She had confirmed what my intuition told me to expect: some people would welcome my presence; others would cling to the rules. To them, the Scriptures were clear: "If anyone comes to you and does not bring this teaching, never receive him into your home or say a greeting to him. For he that says a greeting to him is a sharer in his wicked works." Mom and Dad had somehow found a workable middle ground that allowed them to invite us to their home, but for others there was no acceptable compromise, only patriarchal edicts and time-worn separation.

"Thanks for the warning, Mom, but I expected that," I said. "I'll see you Saturday at the memorial hall."

I channeled my anxiety and excitement into obsessive thoughts over what I would wear. I expected all the Witness women, including Mom and my sister, to make a point of wearing a skirt or dress, just as they did when visiting a Kingdom Hall. That was proper dress code for Christian women. To do anything else would suggest a worldly, almost disrespectful attitude. But I was committed to comfort, not rules. If I was going to be "on display," my pride and ego demanded that I look ravishing, in an effortless sort of way. I had deliberately booked a flight that would give Bob and me just enough time to drive to the service directly after our plane landed. Whatever I wore on the plane would have to carry me through the day. After trying on and rejecting almost every outfit in my closet, I found physical comfort and a nod to my vanity with Italian wool pants and my best bolero jacket.

Saturday came quickly. The alarm went off in the wee hours of the morning, but I was already awake. The early-morning bay fog was receding as Bob and I boarded the plane and settled into our seats. During the two-hour flight to Portland, I went to the restroom five times. I couldn't keep still, filing my nails, pushing back the cuticles, eating stale peanuts, and staring out the window. I wondered who we would see from my dad's "worldly" side of the family—aunts, uncles, and cousins close to my age whom I hadn't seen in over fifteen years. Grandma's brother, my dad's uncle Jess, would be there, keeping things light with off-color jokes in his southern Oklahoma accent. His wife, Aunt Mary, would be there, too, keeping her eye on him, shaking her head and laughing along. They were always kind to me, and the thought of seeing them cheered me up.

Dad had arranged for Ove to give part of the memorial talk. It was his heartfelt nod to the Witness ideology, a chance to spread a little truth and encouragement, no doubt.

After the flight, we picked up our rental car and began the trek toward Tigard. As I drove, I gave Bob the rundown on the relatives and people I thought we would see. I wondered aloud what kind of questions people might ask him, especially my sister. "She might ask you what religion you are."

"What an interesting question," Bob said. "I've never thought about narrowing it down to one. "I haven't been in a Catholic church since I was twelve years old." He looked out the car window for a moment. " If I had to claim one religion, I think I'd want to be a Buddhist."

"Tibetan or Zen?" I asked, trying to anticipate how my sister would respond, then realizing she might not even be aware of the distinctions, just as I had not been until I'd left.

"Does it matter? I'm for any religion that teaches acceptance. How is that for an answer?" Then he got that Irish leprechaun grin that I love. "Or I could tell them I'm very familiar with cults." This was a reference to his past experience as a member of EST's executive management team, the seminal human potential movement that detractors dubbed a cult, though thousands believed it created lasting transformation in their lives.

"Yes, do say that, Bobby." I rolled my eyes, amused. "That will go over brilliantly."

The truth is, I wouldn't have wanted to face the trip without Bob, and I trusted him implicitly to handle with grace and dignity anything that came up. He enjoyed socializing and meeting new people and was skillful at it. I was proud of him, his life, who he was. Over the course of our relationship, he had always been a presence of acceptance for this situation. His career had taken him all over the world, exposing him to a wide variety of religious customs and spiritual practices. He didn't condone my family's actions, but he didn't make them wrong for it, either. He accepted this as their path and knew ranting against it would serve no purpose, least of all for me. He would shake his head at the broad execution of their blind faith, but it was what it was. Here was someone who understood, as I did, that if these people knew any other way to do this, they certainly would. It wasn't our job to convert anyone to reason. We were only there to be ourselves and love everybody the best that we could.

Ten minutes before the service, I steered the car into the funeral home parking lot, which was filled to capacity. Driving to an adjacent lot, I found one of the few remaining spaces. My breathing had become tight and thin.

You have every right to be here. Breathe deeply. Stay present and open.

Bob sat observing me from the passenger seat while I checked my lipstick one last time. Then we looked each other in the eye.

"Shall we?" he said. We walked hand in hand across the

black pavement. It was February, but we did not need overcoats. After a ridiculous forty-two consecutive days of rain, the sun had emerged as a kind friend.

Mom and Dad greeted us in the foyer, where they stood sentry for all visitors. Dad was dressed in a brown pin-striped suit, the lines picking up the silver shimmer of his hair. His blue eyes seemed overcast with gray. He gave me a long hug. "Hi, baby," he said. I relished his affection. Mom hugged me next. Under her wool blazer and skirt, she was a whisper of bones. In hushed tones, I introduced everyone.

"We are so happy to meet you, Bob," my mother said, shaking his hand, exuding the presence of a woman in charge and in control, wanting to affirm a genuine welcome. Dad judged other men by the firmness of their handshake, which was what he received from Bob as he offered his condolences.

"I'm sorry our first meeting is not under more pleasant circumstances," Bob said.

Dad nodded his head in agreement. "We'll take it when we can get it."

"It's a full house in there, but we saved you a seat near the front with us," Mom said. "I'll take you in while Dad stays here."

I looked through the double doors that opened into the main hall. The seats were filled with people facing the front. In the back were a fireplace, two couches that formed a large seating area, a row of serving tables, and an organ, and just to my right was a video projector pouring light onto a wall screen. Three people were standing in back—my sister, Ove, and Uncle Jess—and watching a looping series of pictures of Grandma T. throughout her life.

Ove saw us entering the hall and approached Bob with a warm smile and an extended hand. "Welcome, Bob. I'm Ove," he said. "I'm the *other* son-in-law."

"How do you do?" Bob said. Until that moment, I had never thought of Bob as a member of *this* family. Of course, he'd always felt like *my* family, but I'd not connected that this technically made him a son-in-law, a brother-in-law, an uncle. Lory remained standing at Uncle Jess's side and watched their exchange.

"Please excuse me. I'm a bit distracted right now," Ove continued. "Frank asked me to say a few words here, and I want to focus on what I'm going to say. We'll have more of a chance to visit at dinner." Without saying another word, he gave me a perfunctory kiss on the cheek, then vanished to his seat.

Lory approached us, wearing a long black wool skirt and a loose blazer. "Hi, Bob. I'm Lory," she said, as she shook his hand. A clenched jaw and forced smile betrayed her nervousness. Bob spoke to her in muted tones while I approached Uncle Jess, standing alone and captivated by the passing images of his big sister. My heart was grateful for his presence. Here was one of the family sages, and he had no cause to rebuff me. As I got closer, Uncle Jess looked up through thick square glasses and, after a split second of cognitive reaction, threw open his arms.

"Lindy," he said in a lion-like whisper, wrapping his arms around me with unabashed affection.

I squeezed him back, then pulled back to look at his face, noticing his laugh lines. "I'll introduce you and Aunt Mary to my husband after the service," I whispered.

Mom touched my shoulder from behind, signaling that it was time to take our seats. Every row was filled with people, some whispering to each other, while a tedious melody piped in through the speaker system. Bob and I followed Mom down the center aisle until she stopped, pointing for us to sit down in the middle of the second empty row from the front. As we took our seats, I saw my aunts, uncles, and cousins of my age sitting next to teenagers who shared common physical characteristics—a dimpled chin or deep-set eyes. Many faces brightened as our eyes met. One of my cousins smiled and waved from across the aisle.

I felt a hand on my right shoulder and turned to see my brother, Randy, sitting next to Marlene and Tyler. Sheena wasn't there. Randy had a smile on his face. "You look good," he whispered. Marlene nodded and smiled back at me.

Mission Control, we have contact! Brother and sister just ended a twelve-year silence. Break out the bubbly.

A polished wooden casket dominated the front of the hall, and beside it was the speaker's podium. Bouquets of white lilies and yellow roses sat on either side. I wondered what Grandma's favorite flower was and regretted that I didn't know the answer.

"Remind me what your parents' first names are, again," Bob leaned over and whispered. "You introduced them as Mom and Dad, but it's Ruth and Frank, right?"

I nodded my head. Mom sat down in the row next to Bob and me, and it was then I noticed Lory and Ove were seated behind her, next to Randy. It pleased me that we were seated with the immediate family, but it also added to the off-kilter feeling, fed by the mixture of a solemn occasion, joyful reunions, and gnawing apprehension about what would happen next. Who was talking to me? Who wasn't?

Dad approached the podium and tapped on the microphone. The music evaporated midsong.

"Thank you for coming. As most of you know, I'm Frank, Emma Lee's oldest. We will have two speakers this afternoon. First, Pastor Jess Strickland, Jr.—Emma Lee's nephew and a Baptist minister—will recount her life and times, followed by words of encouragement by my son-in-law Ove Peterson."

And so it went that both men stood in succession and delivered their respective talks. Jess, Jr.—known to the family as Twig—showed his experience as an orator with that comfortable gift of gab. He went year by year, sharing the significant events of Grandma's life and finished by reading aloud the names of her progeny. Upon hearing my name, I felt as if he were speaking of some other Linda Ann, a stranger to these origins, an absence of kinship.

I was listening with only part of my brain. Holding Bob's hand, I was also thinking about the absurdity of the situation—how the end of a life created an opening for me to see my family. Death made it okay for my brother to speak to me, for my sister to give me a hug.

Ove now stood in front of the room, Bible in hand. Perhaps out of respect for Grandma's religious leanings, he never used the name Jehovah. He avoided saying anything about her being in heaven, because this was not something he himself believed. He read from Proverbs about how the day of one's death is better than the day of one's birth, because at death one has a legacy to reflect on. He continued reading how it is better to go into a house of mourning than into a house of celebration. King Solomon, who was credited with writing those words, was encouraging us to use solemn occasions to reflect on our own life. To my ears, Ove was suggesting everyone in the audience take a look at how their lives were stacking up with God, that jealous, judgmental Jehovah who still seemed to be up in heaven, keeping score.

Later that night when we were alone, Bob described the talk as "a little preachy." Near dinnertime, as we stood in her kitchen, Mom asked me if I enjoyed Ove's talk, and I lied and said that I enjoyed it very much, commenting on the calming presence he brought to the room.

"Is 'calming' code for 'boring'?" Bob deadpanned.

As Ove talked about the redeeming power of Christ's sacrifice, how our Savior King had the ability to wash away our sins, I recalled the days when I believed Jesus was the one true liberator and my eternal life depended on his sacrifice. While I remain a huge admirer of his teachings on love, Jesus has become for me an equal presence in a long succession of wise men and women—Buddha, Gandhi, Mother Teresa, the Dalai Lama—who lived and illuminated the human experience. But none of them possessed the power or the responsibility to save me. That was my job. In fact, I didn't *need* an external savior or sacrificial lamb. Only I could save myself. Then came a piercing realization, what my friend Neal calls a "thunderstanding": *I had saved my life. Literally. By leaving this religion, this community, I had saved my life.* The truth of this made me woozy. I was briefly overcome with a fresh awareness of the magnitude of that choice, remembering how scared I was and shuddering as I imagined the narrow confines and unhappiness that would surround me if I'd stayed here.

Tears came to my eyes. My salvation does not depend on hardship and sacrifice, earning approval, and pleasing a jealous deity. It is an internal experience that depends solely on the minute-by-minute choices I make, each and every day. I remembered all those Bible stories of Jesus curing the sick and lame, always with the declaration "your sins are forgiven." I believe he was saying that forgiveness of self and others is the key to our emancipation. Letting go creates the way for a miracle. My freedom is bound up in those split-second choices to look or turn away, open my heart, or close down, love freely, or insist upon conditions. And when he said, "The kingdom of heaven is in your midst," I think he meant that the ability to create our world and our experience is within us—through our perceptions in each moment.

These thoughts reverberated through me as Ove concluded his talk by encouraging us to bow our heads in prayer. Bob and I respectfully complied, but I was too consumed by my own emotional swirl to hear anything he said. We did not echo the "amen" of the audience. In this, we were observers, not participants. Ove sat down. Dad took the podium one last time and invited everyone to gather in the fireside room for refreshments. The Muzak came back on, signaling the program's end.

The cousins in the front row were reaching out to hug me, and I was thrilled to be introduced to their children but preoccupied by the close proximity of my brother. Bob took those moments to introduce himself to Randy, and they were chatting when I turned around. Randy, Marlene, and Tyler were standing side by side, looking at me.

"Randy," I said, sliding both knees onto the seat so I could get close enough to give him a hug. We met for a long embrace, and when I started to pull back, Randy continued his hold. Then I felt the oddest sensation, as if an arrow of energy shot from his heart to mine. It was robust and unexpected, a transfer of grief and regret. It made my eyes sting. As I pulled away and looked him in the eye, I could see he, too, was dewy-eyed but smiling. His smile held an ambivalent mix of desire and reticence, as if he enjoyed the moment but feared he might shatter into pieces if I looked too closely or for too long.

We both took a second to collect ourselves. Like most of the men in the room, he was wearing a suit and tie. His black hair was gray at the temples. Where do we start after twelve years with no communication? My thinking was muddled. I hugged Marlene and shook Tyler's hand. He was the same age as my stepson, Will. The blond hair of his childhood had darkened to a sandy tone; he wore it in the same conservative style as my brother, cut short and parted down one side.

"You've grown up, Tyler," I said.

"I don't really remember you," Tyler said, not unkindly but with the refreshing honesty of youth. It was a difficult thing to hear. The sad truth is, I had no relationship with my brother's youngest child.

"Of course you wouldn't," I said. "The last time I saw you, you were barely five years old. And now you're a teenager."

"Yeah," Randy said, now with a sarcastic grin on his face. "And what a joy it is to have teenagers, right, especially when they're old enough to drive?"

Asking after Sheena, I learned she was feeling the weight of her pregnancy and having mini-contractions. She was home obeying doctors' orders to avoid crowds and stay off her feet.

"We're going to check on her after this," Tyler said. "She lives about a half hour from here."

The crowd had thinned here, near the front. We had not moved from our rows of seats. Most people had gathered in back, near the fireplace and seating area. A rotating crowd gathered to watch the looping slide show of Grandma's life, having ordinary and congenial conversation, but eventually we all stood mute, looking at one another.

"Shall we join everyone else?" Bob asked, raising one arm in that direction. Everyone nodded and disbanded as we made our way back down the center aisle. I was reluctant to leave my brother, but I expected we would have plenty of time to visit at dinner.

Everything hinged on dinner. It would be for immediate

family only. Mom explained that bringing all the aunts, uncles, and cousins together would require renting a large room at a restaurant, and no one had the wallet or energy for that. Now that I knew everyone in my immediate family was speaking to me, at least for that day, I was looking forward to going to Mom and Dad's house for dinner.

Sipping syrupy pink punch from a paper cup, I carried on introducing Bob to my relatives. My intention was to stay long enough to be polite and say hello to all of these distant relatives I hadn't seen in years. Occasionally one of the "good friends of the family" stood at a distance and smiled at me but rebuffed my attempts to engage in conversation. Others walked past without acknowledging me. This included people who'd watched me grow from infancy through school and onto marriage, friends who had always been close to my family and remained so. One of these was a buxom brunette with spindly legs who used to babysit me when she was a teenager. Years later, I watched over her twins and took them out in field service during their summer vacations. She smiled as she passed, grabbed my hand to squeeze it, and, without saying a word, disappeared through the exit.

In contrast, a few of the friends did approach me, friendly as could be, seemingly genuine in their delight at seeing me, eager to meet Bob, nothing amiss. Part of me was crying, and another was laughing at the absurdity of it. None of these people could possibly know anything about my life now, and I saw no reason to take offense, whether they approached me or not. For the moment, I found enough room in my heart for all of it.

Thankfully, the distant relatives were oblivious to all of this, so these interactions were peppered with people who simply saw my extended absence as the natural consequence of living out of state. My parents and siblings were scattered throughout the room, engaged in their own conversations. Years earlier, I'd pressed my mother about what or how she had communicated my excommunication to Dad's side of the family. She said they hadn't told them anything. "We just told them you moved to Chicago. What else would we say?"

That you shunned me. That I exercised my free moral agency and left the religion and my marriage. That the cost of my choice was being expelled. That you cut off communication with me.

It was 3:15 p.m. We had been there an hour and a half, but it felt like five. The group was thinning. Dad approached and encouraged us to come to the house within the hour. "Don't feel like you need to wait for dinnertime," he said. "Just come." Bob and I said our farewells and left through the front door to check in to our hotel and regroup for the evening. As we walked toward the rental car, a cool breeze enveloped my body and I shuddered. It was then that I felt the back and armholes of my blazer soaked wet from perspiration.

C◦◦

Inside our hotel room, Bob unpacked, dressed in black gabardine pants and a sweater, and then sat next to me, signaling it was my turn to get organized. I lingered through several TV commercials, enjoying the reprieve, the lack of intensity, but finally stood and unpacked, too. I started fussing over whether to wear jeans or black pants, putting on one, then the other. I wondered out loud if jeans would be too casual or black pants would be too dressy.

"I can't help you," Bob said. "I don't know the norms of your family."

The norms of my family. What an interesting term.

Black pants it was. We set out to purchase wine at the Fred Meyer in my old neighborhood. Here, memories clashed with reality, reminding me of all that had irreversibly changed. Nothing in the store was as it once was. Produce was where the pharmacy used to be, and wine racks stood horizontal to where refrigeration units once held dairy. Gone were the metal bins holding recycled pop cans. As kids we used to collect beer and soda cans and turn them in here for five cents each, then go to the candy department and buy a handful of Jolly Ranchers. The candy section now housed lottery kiosks, and a lineup of people were holding dollar bills, waiting to enter their magic numbers. I might as well have been in a foreign place.

Our motive for purchasing wine was twofold. First, there was the matter of etiquette and the desire to contribute something, *anything*. My parents had taught me never to show up as an empty-handed dinner guest. Equal to that, I wanted to have some choice in what we drank, as discovering, drinking, and collecting wines is part of Bob's and my lifestyle. In homage to my family, we chose pinot noirs made in Newberg and the Dundee Hills, where both of my parents grew up. If the evening was a complete bust—a fear I had not yet shaken—we would find consolation in a good wine.

I parked on the street across from my parents' house. Their driveway was full of cars, and street parking would allow us an easy exit whenever that time came.

"This is it, Bobby," I said. "This is where I lived from the ages of three to twenty."

My eyes came to rest on the rhododendrons hugging the edge of the living room picture window. This was where Lory, Randy, and I had stood for the photograph that sits near my writing desk, the day my childhood self had imagined the faceless hooded riders coming to get my dad. I remember my urgent need to convince him not to be stubborn, to change his mind, to convince him how much safer he would be if only he'd just believe. *If only. Just believe. Please.* Now I understood how much that was to ask of him. Now there were people in my parents' home worried the faceless hooded riders would come to get *me*. They could come any day now. How foolish we all had been, each in our own way.

Bob grabbed the two bottles of wine, and we walked through the driveway, past several parked cars. The only car I recognized was Dad's Trooper. The living room was lit up, and through the sheer curtains I could make out several people standing around, huddled in pockets of conversation.

We walked through the front door, and I hollered out a hello over the din of voices. My sister was in the living room, visiting with a person I did not recognize. She was wearing the same suit she'd worn to the memorial, and I surmised she had come straight from the funeral home to help my mother prepare. Each free space in the living room held bouquets of flowers that had graced the service earlier. I'd been excluded from helping with any of this, not because I'd journeyed from afar, but because of my status.

Mom and Dad came around the corner from the kitchen. Dad was wearing jeans and leather slippers. Mom had also changed into a black cotton pantsuit that fell loose around her small frame.

"Welcome," they both said, gathering our coats and inviting us to remove our shoes and discard them near the other waiting pairs. Bob slipped easily out of his black loafers. I was wearing high-heeled black boots and hesitated to remove them, which would leave my black pants pooling around my ankles. Struggling for a moment with my vanity, I decided to keep them on. I felt held together by those boots, battened down, ready for what, I could not be sure. Removing them would feel too vulnerable, too casual.

Ove was in the kitchen, speaking to another person I did not recognize. He stood next to my favorite uncle, Jim, Dad's youngest brother, and his wife. Greetings and introductions were made all around. Several bottles of wine and glasses were already set out, to which Bob added ours. Except for the drinks, the counters were cleared, ready to receive whatever food deliveries awaited us from the friends. Bob and I consciously made ourselves at home, opening and pouring our wine, passing glasses around. It was about 5:30 p.m. I looked for Randy but did not see him. I assumed he was in the guest room downstairs, collecting himself for the evening.

Over the next hour, several people came by to drop off food and pay their respects. Some had attended the memorial service; others had not. Without exception, everyone greeted me. Some were cool and reserved and seemed to avoid lingering wherever I happened to be, but no one shunned me outright.

Several people were genuinely happy to see me. "I've thought of you so many times over the years." One woman confessed how jealous her daughter had been when she'd learned her mother would be seeing me. When her daughter was a teenager and I was still considered a good influence, her mother had me study the Bible with her. Over the years, I'd become fond of her daughter as I watched her grow up and get married. It was one of many relationships that had come to a screeching halt when I left the faith. I'd never said a proper goodbye to many of my close friends. Besides not knowing what a "proper goodbye" looked like under the circumstances, it had been all I could do to face the firing squad of family and elders; saying goodbye to my friends would have been a few bullets too many. It probably appeared cold and heartless to my friends, but my lack of contact was a self-protective measure, a hedge against sorrow.

Bob seemed engrossed in conversation with Lory and Ove. I wondered what they were talking about, but the room had grown too loud to eavesdrop and I was being pulled from person to person. "So good to see you." "Where are you living now?" "What exactly does an executive coach do?" This was a cocktail party of just under twenty people. I scanned the room and still didn't see my brother or sister-in-law.

The doorbell rang, and my father urged me to answer it. There on the front porch stood Vince Lloyd and his wife, Sarah. Sarah let out a scream of glee, handed Vince the wooden bowl she was carrying, and gave me a hug. It was the warmest greeting I'd received from anyone there. Joy oozed from her, the way it always had. Vince also hugged me, an owlish grin behind his signature wire-rimmed spectacles. I took their coats, and they disappeared into the living room, greeting everyone else they knew there. Sarah came to find me in the kitchen, and we chatted like the long-lost friends we were. She updated me on their life and two children. It was as if no time had passed and no rules had been broken. Her exuberance for life had always been infectious to me. Her petite frame could barely contain the intensity of her energy, and she made sweeping gestures with both hands as she spoke. I found myself getting lighter and happier with each story she told. I soaked it up like beach sand welcoming high tide. I asked her about all our friends from my former congregation, the one she was still part of, and Sarah gave unbridled and detailed reports on the health and well-being of everyone I could think of.

All seems well here. Like I have, everyone has carried on with life, some moving, some marrying, nurturing their families and communities. We may be guided by a different compass, different beliefs, but our values are similar. Life goes on, and we have all found our unique path.

Vince joined us. It didn't take long for Sarah to slip away, leaving Vince and me leaning against the kitchen counter. Vince had an inquisitive, intellectual mind, and we had always been able to slip into brainy, stimulating conversations with an easy give-and-take. He converted to the religion as an adult and was one of the rare Witnesses of my acquaintance who had a college degree. He held an executive position in the corporate world, so we shared an affinity for the unique pressures of that environment. We were talking about the challenge of raising children. To his dismay, their son, Alex, had not embraced The Truth and had never chosen to be baptized as a Witness. Vince removed his glasses and started polishing them with a handkerchief taken from his rear pants pocket. He was describing what Alex had taught him about free choice. I thought it was an intriguing topic to raise with me, and I wondered what he might be trying to say. Vince wasn't known to indulge in ideal chatter. He always had a point to make. He'd thought he understood free choice before, he said, but he'd come to realize that he'd understood it only intellectually, in theory, not in practice. He wanted Alex to make the choice his god-fearing parents preferred, but doing something to please another isn't freedom. I was tracking with his logic and enjoying our familiar intimacy, how we'd been able to get to the heart of the matter so quickly.

Then a natural pause happened in the conversation. I was rubbing my chin, absorbing what he had just said. Vince put his glasses back on and then pulled out his wallet, removing a business card from its back flap. He handed me the card and said something about "Jehovah's flock." The card read CONGREGA-TION OF JEHOVAH'S WITNESSES above a printed phone number. At the bottom was a second phone number, written in by hand. "The Society has approved a new arrangement for people like you who may wish to get reinstated."

This caught me off guard, and I blanked out for a moment. The boisterous sounds around me dropped to a low din as I descended into a hazy mental tunnel. My throat clenched.

"The handwritten number is my cell phone," Vince said, "if you'd ever like to discuss the new process."

I should have seen this coming. What made me think I could be in a room with all these Witnesses, half of whom are congregation elders, and not get preached to? Damn my naïveté.

Attempting to get my bearings, I set my empty wineglass down on the kitchen counter but continued to hold the business card. Everyone else was staying at a distance, leaving Vince and me to our private conversation.

How many people are in on this?

I folded my arms and then thought better of it. It felt too shut off, too guarded.

Don't blank out now. This is an important moment, a time to take a stand. Whatever I say next will be repeated, along with a precise description of my manner. Can I keep my heart open to this person and appreciate his intent, even as I reject the offer?

"Vince," I said, mindfully breathing and deliberately standing up straight, enormously grateful for the height of those black boots, how tall they made me, how Vince had to look up into my eyes. Sounds were resonating around me again, as I came out the other side of the tunnel. "I appreciate your telling me this, and I will keep your card. But"—and I paused here for emphasis—"I can't imagine ever, ever calling you about reinstatement."

"Really?" Vince said, his eyes drooping at the corners as he stood gaping. His expression jogged loose a faded memory of that same expression from years earlier, when we sat in that back room of the Kingdom Hall with Ross and Jerry, just before Vince pulled out his Bible and condemned me with Scripture. It was a look that seemed to say, *How could anyone with half a brain be so foolish? Armageddon is coming.*

"Really." I felt a smile sprouting up from the clarity and strength I had to voice my feelings without being strident or offended. "If you were to follow me around for a few days, Vince, you might see that I am happy. My life is filled with love, fulfilling work, interesting conversations, beauty, and adventure. I feel a connection to the divine. It's not perfect; I have my struggles like everyone else. But there is nothing to fix. I'm very happy."

Yes. I'm happy. I'm a happy pagan.

"Okay, then." His cheek twitched as he pushed his glasses up the bridge of his nose. "It was good to see you, and I wish you the very best." With that, he slipped away to find his wife and leave. His work was done. It was time to go.

Their departure triggered an exodus, as people realized it was 7:00 p.m. I walked through the cool hallway into my parents' bedroom and scooped up the coats belonging to our guests. Some were made of scratchy wool, others of cold heavy leather. I sat down on the bed, relieved to be alone for just a minute. By the next day, Vince would give a report back to someone in my family, probably Ove or my mom. I was sure he'd been asked in advance to approach me, relieving my family of that obligation. Vince was the logical choice for this assignment since he had counseled me during the breakup of my marriage. Everyone knew that I liked and respected him. There had been a time when I'd considered him a friend. He'd report that he'd done his best, but I was adamant. The story would get passed around like a piece of chipped heirloom china, people shaking their heads in disappointment or dismay. I took a deep breath, trying to shake off a heaviness that pressed down on my shoulders. Returning to the living room, I passed out the jackets one by one.

Mom was in the kitchen, pulling warm platters from the oven. I tossed and plated the salad while Lory set the table. It had been years since the three of us had worked in a kitchen together. Being there gave me an odd sense of belonging. It turned out that Randy was still with Sheena, and Mom did not want to hold up dinner. Uncle Jim and his wife, Paulie, joined us instead. They were gracious people and could provide a buffer, so that Bob and I were not the only "worldly" people.

We gathered at the table. Dad had Ove say a brief prayer to Jehovah. Mom served the meal family-style. We passed tri-tip steak cooked to perfection, au gratin potatoes, and green beans. Wineglasses were filled, and everyone reveled in the feast.

On the surface, everyone seemed calm, even content. A fly on the wall would have observed a traditional family gathering. There was a centerpiece of flowers, salt and pepper, the butter dish, and a basket of bread. I sat between Bob and Ove, around a table just big enough to seat eight knee to knee. Throughout the day and evening, Ove and I were indifferent toward each other. He never spoke to me directly, posing all questions about our life to Bob. I felt no need to ask him any questions. It was the mutual and dispassionate concession of in-laws who wouldn't voluntarily choose one another's company under any other circumstance. Still, I felt low-grade anxiety forming. I wiggled in my chair, legs crossed this way, then the other, slipping my hands under each thigh, looking at my watch. It was dark outside, and the day was slipping away. Unlike Cinderella, I was very aware of the time, unable to lose myself in the night. This was a limited opening, with maybe two or three hours of grace remaining and no glass slipper to leave behind.

The conversation was unambitious yet jovial. We never ventured too deep into emotions or ideology. It had been a long day for everyone. We discussed current property values and how the nearby neighborhoods had changed. Lory told us about her proselytizing at the local women's prison, but only to make a point about crystal meth's stranglehold on the community.

The food was gooey, warm, and solid, and I enjoyed how it filled and grounded me, softening my edges. My watch showed 9:00 p.m. Randy had not returned from his own family mission.

I helped Mom clear the table and bring out dessert. The friends had brought two cakes and a huge tray of cookies.

It seemed like the right time to speak about Grandma, to hear some of the family lore, so I asked Dad and Uncle Jim to tell their favorite stories about her and whether they thought she was a strict mother. They both smiled with the wistfulness of bygone memories and started talking over each other. According to my dad, he was always running from the strap, while Jim got away with murder. "It's true," Jim said. "Mom and Dad spoiled me rotten."

"The youngest always gets away with murder," Lory said, looking at me.

Uncle Jim pushed back from the table as he and Paulie excused themselves to go home. They were the only people that night who asked for our phone number, for use if they happen to pass through the Bay Area. The front door closed behind them. It would have been a natural time for us to leave, too; it was almost ten o'clock, it had been a long day, and everyone was exhausted. But Mom invited everyone to sit down in the living room.

"Maybe for a few minutes," I said. "I was hoping Randy would return before we left."

Bob sat between Dad and me on the couch. Lory and Ove sat across from us on the stone shelf of the fireplace. Mom kicked off her shoes and rested in the wingback chair near the television. Her intensity lessened, the way a fountain ebbs down to a trickle. I figured we had twenty minutes tops; then we'd need to go, not because I felt unwelcome, but everyone was winding down. Bob would leave whenever I was ready. We'd come this far.

No sooner had Mom sat down than she was up again, bringing framed photographs off the walls of the back room, two at a time, and showing them to Bob. There were baby pictures of Lory and Randy, born eighteen months apart, and one of me in fourth grade, wearing a bright yellow jumper, ponytails protruding from each side of my head like branches and tied with fuzzy green ribbons.

"Those were her innocent years," Mom said to Bob. Bob was alternating between sips of wine and respectful nods at each photo. I felt an even larger love for him in that moment, my patient wingman. Mom went back to the room to exchange these photos for another round. A car pulled into the driveway as she returned with a fresh stack of picture frames in her hands. This batch was of Sheena and Tyler from infancy to teens and adulthood. I'd never seen any of them before.

Randy, Marlene, and Tyler walked through the front door. A partition at the foyer made it difficult to see their faces. I'd wanted him to arrive and exclaim, "Good, you're still here!" and join us. Instead they offered a feeble hello to everyone as they walked through the living room and straight to the kitchen. I could hear the refrigerator opening. It was an abrupt entrance that halted our conversation.

Okay. Maybe he's distressed over Sheena or he's simply hungry. Once he eats a few bites, he'll join us.

Lory raised her voice and asked them about Sheena. The answers came between the clank of silverware on plates and the microwave buzzer. She was perfectly fine, Randy said, except for the discomfort of false labor. She was extremely nervous about the delivery. The answer seemed to satisfy everyone in the living room.

Dad started telling Bob the story of how I begged for a puppy when I was twelve years old. I'd taken a 4-H class on dog training through my elementary school and had become obsessed with adopting and training a puppy. He recalled my process of researching the breeds, scouring the classified ads, and begging for a sheepdog, then a husky, then a pointer, and finally settling on a Labrador. After weeks of "begging," a characterization I could not deny, Mom and Dad announced I could have a dog but would have to wait two months, until school let out, for summer. "Dogs—especially puppies—take time," Dad had said, then laid down the law of my responsibility to feed, train, and clean up after the animal.

As Dad relayed his version of this story, Mom and I chimed

in with various corrections or embellishments of his account. Lory, who was seventeen when this happened, encouraged me to choose a dog from the pound, thus saving an animal from probable euthanasia and sparing the family an expensive breeder's fee.

"I did?" Lory smiled with pride and sat up a little taller, realizing her impact on destiny. "I don't remember that."

"That's where I got the idea," I said. "And the day after school let out for the summer, Dad, Randy, and I hopped into the blue Ranchero, drove to the pound, and brought home Shad."

"From the first litter she saw," Dad said to Bob. Shad was a Lab-collie mix who lived to thirteen, keeping Mom company in the years after I left home.

"It was Randy who came up with the name Shad," I said. "The name suited him."

The storytelling created an aperture of kinship that kindled my joy as everyone participated in the telling. At the same time, the contrast with the present was melancholy. Randy could easily hear the conversation from the other room, as he, Marlene, and Tyler sat in silence, eating at the table. He did not contribute any new details, which was unlike him.

The silence between stories was growing, along with my dread of saying goodbye. I knew the death exemption was about to expire. It became clear that Randy was not going to join us. It seemed our conversation at the funeral home was all his conscience would allow. Other members of the family could set aside the rules for one day; Randy could manage only ten minutes. Or maybe he found the whole thing too emotionally confounding to confront. This was not a family reunion but a concession for mourning.

Mom returned from the back room empty-handed and collapsed in the chair, her urge to reminisce waning. Bob looked at me and raised both brows, as if to say, *Enough.* I entertained the idea of speaking up about the absurdity of the situation. *Is this how it will be for the rest of our lives: seeing each other only when someone dies?* How many years would pass before I'd receive another phone call reporting a terminal diagnosis or the need for a deathbed rendezvous? But speaking up felt pointless. It might satisfy some opaque longing to vent, but I could do that on my own time. Truer still, I'd held it together all day, somehow managing to rise to the occasion, and I was afraid pushing past this cordial veil would result in my having an emotional breakdown, tears squirting from my eyes, unable to breathe or speak. To indulge myself felt too extravagant, too risky. I had too much pride to let that happen. In retrospect, it might have been good to let it all out, the sadness and anger, my despair on full display. But I feared it could be misinterpreted as unhappiness or a sign of repentance. Sure, I had regrets, but they were not of a confessional nature.

"It's time to say goodbye," Bob said. "Our day started at four this morning, and you've all had a series of long days, we know. I'm sure we could all use some rest."

Everyone stood. Mom, Dad, Lory, and Ove gathered around me in a semicircle, with Bob off to one side. First, I hugged my sister. "Goodbye, Lory," I said. "It's nice to see you looking so well."

She hugged me back. "You too," she said.

Next I hugged Ove, briefly and with little intensity.

"Thanks, Ove, for taking such good care of my sister," I said.

"You're welcome," he said.

Mom was next. We wrapped our arms around each other and held each other gently, her head resting on my shoulder.

"It was good to see you, Mom." We rocked each other.

"Yes, Lindy, we loved seeing you, too," she answered. Out of the corner of my eye, I could see that Randy, Marlene, and Tyler had emerged from the dining room and were watching us. Bob was following behind me, saying his own goodbyes.

"I wish we could see you all more often," I said.

"Yes, Lindy," Mom said, still holding me. "We'd like that, too. And you know what to do to make that happen."

Disappointment rang through me, and my body felt flushed with heat as I pulled away from her. Even now, she was clinging to her conditions.

This is wack! You look at the sky through a straw. This fanatical behavior is not worthy of you! You used to tell me Bible stories of pagan parents who sacrificed their children in the fires to Baal and shake your head in disgust. Now it is you who sacrifices a relationship with your daughter. And for what? For rules that cannot stand the test of logic or love.

That was what I thought, but it was not what I said. I took a deep breath instead. I would launch into that tearful diatribe later, at the bar with my husband. I just needed to hold it together a few moments longer. I cupped Mom's cheeks in both hands, aware of the needless fears she harbored for my everlasting life. I smiled and shook my head.

Now I turned to my father, the parent who'd given me blue eyes, brown hair, and curiosity about the world. Even when I had my heels on, he loomed over me. He had the sweetest, most melancholy smile. He was just trying to get through this ordeal and squeeze out all the best parts. We would allow ourselves to fully experience our sadness later, in private. We embraced without saying a word.

Then I stood in front of my brother and his family.

"I'm sorry we didn't get to spend much time together," I said. "But I'm grateful for the time we did have . . . for me to see that you're doing well."

Randy's eyes were wide, his face animated with bright red patches on his cheeks, like sections of small countries on a globe. He was anxious for me to leave, to release him from this uncomfortable encounter.

"Yes," he said. Both hands were shoved into his suit pants pockets. Marlene stood near him, a protective sentry. Tyler was still wearing a suit coat and a shy, curious look.

He's heard stories about me, the worldly, renegade aunt who is to be avoided.

I shook Tyler's hand formally, then hugged Randy and Marlene. Bob slipped his shoes back on, and Ove handed us our jackets. I was too warm to cloak myself in wool.

"It's time for you to leave so we can talk about you," Ove

said, and giggled to press home the joke. Everyone else laughed awkwardly. Bob and I just looked at each other.

What a jerk.

"Until we meet again," I said, keeping one hand on the doorknob and waving with the other. The night air gripped and soothed me. Bob grabbed my hand as we walked to the car. I unlocked the doors and slipped behind the steering wheel. Bob got in and pulled his seat belt into place. Looking back toward the house, I saw everyone standing on the front steps, watching us leave. We both waved as I turned on the ignition, put the car in gear, and drove away. The reprieve was officially over.

Death Exemption 2006 had run its course.

Epilogue:
The Death Exemption, 2010

If your everyday practice is to open to all your emotions, to all the people you meet, to all the situations you encounter without closing down, trusting that you can do that, then that will take you as far as you can go. And then you will understand all the teachings that anyone has ever taught.
— Pema Chödrön

Four years passed before I saw my parents again. True to the détente we had worked out over the years, the occasion was another death exemption.

It was a Sunday morning in March. My parents had flown in to the Bay Area the night before. I'd picked them up at their hotel and driven here. I'd presumed the next death exemption would be to memorialize one of them. Instead, I was grieving the well-lived, all-too-short life of my beloved Bob. Mom and Dad had accepted my invitation to attend his service.

His decline was swift and shocking. It began when he took a hard fall in the wee hours of the night, stumbling over a bathrobe belt that had fallen from our bed. His back never felt right after that. He experienced the sensation of his spine being stuck in places, like well-worn piano keys that fail to rise back to their original position. A back specialist was consulted to help us resolve this nuisance. An MRI revealed a spine riddled with a white, cotton-looking substance. Bob didn't need back surgery. He needed an oncologist.

The oncologist arranged for a barrage of diagnostic tests, and twelve days later we learned Bob had Stage Four cancer of the esophagus. We stumbled into the alternate universe of medical care for the seriously ill, a yawning vortex where time contorts and folds inside itself, stretching into a nonlinear black hole.

After reviewing Bob's case with a panel of other doctors, the oncologist said Bob's disease was highly treatable and felt Bob was plenty strong to endure chemotherapy. The graveness of the situation was not lost on us, but, inherently optimistic, Bob and I latched on to the phrase "highly treatable" and proceeded as recommended. We both believed in the body's creative capacity to regenerate and surprise us. We assumed we were in for a lousy six months of treatment, to be followed by a period of rebuilding his strength and well-being. Life would be forever altered, but life would go on.

Instead, Bob died sixty-two days after receiving his diagnosis.

The first, three-day round of chemotherapy was administered in the hospital, and Bob's body accepted the medicine, experiencing just a whisper of nausea, like a passing spell of carsickness. He came home and took to his bed, declining visitors.

Something fierce awakened in me, and I found an inner calm beyond my previous experience. Adrenaline and unconditional love mixed into a potent cocktail of physical strength and mental acuity that allowed me to function on very little sleep. A well-honed meditation practice, prayer, and a daily dose of Ativan carried me, and I sensed we were both being held by divine forces and sources.

A core team of close friends gathered around us and helped me with practical matters and navigating the tsunami of details and decisions demanding attention. One of those friends created a registry on CaringBridge.org, where we posted news of Bob's progress to keep friends and family informed. Every evening I sat at his bedside and read aloud the e-mails and cards that came in from hundreds of people around the world. Bob and I both felt everyone's love at the intuitive level of essence, and that sustained us through some difficult moments.

We had a string of days when rest and optimism prevailed, followed by a series of strenuous complications, two emergency trips to the hospital, time spent in intensive care. His decline was wicked fast. Gaunt from extreme weight loss, Bob's body was no longer a match for the illness or its treatment. Flabbergasted and bereft, I brought him home to the merciful quiet of hospice care. Four days later, he was gone.

We were together eight short years, but our relationship had a timeless quality. Losing Bob knocked me out of time. He was only ever good to me, and we were good together. Despite the awfulness that comes with terminal illness, we shared staggering moments of truth and beauty that mystify me still. Holding the space for his peaceful transition was one of the supreme honors of my life.

The night before he passed away, I had the sudden presence of mind to ask our friend Raz to contact my parents and tell them what was going on. I lacked the emotional bandwidth to call them myself. I required nothing from them. My soul family was providing all the sustenance I could absorb. Raz called them from a back room of my house and invited them to attend Bob's memorial.

They were deeply saddened by the news and asked Raz to give me a hug and assure me of their love.

"I talked to both of your parents individually," Raz said, standing in front of me, holding my hands. "They spoke from their heart, Linda, not their religion." After embracing me, he pulled away and added, "I think they'll come."

Raz was right. The day before the service, he met my parents at the airport and drove them to their hotel. Raz told them I lived in a very special setting and that it would be a shame for them not to visit my home while there. Raz was not aware of Mom's refusal to visit my home years earlier, when I lived in Chicago.

Over two hundred people gathered at the clubhouse of the rustic yet elegant private golf club on Mount Tam, five miles as the crow flies from our house. Bob had many fond memories golfing there as a guest of his close friend Bill, who was a member. Bill arranged for us to have the entire clubhouse for our purposes, including the patios, bar, and great room, which had rugged high beams and a river-stone fireplace on the inside wall. The opposite wall was lined with cathedral-height windows, and beyond that emerald fairways curled off into the woods. A podium and microphone were set in front of the fireplace, and chairs were lined up in long rows.

Outside, the sun was shy with its heat but not its illumination. The air was crisp, and geraniums and petunias tumbled from planters on the patio. Wild turkey and deer crossed the well-groomed span of Bon Tempe Meadow.

The mood of the crowd was tempered by sorrow and the joy of reunion. People who had not seen each other in years were together again; there was the low hum of delight, hugs, "you haven't changed a bit," and expressed longing for happier circumstances.

As I took my place at the podium, the din of voices fell into silence. I scanned the audience and saw my parents among the forsaken, seated in the second aisle at the start of the row. Dad's sport coat was unbuttoned, and his hands rested on each thigh. He was biting his lip. Light reflected off his spectacles, but his concerned gaze and prominent jawline were clear. Mom leaned into him, both hands resting on the handbag on her lap. Thin as always, she barely occupied any space; the bigger personalities surrounding her diminished her presence. Knowing little about my life, they could not have been prepared for the size, sophistication, and unconditional warmth of my community. Their presence was an unexpected consolation to me.

The great room was filled to capacity, and people were standing three deep in back. Bob was a true friend to princes and paupers alike, and the crowd reflected his generous, egalitarian nature. Each person was an echo of his diverse and interesting life as a friend, father, husband, uncle, brother, leader in the human-potential and environmental movements, international management executive, real estate developer, attorney, nonprofit board member, global citizen, and lover of life. I took in the forlorn faces of gifted artists and accomplished writers, house-wives, scholars, spiritual teachers, captains of industry, of our accountant, car mechanic, and home contractor. Over the years, our respective communities had coalesced and I was comforted by the attendance of these, my companions in grief.

Clutching a tissue and getting my balance at the podium, I cleared my throat and heard my gravelly voice float though the sound system. I thanked everyone for coming to comfort one another and celebrate Bob's life. It had been twelve days since Bob's death, and one word kept coming to my mind to describe his essence: luminous. "Luminous," I repeated, with more heft, looking up at the high beams. He was a shimmering, radiant light. Several heads nodded. I shared that once he got clear, Bob was not afraid to die, only sad at leaving us. He had no unfinished business, no grudges, no words left unsaid. He died free of pain, in a state of grace.

I introduced Ann, who was the first of eight people, includ-ing his children, to eulogize Bob, and took my seat in the front row, between Bob's sister and my stepson. The strain of the pro-ceeding weeks had melted twenty pounds off my frame, and I could feel my sit bones press into the seat cushion while Ann opened with an ecumenical blessing.

A sacred, tender reverence filled the room as each person came forward, transparent with deep emotion, and shared their remembrances. Laughter bubbled up many times, reflecting Bob's capacity to dance with the divine without taking life too seriously. Bob was not a religious man, though all who knew him would agree he was a deeply spiritual person, which is to say he was endlessly fascinated by the mysteries of life and pur-sued enlightenment without ever expecting to fully achieve it.

Raz said that while it wasn't always obvious what he was doing, the main point of Bob's life was to peel back the layers from his heart, to more fully express love.

I let the sentiments wash through me and felt deep gratitude for everything Bob taught me about love. Man, did we have fun together. With each story, I saw anew how much he meant to his friends and family. One person said Bob was like the floor—always there, steady, supportive. "You wake up each morning and count on the floor to be there. *It just is.*" My heart tightened with the truth of his absence, and I tamped down the coils of dread swirling in my belly, unable or unwilling to consider the myriad of bleak moments ahead, living without my best friend. This was the first epic transition in my adult life that was not a result of my deliberate intention. Before this, I had thought I understood that life and love are mysterious, not to be controlled, in the same way you know an earthquake is unwieldy and unpredictable. How could it not be? We've all seen the news reports, and I've felt the distant tremors from California fault lines. Until one day you feel bedrock rattling underfoot and realize you're at the epicenter, that nothing is solid, and you comprehend just how vulnerable you are. Something bigger than you is at work, and the only way out is through.

The formal service concluded, and we shared good food, wine, and conversation, which was how Bob would have wanted it. My heart had cracked open, pacified by the outreach of each person. A tender, otherworldly feeling carried me through the day, and I was surprised at my capacity to remember names.

My girlfriends took turns looking after Mom and Dad, without my being aware of it. Every time I glanced their way, I noticed them in conversation with different people. In this way, my parents got a sense of my life now as people from my consulting, writing, spiritual, and volunteer communities came forward. They may not have been Witnesses, but they were all true-blue friends.

After lunch, there were open-mic tributes and a succession of people came forward to tell personal stories about Bob that ranged from poignant to hilarious. Will spoke about how his father always made time for him, and thanked me for everything I did throughout his dad's illness, describing the captain's log, as we called the diary where I tracked his medications, symptoms, and other details.

The whole affair lasted several hours; then people lingered on the sunny patio and in the bar. I sat between my parents as we loitered on a bar couch and I held each of their hands, dazed and tired. They were the only people in attendance who had known me my whole life, yet they understood me the least. Still, it was good to have people there who'd known me before I was the way I am now.

Within the hour, friends and family gathered back at my house for dinner. I was surprised when my parents agreed to come. I didn't question it, just welcomed them in and gave them a tour as others warmed lasagna and tossed a salad. It took Bob's death to bring my parents to my home. (Thanks to the death exemption, that week I also received kind calls from Lory, Randy, and Ross.) They admired the peaceful canyon setting, the artwork, and the clematis overtaking the trellis. Dad said it was good to see that his daughter was well looked after. Following dinner, one of my friends gave my parents a lift to their nearby hotel and I popped a sleeping pill.

The next morning, I awoke to a six o'clock alarm, peeled myself out of bed, stumbled into the shower, and cried. There was one more thing to do before I could allow myself to be strangled by grief: drive my parents to the airport, one hour away. The house was hollow and dark.

Mom sat in the passenger seat, and Dad sat behind her. I could see his face in the rearview mirror. Their advancing age was apparent in their slower movements, in my need to speak loudly to them and repeat phrases several times. The conversation was amiable, covering the weather, service at their hotel, and mercifully few questions about my plans for the future. I could sense their desire and helplessness to assist me. All of my physical needs were met, and I had a community that would keep a protective eye on me.

"Please thank all your friends for taking care of us," Dad said. "Really, Lindy, no one would let us lift a finger."

"I do have great friends."

"That was a beautiful service," Dad continued.

"It made us wish that we had known Bob better," Mom said.

"When you brought him to our house, we could tell he was a great guy," Dad said. "But he was so unassuming, we would never have guessed he was so accomplished."

"And loved by so many," Mom said. "You both are."

"Yes," I said, choking out the next sentence, sensing a well of sadness bubbling to the surface. "I'm still in shock, wondering when I'm going to awaken from this bad dream. He was so special to me." I turned the car toward the airport exit. "I know it hasn't really hit me that he is gone."

My eyes pooled with tears.

I noticed Mom opening her mouth to speak, then stop herself.

"What's on your mind, Mom?"

"Wouldn't it be nice, Lindy, if you could be there, in the New System, to greet Bob when he's resurrected?" She still hoped I would return to the religion so I could survive the inevitable march of the faceless hooded riders and make it into paradise. But her words did not ignite a storm in my heart. I had just lived through Armageddon, and the intensity of that had left me in awe of the mysterious ways in which life unfolds and the inescapable truth that everyone dies eventually. What else could I be sure of anymore? Only the power and presence of love. Under the circumstances, to be angry about anything seemed silly. What did it matter if my mom chose now to preach, which I saw as her way of expressing love? It's easy to forget that parents have unrequited dreams of their own.

"If Jehovah God is going to resurrect anyone," I said, content to play along, "it would definitely be the magnificent Bob Curtis. No question."

Dad was looking out the side window toward a large, empty hangar and the blue DEPARTING FLIGHTS sign.

"Yes, Lindy," Mom continued, looking at me. She went on

about death being full payment for sins, how those who are resurrected will get to start life with a clean slate. "It would be a shame for you to miss seeing Bob again. You obviously loved each other very much."

Bob would have laughed at being characterized a sinner, for indeed he was (by her standards)—and so what? Despite my lethargy, I was amused.

I slowed the car, pulled up to the curb, and turned off the ignition as I thanked them for coming. In that moment, it occurred to me to tell them something more. I turned and leaned against my door to face them.

"I want you to know, Mom and Dad, that Bob never judged you. Many people would be appalled by parents who shun their daughter for leaving a religion."

"We know that," Mom said matter-of-factly, and I realized it took courage for them to have shown up at the service, their reputations preceding them, unsure how they might be received.

"Bob never judged you," I repeated. "He would never shun his own daughter, but he didn't make unilateral assessments about people. He didn't perceive you as wrong or hold your beliefs against you, and that made all the difference to me."

There was a thick silence inside the car. Dad was sitting back in his seat, and Mom was looking at me, waiting for me to say more, but I was tapped out. With every breath I was growing more tired, exhaustion seeping into my body like an invisible ether.

We got out of the car, and I hugged Mom while Dad removed the luggage from the trunk and placed it on the curb. It crossed my mind that I might never see them again, but the idea did not stir tears. I had bigger fish to fry.

Mom urged me to call them if I needed anything. I hugged Dad. I knew I would not call them for help and they would not call me until life brought us another serious illness or death exemption.

I got into the car and pulled into the far exit lane, then glanced into my rearview mirror to see Mom and Dad standing at the curb, watching me drive away.

Acknowledgments

This book was years in the making and I could not have completed it without the support and encouragement of some very special people. My heartfelt gratitude to:

Bob, for your intelligence, humor, and boundless love and generosity, before, during, and after.

Angeles Arrien, for lending me your cherished terrapin rattle at a very difficult time and helping me discover how to begin again. The depths of your wisdom and generosity astound me and I am deeply grateful for your humility and encouragement to build upon your own work with honorable closure. One of my most cherished possessions is your handwritten note, "It is in the DNA of the human spirit to end well."

Adair Lara, for the memoir-writing classes you taught in your living room, believing this story should be told, and helping me find where it began.

Leslie Keenan, for being an extraordinary writing coach and helping me map the through-line of this tale. Also, for the chocolate.

Scribe Tribe (a.k.a. Rachel, Jeffrey, Mary, Marilyn, and Wendy), for your kind and incisive feedback on my early drafts and holding all of our work with tenderness.

Diane Petrocelli and her team at Book Passage, for being a beacon of creative inspiration in this community and giving Scribe Tribe a gathering place year after year.

Carol Ann, for your relentless belief in me and your big, beautiful heart.

Tracy, for your friendship, fierce loyalty, and always holding me in love.

Lanie, for the laughter and hikes and travels and code words and love. You are a true friend who has stood by me and for me since the day we met.

She Writes Press—Brooke Warner and associates, I am deeply grateful for your love of good writing and ushering in a new era of publishing with your passion, courage, and innovation. Keep going!

Depature Lounge Readers, for trusting me with your own stories of closure so we can all learn together.

Finally, the many people around the world with whom I have had the privilege of working over the years are too numerous to mention by name, but they are woven into the fabric of this book and its message. This memoir is intended to share the lessons, love, wisdom, and inspiration that they have contributed to me.

About the Author

Linda Curtis is an author, teacher, and keynote speaker whose life experience has granted her expertise on the subject of endings, large and small. As a champion of Honorable Closure—a learned process that honors endings, exits, and good-byes as a natural and dynamic part of our human experience—she mentors individuals, executives, and teams in transition, supporting them from unfinished business to dignified completion. She is a Master Mindfulness Teacher at the Google-born Search Inside Yourself Leadership Institute and an accredited ICF coach.

Linda lives in Marin County, California. She's a hiker, a yogini and an avid cyclist who loves celebrating life with friends and chosen family, while enjoying the jammy notes of a fine cabernet.

Learn more about her work at www.lindaacurtis.com.

Author photo © Abigail Huller

Selected Titles from She Writes Press

She Writes Press is an independent publishing company founded to serve women writers everywhere. Visit us at www.shewritespress.com.

Uncovered: How I Left Hasidic Life and Finally Came Home by Leah Lax. $16.95, 978-1-63152-995-5. Drawn to their offers of refuge from her troubled family and their promises of eternal love, Leah Lax becomes a Hasidic Jew—but ultimately, as a forty-something woman, comes to reject everything she has lived for three decades in order to be who she truly is.

The S Word by Paolina Milana. $16.95, 978-1-63152-927-6. An insider's account of growing up with a schizophrenic mother, and the disastrous toll the illness—and her Sicilian Catholic family's code of secrecy—takes upon her young life.

Fourteen: A Daughter's Memoir of Adventure, Sailing, and Survival by Leslie Johansen Nack. $16.95, 978-1-63152-941-2. A coming-of-age adventure story about a young girl who comes into her own power, fights back against abuse, becomes an accomplished sailor, and falls in love with the ocean and the natural world.

Learning to Eat Along the Way by Margaret Bendet. $16.95, 978-1-63152-997-9. After interviewing an Indian holy man, newspaper reporter Margaret Bendet follows him in pursuit of enlightenment and ends up facing demons that were inside her all along.

The Coconut Latitudes: Secrets, Storms, and Survival in the Caribbean by Rita Gardner. $16.95, 978-1-63152-901-6. A haunting, lyrical memoir about a dysfunctional family's experiences in a reality far from the envisioned Eden—and the terrible cost of keeping secrets.

Not Exactly Love: A Memoir by Betty Hafner. $16.95, 978-1-63152-149-2. At twenty-five Betty Hafner, thought she'd found the man to make her dream of a family and cozy home come true—but after they married, his rages turned the dream into a nightmare, and Betty had to decide: stay with the man she loved, or find a way to leave?